Religion, Language and Power

Routledge Studies in Religion

Religion, Language and Power

Edited by Nile Green and Mary Searle-Chatterjee

Routledge
Taylor & Francis Group

New York   London

First published 2008
by Routledge
270 Madison Ave, New York, NY 10016

Simultaneously published in the UK
by Routledge
2 Park Square, Milton Park, Abingdon, Oxon OX14 4RN

Routledge is an imprint of the Taylor & Francis Group, an informa business

© 2008 Taylor & Francis

Typeset in Sabon by IBT Global

Library of Congress Cataloging-in-Publication Data

Religion, language and power / edited by Nile Green and Mary Searle-Chatterjee.
    p. cm. — (Routledge studies in religion ; 10)
    Includes bibliographical references and index.
    ISBN-13: 978-0-415-96368-8 (hbk)
    ISBN-10: 0-415-96368-0 (hbk)
    ISBN-13: 978-0-203-92685-7 (ebk)
    ISBN-10: 0-203-92685-4 (ebk)
1. Religion. 2. Religion and sociology. 3. Language and languages—Religious aspects. I. Green, Nile. II. Searle-Chatterjee, Mary.

BL50.R42665 2008
200—dc22   2007047631

ISBN10: 0-415-96368-0 (hbk)
ISBN10: 0-203-92685-4 (ebk)

ISBN13: 978-0-415-96368-8 (hbk)
ISBN13: 978-0-203-92685-7 (ebk)

I sell here, Sir, what all the world desires to have – Power.
—Matthew Boulton, Birmingham industrialist, 1776

Contents

PART III
Struggling for the Self

Preface and Acknowledgments

Religion, Language and Power had its immediate origins in a series of intellectual 'retreats' in which colleagues working in Religious Studies at the University of Manchester gathered both in the department and in the genial setting of Gladstone's memorial library at Hawarden in North Wales. The idea of these gatherings was to share the perspectives brought by the divers expertise gained from working with materials ranging from contemporary Arabic writings to early modern English texts and premodern Sanskrit documents. One of the ground rules for the gatherings was to try to think beyond the category of 'religion' by which our expertise was usually organised and to think of our respective fields as instead being organised on the more sociologically and historically tangible criterion of language—that is, of books, conversations, or discourses shared between particular people in particular places. In the long debates in the leather chairs of Hawarden, we circled around some fundamental questions: Does 'religion' have any use as an analytical category? Does 'religion' exist, or is it merely a cipher for the operation of hegemony through the texts, persons, and places of power? Is what usually passes as 'religion' in substance the operation of language and power in human society?

This collection offers the fruit born from that cross-fertilisation of ideas. It is a strange fruit perhaps, since it might be said that it is only the existence of a university department of 'Religious Studies' that could have brought specialists working with such a miscellany of materials together. Be that as it may, the first gathering at Gladstone's library was also a culmination of several years of more ad hoc cross-fertilisation on the stony ground of the departmental corridor (as well as the better watered pastures of the nearby Kro-Bar, which also deserves a shout-out in the credits). For all the heterogeny of our expertise, a certain commitment to contextualised and politically-informed analyses of 'religion' allowed us, as it were, to speak in the same language. At the same time, the common stimulus of a number of other events that stood out from the run of the departmental calendar was also important in allowing us to think together. But there have been other stimuli as well and the collection as a whole aims to respond to Richard King's call in *Orientalism and Religion* (London: Routledge, 1999) 'to "transgress the boundaries" imposed by normative Western models of "religion" . . . [by] an interrogation and displacement of Western (Judeo–Christian/secular) paradigms of what "religion" is' (p. 210).

So much for genesis—now for the chronicle of individual efforts by way of acknowledgements proper. The editors wish to thank George Brooke for initially encouraging Mary Searle-Chatterjee to organise the first workshop in December 2004, which set the project in motion. The third of these prime-moving archons was Alan Williams, who helped take the project forward by locating funds with the help of Graham Ward for the two residential workshops at St. Deiniol's Library in Hawarden in May and October 2005, and in turn organising them (and us) with characteristic wit. The workshops were all the stronger for several presentations that for the presenters' own reasons were not turned into chapters for the final book. On this count, we would like to thank Roger Ballard, Kate Cooper, F. Gerald Downing, Michael Hoelzl, Dermot Killingley, and Graham Ward. Each of the individual chapters was circulated between the other contributors, so a collective debt of thanks is due all round. However, several colleagues also gave up their time to read drafts of the editors' introduction and provide incisive comments, particularly Jeremy Gregory and John Zavos. Thanks are also due on this count to Ursula Sharma and to Routledge's three anonymous readers. The responsibility for the remaining flaws is of course the editors' own.

We are grateful to the University of Chicago Press for permission to quote from Jonathan Z. Smith's *Imagining Religion: From Babylon to Jonestown*; to Polity Press for permission to quote from Pierre Bourdieu's *Language and Symbolic Power*; and to Prometheus Books for permission to quote from Ibn Warraq's *What the Koran Really Says: Language, Text and Commentary*.

Nile Green and Mary Searle-Chatterjee

Manchester, September 2007

Religion, Language and Power
An Introductory Essay

Nile Green & Mary Searle-Chatterjee

If we have understood the archaeological and textual record correctly, man has had his entire history in which to imagine deities and modes of interaction within them. But man, more precisely western man, has had only the last few centuries in which to imagine religion. That is to say, while there is a staggering amount of data, phenomena, of human experiences and expressions that might be characterised in one culture or another, by one criterion or another, as religion—*there is no data for religion*. Religion is solely the creation of the scholar's study. It is created for the scholar's analytic purposes by his imaginative acts of comparison and generalization.[1]

ORIENTATIONS

In the paragraph quoted, Jonathan Z. Smith argues that 'religion' should be seen more as a heuristic category than a social reality. But the genie of 'religion' has escaped the scholar's bottle and over the last two centuries the discourse of 'religion' has wrought major social changes not only in Europe but throughout the world. In spite of this, commentators and scholars of 'religion' are often blind to the political implications of their 'packaging' of other people's beliefs and practices through their reification of the category of 'religion'. As we show below, such inadvertent reification is part of the genealogy of Religious Studies and its marking of a distinct proprietary territory of 'religion.' The influence of positivist models of 'objective' knowledge has also contributed to scholars' neglect of the political dimensions of the raw material from which they have constructed the discourse of 'religion' in general and the totalitarian architecture of the 'World Religions' in particular. Such traditional forms of scholarship assumed that 'religious' language and texts are politically neutral rather than expressions (or claims or disguises) of relations of power.[2] 'Canonical' or 'sacred' texts were positioned as touchstones of definition, while 'key insiders'—typically literati or lay persons associated with scripturalist trends—were identified as the most appropriate sources for evaluating the meanings of texts and actions. By resorting to texts and persons (who were in fact engaged in all manner of scrambles for power), it was thought that an 'objective' description could be given of the proper constituent elements of any particular 'religion', which could then be identified by its key texts, experts, and institutions and kept distinct from the constituents of other 'religions' or their compound forms of 'Indian religions' or the 'Judeo-Christian' tradition. All such scholarly formations are intrinsically ideological, and often blatantly ahistorical to boot.

In such ways, a bridge was made between an abstract category of 'religion' and the human world of practice and belief: 'religion' could be used as a means of identifying persons, places, and societies. Linguistic realism became the order of the day, hesitant to problematise the relationship between labels and persons, signs and referents. As a result of this lack of attention to the social life of words, it has been assumed that such group labels as 'Hindu', 'Christian', or 'Muslim' can be accepted at face value, as simple referents to existing social groups rather than as performative or transformative categories used for particular purposes, as labels capable even of bringing into being groups to which they claim only to refer. Written or oral texts were thus seen as 'sources', passive media that shed light on the inner world of 'belief' or the outer world of 'events', ignoring the agency and power of such texts to make 'moves' in the world, and so to reshape it.[3]

With its ancestry in the missionary, mercantile, and colonising projects by which Europe gained its knowledge of the wider world, Religious Studies has in such ways served to amplify voices at centres of power (whether in Europe or elsewhere) that have attributed or imposed standardisation of practice and belief. During the twentieth century the most influential case of scholarly classification acting as a tool for the intellectual legitimisation for the forces of 'religious' uniformity was the model of the 'World Religions'.[4] This model implicitly assumes that religious activity and belief can be understood independently of the contexts in which they appear. Religion is taken to be a separable and definable phenomenon that has crystallised into about six distinct major faiths with specific institutions and literatures.[5] In the case of Islam, the World Religions model has led to an acute and unanticipated collusion of academic and 'reformist' Muslim discourses in that almost without exception the form of religion presented in academic primers on Islam is indistinguishable from the textualist, normative, and Arabocentric vision of Islam promoted by many Muslim reformist groups; in other words a 'Protestant' Islam.[6] Similar trends are observable in the case of other 'World Religions' such as Buddhism and Hinduism, and are partly located in the Protestant intellectual genealogy that Religious Studies shares with the administrators and commentators of the British Empire and its American heir.[7] 'Beginnings' thus always count more than 'ends'; 'scripture' has authority over practice; a 'canon' and a clear articulation of orthodoxy are to be distinguished from the jarring incoherence of the masses; 'superstition' and 'idolatry' are to be relinquished in the name of 'true religion'. Given the axiomatic orientation of this Protestant tradition towards written textuality rather than the spoken word, language (and particularly the contextual study of language use) needs to take the centre stage of any critique of its legacy, the effects of which have been magnified with the return of 'religion' to the spotlight in a new imperial age. Religious Studies specialists increasingly work in a context in which publishers, readers, and the media at large expect responses in terms of such a framework. Invitations to appear on radio or television programmes on 'religion' are often withdrawn if academics refuse to give themselves or their subjects a tidy religious label. This is an example of the consequences of a type of representational discourse that functions to deny individuality and agency.[8]

In earlier work, Manchester scholars have shown how with its conventional packaging of 'World Religions' the current discourse of 'religion' distorts understanding of South Asia in past and present.[9] The reified images of 'Hinduism' and 'Islam' in standard textbooks bear little relation to practice and cognition on the ground, which defy the neat and discrete criteria of the World Religions model. The intellectual collaboration on which *Religion, Language and Power* is based extends these insights beyond the Indian subcontinent in order to explore the workings of religious language and labelling in Europe, China, and the Middle East. Here the contributors to this collection reflect a growing awareness among other scholars that whether in Western Asia or Eastern Europe the supposed social and intellectual frontiers of 'religions' have often been invisible to those we might too easily label with the distinct categories of Muslim, Jewish, and Christian.[10] From India to the Balkans and Israel/Palestine, in the twentieth century the concept of religion as a means of social categorisation had radical consequences on social practice in a manner comparable to the model of the linguistic nation in the previous century. 'Religion' has functioned as an ideological 'move', a word in action rather than a neutral hermeneutic category. In this volume our aim is to show that an apolitical approach to the language of 'religious' texts is unsatisfactory, since it misses the very trick that the discourse of 'religion' pulls. Our contributors are mainly historians and linguists who work in the field of Religious Studies and in this volume they explore the power that lies within and around 'religious' language. The instances of language use that are examined in *Religion, Language and Power* are drawn from a wide range of places and languages, from India and Iran to America and China, from Sanskrit and Persian to English and Chinese. These examples are examined in order to assess the global consequences of understanding—and misunderstanding—political practices and social identities wrought through the language of 'religion'.

ON RELIGION, LANGUAGE AND POWER

In Roman Latin, the word *religio* did not generally apply to an imagined hypostasised entity, or to an inner realm of 'belief', but was used relationally to refer to respect for the ordered public world of established tradition.

Religio was thus contrasted with the private and selfish world of *supersti-tio*; it was not contrasted with the 'secular' as it is today.[11] At first, 'Christianity' was not seen by Romans as falling into the domain of *religio*, nor did Christians and Jews consider themselves to belong to *religiones*. But by the third and fourth centuries of the Christian era, Christians had succeeded in redefining *religio* to emphasise belief and exclusivity.[12] Yet after the fall of the Roman Empire in the west, *religio* and its cognates were little used for nearly a thousand years. The 'religious' were only those of unusual piety, such as monks. 'Religion/religions' only began to develop its current meaning in the early modern era, slowly expanding its remit to become a means of classifying communities, societies, and more recently whole 'civilisations'.[13]

Wilfred Cantwell Smith argued that until modern times, no language contained the idea that the whole world can be divided up into neatly labelled, clearly separable, and countable 'religions' or 'sects'. He considered that Arabic is a partial exception to this, in that the word *din* has long been used along with *nizam* to indicate some kind of system.[14] During the 'Abbasid period (750–1258), Arabic scholarship evolved a system for the categorisation of 'sects' (*firaq*) and 'religious' communities (*madhhab, milla*) to make sense of the diversity of intellectual and social practice that they encountered through the expansion of 'Abbasid military and commercial power across much of Asia.[15] Ranging between plain curiosity and a polemical will to power, such scholarship included the *Book of India* of al-Biruni (d. 1048) and the great heresiographical compendium of al-Shahrastani (d. 1153). 'Islam' may then be said to be something of a special case in developing a label for itself from within because it emerged in a context of encounter with other traditions in a range of commercial, scholarly, and military settings.[16] Certainly, Islamic legal categories constituted communities in what might be regarded as a 'religious' framework, so that such complex multicultural polities as the Ottoman empire could administer their different peoples under the framework of the 'religious' community or *milla*. But insofar as access to this legal status was dependent on any group being recognised as a 'people of the book' (*ahl al-kitab*), it is the nexus of power and written language rather than 'religion' per se that offers a more helpful mode of understanding this process of categorisation. After all, even the animist groups with whom Muslims came into contact in Inner Asia and Africa would usually be regarded by modern commentators as having a 'religion'. But unlike Jews and Christians (and the Zoroastrians and Hindus at times accepted as *ahl al-kitab*), what such groups did not possess was a *book*. Recognition as a legitimate 'religion' was in this way incumbent on access to written language, since in the legal framework of Shari'a at least, groups received the protection of law through demonstrable possession of a prophetic book. For the *ahl al-kitab*, 'religion' was thus a corollary of writing that in turn lent the prestige of recognition and protection by the legal apparatus of the state.[17] At a comparative level, what is therefore clear is the centrality of written language to the legitimacy of recognition. This emphasis on what we might term the paper credentials of religiosity was one that Muslim scholars shared with their Christian counterparts in an echo of the historical interconnections of Christian and Islamic knowledge systems, a common culture of paper and pen that would render the scholarly *'ulama* class the natural informants for early Orientalists searching for the key constituents of the Islamic 'religion'. Whether in the 'Abbasid or Roman spheres, intellectuals in other world empires formulated their own responses to the encounter with difference, each response stamped with the imprint of power and—as stylus, pen, and eventually print technologies developed—of writing.[18]

Building on Foucault's specific use of the term, in *Religion, Language and Power* we treat the language of 'religion' as discourse, that is, as a range of social practices and investigations, in talk and writing, that bring into being new ways of classifying and linking experiences and people, so creating new versions of 'reality' that in turn produce specific social and political effects.[19] Talal Asad has done more than anyone to show that the language of religion is such a discourse. As early as 1993, Asad charted the genealogy of the English term 'religion', pointing out that current understandings of it emerged in polemical and political contexts of social and intellectual change in early modern Europe.[20] He argued that this usage was part of a new discourse that functioned to isolate and capture a discrete domain—newly classified as 'religion'—that made it easier for commerce to break free from traditional moral values and hence to evolve into capitalism. The appeal of the new idea for those who were consciously pious, or aligned to the ecclesiastical system, was that it promised a demarcated and protected zone of 'religious' belief and practice, safe from the predations of scientists, atheists, and governments. The development of the discourse of religion in early modern and Enlightenment Europe was less a hermeneutic extrapolation from the experience of the world than an attempt to re-think and re-order society, in effect relativising the truth-claims of the Catholic and Protestant churches in an attempt to separate political agency from a clerical class that based its authority on claims of divine sanction. Ultimately, this notion evolved into ideas of 'religious freedom', based on the implicit assumption that the state did not interfere with religion because religion did not interfere with the state, since 'true religion' was by definition nonpolitical.[21] In this way, a sphere of 'politics'—of executive social agency—could be kept free of ecclesiastical influence, in time replacing the old conceptual alliance of the pope and emperor with 'rational' polities based on a new triumvirate of science, commerce, and suffrage.

Debate continues about the precise timing and combination of factors that led to the emergence of this new discourse and its connection with the reification of 'religions'. Some authors push it back as far as the thirteenth century, though comparisons are complex since the word 'religion' has been used in several different ways with different frequencies since its earliest usage.[22] It may be argued that the efforts of scientists in the eighteenth century to classify plants and animals into genus and species influenced thinking in the human sciences, so that once 'Religion' was conceived as a separate phenomenon it was natural to classify 'religions' in the plural in the manner of subspecies. From the seventeenth century, the new plurality of 'religions' was strengthened in Britain by the efforts of Dissenters to gain recognition and toleration of their beliefs, a pluralisation that was in turn hastened on the European mainland by revulsion to the 'wars of religion'.[23] An ever further list of other 'religions' was then gradually generated from the interaction of this European notion with communities and practices encountered in the wider world through commercial and imperial expansion.

In more recent work on the development of the plural category of 'religions', Asad placed greater emphasis on this role of increased encounters with a wider range of peoples with different beliefs and customs that came about through colonialism and the growth of trade.[24] Since the early modern period, European and then American power has led to the diffusion of these categories among peoples speaking other languages, so that the discourse of 'religion' can no longer be regarded as an alien intrusion but rather as a transformative concept adapted to a wide variety of settings. Even when such an originally alien term is embraced rather than imposed, the effects may be similar. Given the textualist paradigms of knowledge common to all Europe's pioneering Orientalists from the Jesuit travellers to India, Japan, and the Americas onwards, their selection of local informants showed a strong bias towards those whom they considered as exponents of the 'scriptures', working on the assumption that, among the 'higher races' at least, the norms of canon and textuality were universal.[25] The collaboration of European scholars with their native informants in other parts of the world—the forgotten lamas, pandits, and mullahs at the dawn of Religious Studies—gave authority to distinct social groups in Asia.[26] In a range of colonial societies the work of such empowered collaborating groups in turn contributed to the process of 'packaging' or reification that would become a truly global discourse on religion. The religious reform movements that swept across colonial India and Ceylon are perhaps the most vivid example of this, as an Anglophone Asian middle class sought to re-envisage Indian cultural and political practice in accordance with the precepts of the new discourse of 'religion'.[27] Similar processes were seen in such regions as China and the Middle East, as Francesca Tarocco and Andreas Christmann show in this volume. In their global reach, such processes are connected to the expansion of what the historian Christopher Bayly has termed 'imperial religions', the large-scale formations of modernity that promoted printed scriptures and new programmes of the 'uniformity' of body and mind.[28]

Talal Asad's work on the discourse of religion in the English language has been continued in debates generated by Richard King's study of the modern contexts in which the English category of 'mysticism' emerged and of its implications for the 'packaging' of 'Buddhism' and 'Hinduism'.[29] King showed that when we speak of 'religion' as if it were a distinct entity or realm we are being directed to put aside considerations of context and politics, of the state and the individual, with the latter ultimately ceasing to have any capacity for independent reason or agency. Religion rules persons rather than vice-versa and becomes an agent of irrational behaviour based on literal or 'fundamentalist' readings of scripture. The legacy of these colonial definitions was the location of 'bad religion' in the East (and reasonable religion in 'the West', a term that has survived the demise of its antonym), which continues to legitimise a range of colonial projects today. When Tony Blair was widely reported to be reading the Quran in order to understand Middle Eastern politics in the wake of September 11th 2001, his actions represented the culmination of this formulation of 'orientals' as driven by religion, and of religion in turn as driven by scripture. If such formulations are to be given such credence at governmental levels, then it is all the more important that scholars examine the nature of the power with which such 'scriptural' texts are credited. The recent expansion of 'religion' into the realm of foreign policy highlights the need for the kind of critical approach towards the discourse of religion that is adopted by the contributors to this volume and the importance of their essays in exploring alternative discursive formations across a range of linguistic settings.

By sidestepping the presuppositions of a 'religions' discourse to highlight the roles of discursive power, it is possible to approach the conceptions of groups that did not succeed in securing ideological dominance. While it is important to study the work of literati (partly because of the power of the elites that patronise or constitute them), over-reliance on written texts can obscure the discursive strategies and alternative forms of group-labelling used by subordinate groups that have been unable to control public representations. A hermeneutics of suspicion is therefore a guiding principle for several of our contributors, who follow the lead of the Subaltern Studies collective of historians of India in reading their chosen texts 'against the grain' as well as in seeking out lesser-known material. Although it is always more difficult to ascertain the views of dominated groups of any kind, it is also possible to approach 'subaltern' life-worlds by ethnographic research and the use of the oral medium of the interview.[30]

Dominant groups that are successful in attributing labels to others adopt a strategy that may facilitate action on the part of their supporters or passivity in the face of injustice. One of the goals of this volume is to differentiate between such different types of discursive strategy and to relate these to the differing social locations of the groups in question. Postcolonial criticism has sought to take apart the hegemony of colonial power, and as a result initially showed little interest in the discursive strategies of dominated 'underdogs', whether interpreted as colonised 'nations', doubly subordinate groups from within such nations, or marginal voices from the earlier, typically written, historical record. The work of the Subaltern

Studies historians has done much to redress this, as has Homi Bhabha with his account of the mimicry of comprador elites.[31] But in the field of Religious Studies, less interest has traditionally been shown in nondominant groups, partly due to Religious Studies' traditional concern with writings seen as 'canonical' and so thought to embody the key principles of the 'World Religions'. In recent decades this has changed with the recognition that normative and dominant discourses are themselves shaped through the dialogical encounter with their rivals, whose histories are suppressed and concealed in the lost contexts of such textual utterances.

It is important now to define our understanding of power, and its relationship to language.[32] Our basic conception of power is an inclusive one, as the ability to influence the bodies and minds of other men and women, typically by means of superior access to physical, cultural, or human resources. Power shows itself in various ways as explored in such concepts as Marx's 'means of production', Gramsci's 'hegemony', Bourdieu's 'cultural capital', Foucault's 'episteme', and the colonial cultural complexes described by Fanon and Said.[33] In line with the approach of our contributors, we suggest that power must always be understood relationally in the struggles between individuals for the assets of their environment. Power in this sense is always expressed in different degrees and must ultimately be measured in terms of how many minds and bodies can be swayed. The institutions of modernity (particularly the modern state and its apparatus of prisons, laws, bureaucracies, schools, academies, etc) thus afford a particularly efficient means of monopolising power. It is the co-emergence of modernity with European colonialism that has led scholars to be so concerned with questions of power in a whole range of colonial societies. But while lacking the hegemonic potential of the modern state, premodern and early modern formations of power have received less attention from scholars, particularly with regard to the extra-European world. For this reason, the essays in this volume pay attention to the relationship between religion, language, and power in pre- and early modern as well as fully modern settings.

Building on the work of Foucault and Said, we distinguish between the power-*within*-language and the power-*behind*-language. For power does not only surround communication acts, standing behind it as an *éminence grise*, but also infiltrates language to enter within communication itself. As Pierre Bourdieu explained, in spite of appearances the languages we use to communicate with one another are far from 'natural' or 'transparent' media of communication, and different languages form specific political contexts of their own. In order to extrapolate the relationship we posit between power within and power behind language, Bourdieu takes us a step further:

> It is necessary to distinguish between the capital necessary for the simple production of more or less legitimate ordinary speech, on the one hand, and the capital of instruments of expression . . . which is needed

to produce a written discourse worthy of being published, that is to say, made official, on the other. This production of instruments of production, such as rhetorical devices, genres, legitimate styles and manners, and more generally, all the formations destined to be 'authoritative' and to be cited as examples of 'good usage', confers on those who engage in it a power over language and thereby over the ordinary users of language, as well as over their capital.[34]

In exploring the triangulation of religion, language, and power we therefore need to be aware of the contiguous flow of power-behind-language and power-within-language. Power-within-language might at first suggest an analysis of the criteria of rhetoric that traditionally formed the foundations of literary appreciation, from the poetics of Aristotle right through to the modernist New Criticism of I. A. Richards. Such *ars rhetorica* certainly can conjure an ethereal form of power capable of influencing the thoughts and deeds of the listener; early Arab literary critics thus spoke of the 'sorcery' (*sihr*) of poetic language.[35] But despite their value, we do not wish here to foreground such approaches. Instead, our approach resembles Quentin Skinner's idea of linguistic action as a way of 'doing things'.[36] Rhetoric in this sense serves not merely as the decoration of a text but as the modality through which texts are able to make 'moves', both in the strategic sense of playing against other voices of argument and in the physical sense of provoking action in the world. Rhetoric can therefore be seen as a form of action through which language—whether in terms of an oral or written speech act—finds its connection to the world. In this way, power-within-language is able to work outwards into its contexts.

Through this model we are able to see the two-way movements of power, both out of contexts into texts and out of texts into their contexts. This recognition of the historical agency of writing helps steer the insights of critical theory in directions that are workable for both social scientists and historians. At the same time, such recognition of the formative agency of language helps break down the sterile dichotomy of texts and practices in order to recognise their interdependence. Insofar as we assume that whatever power any discourse possesses derives from and is directed towards the social world of human life, power-within-language must ultimately always derive from the same human sources as power-behind-language. Despite their common frame of reference in the human world, the distinction between these two guises of power as 'within' and 'behind' language seems worth making, in that it enables us to sufficiently estrange ourselves from our familiar linguistic media (whether English, Hebrew, or Chinese) so as to recognise the political genealogy that inevitably lies behind the capacity of any language to be comprehensible to any but the smallest units of social organisation.

As Bourdieu suggests, the most important aspect of power-within-language is often the choice of language itself. Whether learned or vernacular, there is nothing intrinsically natural about the choice of any language as a medium of communication. Even the rise of the so-called vernacular languages of Europe and Asia was facilitated by the sanction of the nation state. Any language—and above all any learned or scriptural language—that proves successful in the linguistic marketplace of rival media of communication must participate in the struggle of politics in order to be rendered legitimate.[37] A language must conquer new hands and tongues; it must see itself written and hear itself spoken; it must not be repulsed but acquiesced to. A language must be shared or else it has lost its campaign. It is therefore essential that we recognise the political preconditions behind the apparent normality of communication in any shared language. Such regulations of access and 'normalcy' are no less important with regard to languages whose use is restricted to subgroups, such as the Hebraic and Sanskritic traditions that are also discussed in this volume.

However, it is writing that allows the powers of language to work their high magic on a scale that outstrips the shorter reach of human life. In contrast to the protean qualities of life in the world, written language shows an opposing tendency towards stasis. Written language is fixed, even as its meanings are not. While people, societies, and the contexts that shape them all change, written language has the ability to remain constant, failing or refusing to keep pace with the transformations of the world around it. Engaging with texts is therefore a perilous pursuit; the stasis of writing suggests a stasis of meaning that is actually impossible.[38] Many communities of readers—especially when dealing with 'religious' texts or 'Scripture'—read in the transcendent mode, denying the temporalities in which both writing and reading are always embedded.[39] This is a propensity that is inherent to writing itself, for with the loss of its originating context any act of writing is a form of communication which encourages such transcendent responses in the reader. Since the context of writing is usually irrecoverable without extreme effort (historical, hermeneutic, archaeological), texts appear to speak out of time. And like any other attribute of divinity, such timelessness is a form of power. If speech acts or contemporary acts of writing reveal the limitations of their contexts all too easily, texts that constitute 'tradition' or 'canon' are conversely empowered by the concealment of their originating context. Through such lost contexts and transcendent readings, written communication thus bears an asymmetrical power relationship to spoken communication; simply put, written language is more powerful than spoken language.[40] This power of writing is manifested in an almost limitless range of cultural settings, from the Jewish and Sikh veneration of the physical presence of holy writ to the role of the printing press in the European Reformation and the potency of written Arabic talismans among the nonliterate peoples of the African Sahel.

This power of written language is particularly clear in texts that are considered to be authoritative through their alliance with influential subgroups within a given community, in other words these same texts of tradition and canon. Such texts may be rule-books of prescribed social practices or the templates of collective memory that we usually term as history. From a sociolinguistic perspective such texts need not necessarily be 'scripture' in the theological sense, but can include any text making claims about the nature of society that is upheld through time as a model of normative values. Hence, the 'scriptures' of different societies have ranged from the battle stories of Homer to the parables of the Gospels and the incantatory liturgies of the Zoroastrian Gathas. The formative process behind the empowerment of these documents is fundamentally social and as such external to the text itself. In contrast to power-within-language, that is, power that reaches out from a speech act into its contexts, this is power-behind-language, that is, power that seeps into a speech act from its enclosing social contexts so as to endow it with the megalithic weight of authority. In the case of such power-behind-language, there is therefore an arbitrary—even absurd—quality to the encounter between normative 'scriptural' writing and its readers, in extreme cases forcing individuals, groups, or entire societies to remodel their inner and outer lives in accordance with a text whose original formative context has long disappeared as tradition carries a text far away from the time and place of its originating context. New Jerusalems—or Ayodhyas, or Medinas, or Shangri-Las—are re-invented in attempts to make past and present time collapse through the mediation of texts. Paradoxically, through the power of such traditionally or canonically normative writings, what is present is therefore shaped by what is absent.

A subsidiary form of this process is seen in the power of different genres, usually but not exclusively of a written kind. Nurtured in response to the particular needs of specific social contexts, in any given tradition genres eventually fossilise and so standardise and structure the self-expression of subsequent communications, from sonnets, jokes, and hagiographies to telephone directories and prayers. The absent or lost context that has formed any successful genre in the global history of language thus shapes and constrains any subsequent user of the genre's depiction of the present world.

The approach of the contributors to *Religion, Language and Power* thus stands in distinction to those trends of textualism that uproot language into transcendental realms of meta-communication. What is more, this firmly contextualist approach challenges the reading and writing strategies that underlie the composition and reception of religious texts themselves, whose utterances are frequently made in a declamatory, prescriptive, or universalising register. The set of overlapping methods explored in this volume proposes a reading of texts against the grain so as to alert us to the masked ideologies behind 'religious' language. For the characteristic rhetoric that may be said to define 'religious' language can be said to be an aggrandised reflection of the political contexts of its utterance. In other words, the transcendental and universalist character of religious discourse needs to be understood as the rhetorical corollary of struggles for authority, whether conceived as obedience or truth. Yet language is no simple cipher for the actual possession of power, and its use may often reflect bids by the powerless to acquire authority. Our working sense of power is therefore a relational one that stresses the constant realignment of interpersonal and intergroup relations that creates the perpetual shuffling of power that is the daily bread of history. A common theme to several of the essays in this collection is therefore the interrogation of the claims to authority that underlie specific forms of language that are often accepted uncritically in Religious Studies, as well as of the contextual foundations that underlie those claims.

CLASSIFYING OTHERS AND NAMING THE SELF

As well as examining the role of 'religion' as a discourse, *Religion, Language and Power* also focuses on two other important aspects of language that are the naming and classifying of other groups of people (a process that often relates to the exclusion and denunciation of particular social groups) and the articulation of a language of the self. Edward Said forced his readers' attention to the contribution of Orientalist scholarship to the process of constructing the 'Oriental' as the shadowy antithesis of the European, who was imagined as more rational, disciplined and in command of his destiny, arguing that the dichotomous labels of 'Orient' and 'Occident' did more to create a sense of European identity than shed light on the people being written about.[41] Said built on the insights of structuralism, in which words, concepts, and identities are seen to be defined in relation to other components of a communicative or cultural system, as being that which is not the 'other'. Like Said, later writers in the field of postcolonial studies have focused on dichotomies in European images of the 'other', of 'the West' versus 'the Rest'.[42] Stuart Hall described 'identity formation as the marking of symbolic boundaries' that 'require what is left outside to consolidate the process.'[43] Like other postcolonial writers, we also therefore look at the naming and ranking of others, whether dichotomously or otherwise. However, in learning the lessons of postcolonial criticism, we also look at discursive practices from beyond the reach of European colonialism, examining other earlier centres of power and their own representative practices. For while the reach of the European colonial enterprise was unprecedented in its scope and its technologies of representation and knowledge, it was by no means the first formation of power to write about or mis/represent the 'others' brought into its political embrace. Issues of power are in this sense an integral part of any act of communication, and particularly of description. For these reasons, most of the essays in *Religion, Language and Power* look at the discursive strategies used as groups position themselves in relation to others through the construction of labels of group identity of a kind that English-speakers would see as 'religious' or 'religion-like'. Nonetheless, most of our contributors look at languages in which the operative discourse is not the European notion of 'religion'. Radically expanding the insights of postcolonial theory, by these means the essays show that the 'packaging' and ranking processes described by such scholars as Said and Hall have been produced in a variety of discursive settings beyond those of 'religion', 'orientalism' or modern European imperialism. Many of the texts under scrutiny in this collection voice the claim that the speaker belongs to a group that is superior, whether in terms of reasonableness, refinement, or morality. Our contributors' work in this way undermines any simple notion of an East/West dichotomy, while showing that the use of stereotyped and derogatory labelling for distancing other people is a two-way process that may be employed by those who resist power as much as by those who possess it. The 'strategic essentialism' to which Gayatri Spivak refered is in reality a process found in many different periods and social locations.[44]

Reification of one's own practices and beliefs is a constructed and strategic claim to unity and continuity. This is so because the reifier attempts to harness the power of ritual, myth, and memory to justify and bolster his or her own perceptions and interests. Such strategies are by their nature antihistorical, claiming transcendence over contingency, eternity in place of temporality. Reifying the notion of religion and defining its expressions as properly nonpolitical makes it easier for unwelcome or rival groups to be excluded and devalued, whether by governments or other gate-keepers. If the constitution of a country guarantees 'freedom of religion' or gives privileges to groups defined as 'religious' (as is the case in Britain and the United States), the people who control the definition of 'religion' and police the list of recognised 'religions' are powerful indeed. This has been previously demonstrated in Malory Nye's account of the struggle of ISKCON ('Hare Krishna') supporters to gain planning permission for the expansion of a major temple outside London, but the process may be observed in numerous other settings.[45] The allocation of badges of membership is thus a political tool and act. The definition of 'religion'—and the right to use and define 'religious' language—is more than academic pedantry; it is part of the politics of everyday life. With the recent emergence in several countries of new laws policing speech acts that incite 'terrorism', the definition, constraints, and limits of 'religious' language have come under renewed state scrutiny and control. Apolitical definitions of 'true religion' have become law, and 'religious' language the business of the state and its human and electronic informants.

It is sometimes suggested that state-empowered or other dominant groups are less likely to develop labels for themselves than for others, that their own identities are more likely to be implicit. The dominant 'self' may even be regarded as the transcendent viewer of 'others' and, hence, as not requiring explicit labelling or definition at all. In this vein, Richard Dyer argued that while 'whites' defined others, they rarely saw any need to define themselves.[46] Several of our contributors similarly suggest that reification of others rather than of the self may indeed be more common among dominant or elite groups (including the learned or literate), as Said also implied. Such attempts to claim the implicit and unmarked 'norm'— whether conceived in terms of middle ground, 'reason', or otherwise— form a standard process of the articulation of orthodoxy. Self-labelling may then be carried out with less rigidity. Yet outside the categorising realm of language, life is fluid and individuals foreground different elements of their own identities and self-labels according to context. Humans are continually engaged in creatively reinterpreting the worlds they experience as they re-ally themselves with different collections of people in the process of constructing what Stuart Hall preferred to call identifications rather than identities, so emphasising the dynamic nature of the constant and dialogical shifting of identity.[47]

Many postcolonial writers have been influenced by the structuralist emphasis on binary classification classically espoused by Lévi-Strauss and have as a result focused on the particular and stark dichotomies of colonial thinking about social identities. However, the interactive construction of 'others' and 'selves' may be more complex than this and not just the result of fixed and simple dichotomies between a uniform self and its other. Such binary approaches to the labelling of 'others' and the analysis of texts have been over-emphasised, since they do little to explain how discursive change of the kind described by several contributors to this volume may occur. Said's dualistic emphasis on the role of 'others' in defining the self was somewhat at odds with Foucault's notion that the power in a discourse is always diffused (however unequally) and constantly in struggle with other forms. Irene Gedalof also criticised binary approaches in her discussion of Indian and Western feminisms, and pointed out that identities are neither singular nor multiple since they are intimately linked in ever-changing ways.[48]

The interactionist approach adopted by the contributors to *Religion, Language and Power* enables us to avoid the trap of seeing the cognitive structures of labelling as static patterns of contrastive relations unaffected by changes in political context. The creative development of a new intermediate label may enable a rival group to redefine the field of debate (and perhaps even develop a new discourse) and so facilitate change, since the use of labels can only be understood in terms of narratives and not only in terms of sets of categories. Labels are therefore signs that take their meaning from a wider body of discourse or 'grand narrative' (such as modernity, progress, or 'true religion'). New wholes may also be created by selecting an element of an opponent's symbolic narrative and recombining it to work against them. To use the jargon of Durham and Fernandez, liberating potential thus lies in the use of metonymy to enable diachrony.[49]

THE MANCHESTER APPROACH: TEN ESSAYS

The first three essays in *Religion, Language and Power* examine some of the different ways in which the discourse of religion has been exported from Europe to the wider world. Given the contemporary importance of our topic, the opening essay by John Zavos deconstructs the current global discourse of 'religion' as echoed in the World Parliament of Religions. Drawing on the work of Asad and King, Zavos catches contemporary 'religion' in the making, exploring the political implications of the English-language discourse of religion in the context of concerns about terrorism at the World Parliament of Religions held in Barcelona in 2004 shortly after the Madrid train bombings. The essay analyses English-language use at the 'parliament' to unearth the ways in which an agreed—and substantively American—language of religious legitimacy is used in an attempt to police 'true religion' at a global level. Zavos examines the strategies used at the 'parliament' to address the issues of 'fundamentalism' and 'extremism', arguing that these strategies are indicative of broader developments in the ways that the relationship between 'religion' and political violence is conceptualised. By conceiving 'religion' as a discourse, Zavos then argues that we can see the 'parliamentary' debating processes as social technologies—'technologies of faith'—which serve to instantiate religion as a discrete yet integral feature of modern society, characterised by a celebration of difference, but in fact underpinned by an established agenda about what constitutes 'religion'.

In the second essay, Francesca Tarocco turns to China to look at how a new generic term for 'religion' or *zongjiao* emerged through a process of cross-cultural translation, borrowing, and accommodation between China and Europe. Rhetorical 'labelling' and self-representation in a 'religious' context became especially relevant in the late nineteenth and early twentieth century, a time of great political unrest but also of heightened intercultural exchange between the Chinese of the metropolitan and semi-colonial areas and Christian missionaries and European merchants and revolutionaries. Here the term 'translation' is used both in the conventional sense and in the extended sense suggested by Tony Stewart's study of lexical and metaphoric borrowing in the context of 'religious' encounters, which argues that when a translation is successful the new term carries another conceptual world as part of its semantic baggage. However, Tarocco's essay also reveals the political power that lies hidden behind the category of *zongjiao*, for whatever is not regarded as properly a part of *zongjiao* cannot be 'true religion'. It can only instead be 'superstition' (*mixin*), which the Chinese state is committed to suppressing all forms of.

In the next essay, Andreas Christmann looks at the interaction between the European discourse of 'mysticism', its use to define 'Sufism' or *tasawwuf* and the responding attempts of Muslim scholars to recapture the discourse of *tasawwuf* in postcolonial Egypt. Christmann examines a body of literature that emerged in early twentieth-century Egypt among Arab academics seeking to challenge models of 'Islamic mysticism' developed by European Orientalists. In so doing, Egyptian scholars invented the neologism *al-tasawwuf al-islami* or 'Islamic Sufism' in explicit contradistinction to the model of universalist mysticism promoted by Western scholars from the late nineteenth century onwards. Rather than labelling the literature of 'Islamic Sufism' as atavistic, apologetic, or essentialist, Christmann's essay places it into the context of postcolonial Egyptian society and explains it as an attempt to control a revival of 'religion' in the Middle East during a time of the increasing pluralisation of neo-Islamic groups and revivalist movements. Along the way, the essay surveys the evolution of the discourse of 'mysticism' and of Sufism as 'Islamic mysticism' in Europe and North America as a necessary preamble to understanding the Arabic literature of 'Islamic Sufism' that responded to it. Finally, Christmann positions his discussion in the larger general debate on Egypt's Islamic revival.

The next section sees a shift of historical focus to analyse the language of power and 'religion' in a number of pre- and early modern settings. In the first of four essays dealing with the labelling of the religious other, Philip Alexander analyses the emergence of a 'vocabulary of orthodoxy' in Hebrew, and the attempt to use that vocabulary to establish the spiritual hegemony of the Rabbinical movement. The essay shows that though dominant (if only precariously) among Jews by 70 CE, Rabbinic discourse was nonetheless weak in self-designations and Alexander suggests that this might have been because the Rabbinical movement was attempting to lay claim to the middle ground of debate. The essay also compares two other groups within early Jewish society and makes suggestions about the way language is used to assert, establish, and subvert power. After looking at these other early Jewish groups, the Descenders to the Chariot and the Dead Sea Community, Alexander reflects on the possibility of generalising about the relationship between power and language within religious traditions. He argues that groups that are making a bid for power by using persuasion adopt transparent labels, while the marginalised or powerless adopt opaque labels as a protective device. Alexander suggests that there are scales of vilificatory labelling, such that vilification often (though not always) declines as groups become more politically secure.

In the following essay, Jacqueline Suthren Hirst shows that while in different eras the actual persons conceived as an 'opponent other' in Sanskrit writings changed dramatically, these different people were nonetheless referred to by the same terms. A focus on the power-within-language and a refusal to take for granted the categories of the current discourse of the 'World Religions' enables Suthren Hirst to show how competition for students and prestige influenced the way the Indian Advaitin philosopher Shankara (*fl.* c. 700 CE) drew the boundaries between Vedic-inspired and non-Vedic schools. Those schools to which Shankara attributed the respectability and prestige of being labelled as 'Vedic' did not necessarily have their roots in the 'canonical' texts of the Veda. Moreover, Shankara's list also diverged from that which would later become accepted in the 'World Religions' model. Because Shankara's boundaries were differently drawn, Buddhist groups and ideas were central to the Sanskritic world of discourse in which his school negotiated its position, while groups that would now be called 'Hindu' were pushed out of the Vedic fold. Suthren Hirst also makes use of the important distinction between 'ignored others' and 'opponent others' to show how a particular discursive sphere in Sanskrit literary culture could treat some groups (or topics) as beyond the bounds of debate. The silences in texts can therefore be no less revealing than the written word.

Continuing this exploration of the language of antagonism, Alan Williams begins his study of how polemical Zoroastrian writings in the Middle Persian or Pahlavi language insulted non-Zoroastrian 'others' by attacking the notion of 'sacred language' that scholars of religion so often fall back on through an uncritical reflex. Williams considers religious language as if on two axes. At one extreme of this language scale is 'sacred language' and 'high' (or divine) speech, together with all the claims made about such language by religious traditions. At the other extreme is 'low' speech, comprising execration, insults, and calumny, and in particular the names 'religious' groups call one another. By recourse to a discussion of the dualistic Zoroastrian scheme of thought and language, Williams argues that understanding the constructed and contextually ramified nature of religious 'unsacred language'—in particular that of insults and hostile speech—enables us to see 'religious' language as a continuum of a constructed and contextually ramified discourse. This expands our notion of 'sacred language' by disclosing the ideological power invested in and unleashed by such language across its entire spectrum from high use to low abuse.

This theme of abuse in also taken up in Jeremy Gregory's essay on English language use among early modern Anglicans. Gregory explores the ways in which the Anglican Church represented both itself and its rival Christian denominations as part of its efforts to maintain its dominant position in English society and its attempts to gain power across the Atlantic in colonial America. In particular, Gregory examines how the Church portrayed and labelled its Christian competitors as 'enthusiasts' by the use of stock descriptions in the public sphere, primarily through the medium of print culture such as sermons, tracts, and pamphlets. The essay describes how John Wesley attempted to escape the constraints of the dominant polarity of labels in his day by developing a new term, 'zeal'. But how quickly can such changes of labels be adopted? Gregory observes that the linguistic armoury deployed in the language of the 'other' remained remarkably constant in eighteenth-century England, even though the actual social target shifted. Hurling insults was thus a kind of transferable skill.

The final three essays in *Religion, Language and Power* turn the focus away from the labelling of the 'other' to explore the evolution of a vocabulary for the self. Todd Klutz turns our attention towards the core of the issue by exploring the emergence of the earliest surviving recorded use of the label *Christianos* (Christian). Although originally a Greek term, this first appears in Christian writing of the early decades of our Era. The term *Christianismos* (Christianity) only came later. The terms are often understood to be semantically homogeneous and lacking in significant variation. Klutz argues against this, by applying select concepts borrowed from systemic linguistics and Bakhtinian discourse analysis to demonstrate that the meaning of *christianos* in texts from the first two centuries of the Common Era was far more polyvalent and unstable than is normally suggested. Linguistic criticism of the key passages in the Acts of the Apostles is employed to shed light not only on the social groups by which the earliest Christians comprised a form of anti-society, but also on the neglected differences—and lost contexts—in which the Acts of the Apostles and was composed.

In the next essay in this section, Mary Searle-Chatterjee examines the term 'Hindu' in Hindi usage in modern India. She presents a case where although the language of self-labelling has changed, the defining and opponent 'other' has not. For Dalits—the 'lowest' castes in India—the key 'others' have remained the 'high' castes, even though the labels used for them have sometimes been reversed. She shows that in North India usage of the term 'Hindu' cannot be understood without a caste/class perspective, nor without an awareness of the discursive power of the colonial state. She argues that both the denotation and connotation of the word 'Hindu' vary according to caste, while language use changes dialogically as status groups develop new labelling strategies and representations of 'others' as part of their struggle to gain recognition for feelings of self-worth or even superiority. The conventional Euro-American use of the label 'Hindu' does not correspond exactly to any of these Indian meanings on the ground, though it is notably closer to the use of the term by powerful 'higher' castes. Finally, Searle-Chatterjee asks whether there is any kind of cultural commonality underpinning the struggle for control of the word 'Hindu' in contemporary India.

In the final essay, Nile Green explores the dialogical foundation of a 'religious' language for the self as a two-way process. On the one hand, the adoption of common idioms and genres has made the histories of certain groups conform to the norms of others. On the other hand, this shared language serves to undermine hegemony by disguising local social systems or cultural practices in the respectable idioms and genres of the powerful. Green argues that Sufism (*tasawwuf*) may be understood as such a powerful and respectable discourse, comprising a lexicon of Arabic terminology whose common usage served to disguise (and thence either dignify or preserve) what were often heterogeneous cultural practices. Building on the role of this 'Sufi lexicon', he then explores the related role of prestigious and transregional literary genres in the same process. Through case studies of the self-histories written by Afghans and Kurds in Persian rather than in their own Pashto and Kurdish languages, he argues that the depiction of Kurdish and Afghan life was distorted by the gravitational pull of the past as tradition preserved in norms of language, idiom and genre associated with the politically and culturally dominant groups among whom Afghans and Kurds lived in India and Iran.

While taking the work of Asad and King on the English discourse of religion as a starting point, most of the contributors to *Religion, Language and Power* move away from English to look at discourses in other languages that are all too easily taken to refer to the same semantic field ('religion'). These other linguistic modes of knowing the world have been marginalised through the intellectual hegemony of the English language and its own locations of power. Our purpose in this volume is not therefore to 'translate' the English discourse of religion, but to further unsettle it from its zenith and so ultimately relativise it. Timothy Fitzgerald has already attempted to do something similar, using material from India and Japan to argue that because the English word 'religion' is irredeemably constrained by its Christian theological origins, it is a hindrance to analysis, whether of English-speaking cultures or of others.[50] Fitzgerald attempted to solve the problem by proposing a shift to terms such as 'symbol' and 'culture', which he argued are less linguistically parochial and ideologically loaded. But such open-ended terms seem to get us no further than 'religion' does and many of our contributors are unsatisfied with Fitzgerald's approach. The essays collected here therefore aim to bring the contextual study of language to centre stage, by suggesting that power is expressed most effectively through the conscious and ostensibly logical order that language projects onto the world.

Our project, then, contains echoes of postcolonial studies, in that it aims to provincialise European categories of analysis. But the essays are also intended to allow readers to look beyond the usual remit of postcolonial scholarship, which in its emphasis on the English language and modern European imperialism has a self-contradictory tendency towards parochialism in its own right. In order to provincialise current Euro-American assumptions—even fashionably 'postcolonial' ones—a comparative approach is therefore essential, and we hope that the essays in *Religion, Language and Power* provide this by looking at language usage in many parts of the world at many periods. Each chapter examines snapshots of the words used by particular groups at specific moments in talking about and labelling what current English usage would conceptualise as 'religious' groups. In this sense while the contemporary English concept of 'religion' lingers on as an implicit organising category, we do not assume that it is an organising category for the people we write about, who might not recognise such categories as cultural, linguistic, legal, ethnic, and religious in the way that English-speakers do today. In these ways, the ten chapters collected here provide the historical contexts of a range of different discourses and systems of classifying groups in various languages. As such, *Religion,*

Language and Power is part of a larger de-reifying moment—or even move-ment—that aims to weaken the purchase of the dominant discourse of 'reli-gion' by which we are increasingly constrained.

NOTES

1. J. Z. Smith, *Imagining Religion: From Babylon to Jonestown* (Chicago: University of Chicago Press, 1982), p. ix. We are grateful to Alan Williams for bringing this work to our attention.
2. N. Smart, *The Phenomenon of Religion* (London: Macmillan, 1973). See also the critiques of this approach in G. Flood, *Beyond Phenomenology: Rethinking the Study of Religion* (London: Cassell, 1999); R. McCutcheon, *Manufacturing Religion: The Discourse of Sui Generis Religion and the Politics of Nostalgia* (Oxford: Oxford University Press, 1997).
3. K. Palonen, *Quentin Skinner: History, Politics, Rhetoric* (Cambridge: Polity, 2003). On a similar approach to South Asian textual practices, see R. Inden, "Introduction: From Philological to Dialogical Texts", in R. Inden, J. Walters, & D. Ali (eds.), *Querying the Medieval: Texts and the History of Practices in South Asia* (Oxford: Oxford University Press, 2000), pp. 3–28.
4. T. Masuzawa, *The Invention of World Religions, or, How European Universalism was Preserved in the Language of Pluralism* (Chicago: University of Chicago Press, 2005).
5. T. Fitzgerald, "Hinduism and the World Religions Fallacy", *Religion* 20 (1990), pp. 101–108.
6. For a critical assessment of the validity of this term, see R. Loimeier, "Is There Something like 'Protestant Islam'?", *Die Welt des Islams* 45, 2 (2005), pp. 216–254.
7. W. Sweetman, "'Hinduism' and the History of 'Religion': Protestant Presuppositions in the Critique of the Concept of Hinduism", *Method and Theory in the Study of Religion* 15 (2003), pp. 329–353. For the Protestant influence on Buddhist reform, the foundational study is G. Obeyesekere, "Religious Symbolism and Political Change in Ceylon", *Modern Ceylon Studies* 1, 1 (1970), pp. 43–63.
8. R. O'Hanlon, "Recovering the Subject: *Subaltern Studies* and Histories of Resistance in Colonial South Asia", *Modern Asian Studies* 22, 1 (1988), pp. 189–224; E. W. Said, *Covering Islam: How the Media and the Experts Determine How We See the Rest of the World* (London: Routledge & Kegan Paul, 1981).
9. R. Ballard, "Panth, Kismet, Dharm te Qaum: Four Dimensions of Punjabi Religion", in P. Singh (ed.), *Punjabi Identity in a Global Context* (Delhi, India: Oxford University Press, 1996), pp. 7–37; N. S. Green, "Oral Competition Narratives of Muslim and Hindu Saints in the Deccan", *Asian Folklore Studies* 63, 2 (2004), pp. 221–242; M. Searle-Chatterjee, "Religious Division and the Mythology of the Past" in R. Bradley & C. Humes (eds.), *Living Banaras: Hindu Religion in Cultural Context* (Albany: State University of New York Press, 1993), pp.145–158; and particularly J. Suthren-Hirst & J. Zavos, *Teaching Across South Asian Religious Traditions*, Special Edition of *Contemporary South Asia* 14, 1 (2005).
10. See e.g., D. Eickelman, *The Middle-East: An Anthropological Approach* (London: Prentice Hall, 1981); J. W. Meri, *The Cult of Saints Among Muslims and Jews in Medieval Syria* (Oxford: Oxford University Press, 2002); H. T. Norris, *Popular Sufism in Eastern Europe: Sufi Brotherhoods and the Dialogue with Christianity and 'Heterodoxy'* (London: Routledge, 2007).

11. On the connection of religion and *religio*, see B. Saler, "*Religio* and the Definition of Religion", *Cultural Anthropology* 2, 3 (1987), pp. 395–399. For an analysis of the roles of language and empire in understanding the Asian religious cults of the Roman Empire, see J. L. Lightfoot, *Lucian: On the Syrian Goddess* (Oxford: Oxford University Press, 2003).

12. K. Cooper, "'Religio' and a Relational Approach to Latin Christianity" (unpublished paper, 2005); R. King, *Orientalism and Religion: Postcolonial Theory, India and the Mystic East* (London: Routledge, 1999), pp. 35–38.

13. We refer of course to S. P. Huntington, *The Clash of Civilizations and the Remaking of World Order* (New York: Simon & Schuster, 1996).

14. W. Cantwell Smith, *The Meaning and End of Religion* (Minneapolis, MN: Fortress, 1962), p. 80. While Cantwell Smith's pioneering work in deconstructing the terms 'religion/religions' has been enormously valuable and influential, it neglected the role of power.

15. For an overview, see J. Waardenburg, *Muslims and Others: Relations in Context* (Berlin: de Gruyter, 2003), Chapters 3 to 8.

16. See also C. W. Ernst, "Islam as Religion", in C. W. Ernst, *Following Muhammad: Rethinking Islam in the Contemporary World* (Chapel Hill: University of North Carolina Press, 2003).

17. The revisionist historians Patricia Crone and Michael Cook even argued that the Quran was itself a late Arab imitation of the hallowed 'book' of the Christian Byzantine Empire, created during the 'Umayyad era to place Arabs on a level civilisational status with Greek-speaking Christians. See P. Crone & M. Cook, *Hagarism: The Making of the Islamic World* (Cambridge: Cambridge University Press, 1977).

18. J. Bloom, *Paper Before Print: The History and Impact of Paper in the Islamic World* (New Haven, CT: Yale University Press, 2001); A. Gaur, *Literacy and the Politics of Writing* (Bristol: Intellect, 2000); R. Finnegan, *Literacy and Orality: Studies in the Technology of Communication* (Oxford: Basil Blackwell, 1988).

19. M. Foucault, *The Archaeology of Knowledge and the Discourse on Language* (New York: Pantheon, 1972). Discourses in the Foucauldian sense determine what things can be said, and heard, and thus do a particular kind of cultural work in shaping thinking and producing effects that are a source of opportunity for some groups.

20. T. Asad, *Genealogies of Religion: Discipline and Reasons of Power in Christianity and Islam* (Baltimore: Johns Hopkins University Press, 1993).

21. G. Ward, *True Religion* (Oxford: Blackwell, 2003).

22. See references in W. Sweetman, *Mapping Hinduism: 'Hinduism' and the Study of Indian Religions, 1600–1776* (Halle, Germany: Franckesche Stiftungen, 2003).

23. K. Cameron, M. Greengrass, & P. Roberts (eds.), *The Adventure of Religious Pluralism in Early Modern France* (Oxford: Lang, 2000).

24. T. Asad, *Formations of the Secular: Christianity, Islam, Modernity* (Stanford, CA: Stanford University Press, 2003), p. 35.

25. For different approaches to canon, see P. R. Davies, "The Dimensions of Canon", in P. R. Davies, *Scribes and Schools: The Canonization of the Hebrew Scriptures* (London: SPCK, 1998); L. Patton, "Afterword", in L. L. Patton (ed.), *Authority, Anxiety and Canon: Essays in Vedic Interpretation* (Albany: State University of New York Press, 1994), pp. 309–316.

26. C.A. Bayly, *Empire and Information: Intelligence Gathering and Social Communication in India, 1780–1870* (Cambridge: Cambridge University Press, 1997). Similarly, Mohamad Tavakoli-Targhi has shown the historical 'amnesia' which has suppressed the role of Asian intellectuals in the formation of

the scientific and academic enterprises which 'Orientalism' would claim as the prerogative of Europe. See M. Tavakoli-Targhi, *Refashioning Iran: Orientalism, Occidentalism, and Historiography* (Basingstoke: Palgrave, 2001).

27. On India, see K.W. Jones, *Socio-religious Reform Movements in British India* (Cambridge: Cambridge University Press, 1989).

28. C.A. Bayly, *The Birth of the Modern World, 1780–1914: Global Connections and Comparisons* (Oxford: Blackwell, 2004), Chapter 9.

29. King (1999).

30. G. Omvedt, "On the Participant Study of Womens' Movements", in G. Huizer & B. Mannheim (eds), *The Politics of Anthropology: From Colonialism and Sexism Toward a View From Below* (The Hague: Mouton, 1979), pp. 373–393 and G. Spivak, "Can the Subaltern Speak?", in C. Nelson & L. Grossberg (eds), *Marxism and the interpretation of Culture* (Urbana: University of Illinois Press, 1988), pp. 271–313.

31. H. Bhabha, "Signs Taken for Wonders: Questions of Ambivalence and Authority under a Tree outside Delhi, May 1817," *Critical Enquiry* 12, 1 (1985), pp. 144–165.

32. For alternative explorations of the language/power and religion/language interface in colonial and postcolonial India, see P.R. Brass *Language, Religion and Politics in North India* (Cambridge: Cambridge University Press, 1974) and R. Puniyani (ed.), *Religion, Power and Violence: Expression of Politics in Contemporary Times* (Delhi: Sage, 2005).

33. S. Westwood, *Power and the Social* (London: Routledge, 2002).

34. P. Bourdieu, *Language and Symbolic Power* (Cambridge: Polity Press, 1991), pp.57–58.

35. J.C. Burgel, *The Feather of Simurgh: The 'Licit Magic' of the Arts in Medieval Islam* (New York: New York University Press, 1988).

36. Palonen (2003), Chapters 3 and 6.

37. See the discussion of 'linguistic domination' in Bourdieu (1991), pp.45–46.

38. J. Evans, *Paul Ricoeur's Hermeneutics of the Imagination* (New York: Peter Lang, 1995).

39. On the transcendent quality of written traditions, see also N.S. Green, "Emerging Approaches to the Sufi Traditions of South Asia: Between Texts, Territories and the Transcendent", *South Asia Research* 24, 2 (2004), pp. 123–148.

40. For a survey, see J. Goody, *The Power of the Written Tradition* (Washington: Smithsonian Institution Press, 2000). For specific case studies of the power of writing in colonial Africa and India, see A. Skaria, "Writing, Orality and Power in the Dangs, Western India, 1800s-1920s", in S. Amin & D. Chakrabarty (eds), *Subaltern Studies: Writings on South Asian History and Society*, vol. 9 (Delhi: Oxford University Press, 1996), pp. 13–58 and M. Twaddle, "The Bible, the Qur'an and Political Competition in Uganda", in N. Kastfelt (ed.), *Scriptural Politics: The Bible and the Koran as Political Models in the Middle East and Africa* (London: Hurst & Company, 2003), pp. 139–154.

41. E.W. Said, *Orientalism: Western Conceptions of the Orient* (London: Penguin, 1991 [1978]).

42. S. Hall & B. Gieben (eds), *The Formation of Modernity* (Cambridge: Polity Press, 1992), p.277.

43. S. Hall, "Introduction: Who Needs Identity?", in S. Hall & P. du Gay (eds), *Questions of Cultural Identity* (London: Sage, 1996), p.3.

44. G. Spivak, "Practical Politics at the Open End", in S. Harasym (ed.), *The Post-Colonial Critic* (New York: Routledge, 1989), pp. 95–112.

45. M. Nye, *Multi-Culturalism and Minority Religions in Britain* (London: Curzon, 2001).

46. R. Dyer, *White* (London: Routledge, 1997).
47. Hall & du Gay (1996).
48. I. Gedalof, *Against Purity: Rethinking Identity with Indian and Western Feminisms* (London: Routledge, 1999).
49. D. Durham & J.W. Fernandez, "Tropical Dominions: the Figurative Struggle over Domains of Belonging and Apartness in Africa", in J.W. Fernandez (ed.), *Beyond Metaphor: The Theory of Tropes in Anthropology* (Stanford: Stanford University Press, 1991), pp.191–209.
50. T. Fitzgerald, *The Ideology of Religious Studies* (Oxford: Oxford University Press, 2000) and King (1999).

Part I
Exporting 'Religion'

1 Dialogues on Religion and Violence at the Parliament of the World's Religions

John Zavos

INTRODUCTION: THE DISCOURSE OF RELIGION

In her account in this volume of the making of religion in modern China, Francesca Tarocco examines the processes through which the neologism *zongjiao* emerged and became established as a Mandarin translation of European terms for religion. The coming of *zongjiao* reflects a broader development: the conceptualisation of what is termed 'the Chinese religious world' in a context of modernity. Three 'systems' of teaching—Confucianism, Taoism, and Buddhism—are identified as establishing the contours of this world, and practices identified as extraneous to these systems, or cutting across the boundaries being established between them, are increasingly perceived as marginal. Tarocco goes on to explain how such practices have been understood by the state in contemporary China as *mixin*—that is, superstition or folk practices. In being identified as such, these practices are precisely produced in relation to the Chinese religious world—as being outside, or specifically *not* religious. This scenario points up a number of significant issues in relation to the interaction of religion, language, and power. In the first instance, it emphasises the importance of historical contextualisation for an understanding of 'religion' and its meanings; secondly, it demonstrates the dynamic role played by language in the shaping of (religious) social realities; thirdly, it provides us with an indication of the impact of global processes—global cultural interactions, global political dynamics—in the shaping of more recent social realities; and fourthly, it points to a specific process of inclusion and exclusion as an important indicator of the relations of power at work in the articulation of religion. These are all issues which will be addressed in the present chapter, in which I will focus on the way religion is articulated in a contemporary environment with a self-image of global importance: the Parliament of the World's Religions, 2004.

Following the centenary celebration of the original 1893 Parliament, in Chicago in 1993, the Parliament of the World's Religions now takes place on a rough five yearly cycle. The 2004 session was preoccupied with the issue of political violence, and in particular the incidents of September 11,

2001 in the United States, and the train bombing in Madrid, Spain on March 11, 2004. The perpetrators of these incidents are often character-ised as 'fundamentalists' or 'religious extremists'. In this characterisation, intense religious feeling is associated with political violence: an association that was clearly of concern to many at the Parliament. More broadly, we can identify 'fundamentalism' or 'religious extremism' as what we might call the sharp end of a widely recognised 'resurgence of religion' in global politics.[1] Religion is currently recognised as a critical factor in developing global politics. How would the delegates at the Parliament respond to this trend? How would the apparent association between religion and violence be addressed?

Taking a lead from the points identified in Tarocco's discussion, I want to frame my examination of the dialogues on these issues at the Parliament with the idea of religion as a historically contingent discursive practice. Discourse, Stuart Hall reminds us, is 'a language for talking about—a way of representing the knowledge about—a particular topic at a particular his-torical moment'.[2] He draws on the work of Laclau and Mouffe to explain that this representation of knowledge about a particular topic depends on a 'systematic set of relations' that enables language to be meaningful in any particular context. Their example is the kicking of a spherical object, which may only be interpreted as playing football if this physical act is located within a systematic set of relations (including, but not exclusively, linguistic relations) which construct it as such. 'The [spherical] object is a football only to the extent that it establishes a system of relations with other objects, and these relations are not given by the mere referential mate-riality of the objects, but are, rather, socially constructed'.[3] This, then, is what they called a discourse of football—a socially constructed set of rela-tions between a variety of objects, actions, and ideas.

In a similar way, we can locate a discourse of religion. This is of course not a new idea, but it is worth restating because of the emphasis it places on the role of power in the representation of knowledge as religion.[4] Michel Foucault's studies of discourse complexify our understanding of the opera-tion of power. Discursive power, he says, is 'not something that is acquired, seized, or shared, something that one holds on to or allows to slip away; power is exercised from innumerable points, in the interplay of nonegalitar-ian and mobile relations'.[5] How can we begin to understand and identify the way in which religion is implicated in this diffuse operation of power in contemporary political and social contexts that are increasingly globalised? In the first instance, we need to remember that as with football, religion-as-discourse may be understood as a socially constructed set of relations between a variety of objects, actions, and ideas. The process of identifying particular objects, actions, and ideas as religious (referring back to Tarocco, that which constitutes *zongjiao*), and other objects, actions, and ideas as not religious (*mixin*), is therefore a significant process because it involves an exemplification of power in a given historical context. Similar processes are evident in the identification of different kinds of others in Shankara's work, as explored in Jacqueline Suthren Hirst's contribution to this volume.[6] I argue that identifying such processes here enables us to establish some co-ordinates in a matrix of contemporary power relations, and so provide some indications of the dynamics of religion as a discourse bound up with these relations.

In the context of modernity, the dominant discourse of religion is marked by two particular paradigms. First, that through which our understanding of religious objects, actions, and ideas is configured by the identification of World Religions; that is, discrete systems of belief and practice that organise a person's religiosity and identify them in relation to the adherents of other World Religions.[7] Secondly, that paradigm which identifies the religious as nonsecular, a form of human experience that is somehow removed from the secular domain of economics, politics, and rational organisation.[8] In the perception of a relationship between religion and contemporary violence and the dialogues that ensued at the Parliament of the World's Religions, we can see these paradigms at work. First, the idea of 'World Religions' underpins the anxiety over violence. One particular World Religion is consistently and painfully associated with 9/11 and 3/11, and chronic political violence across the globe is often associated with antagonism between adherents of different World Religions (Palestine/Israel; Pakistan/India; communal violence in Nigeria, Sri Lanka, India, Bosnia, East Timor, and so on). Secondly, the so-called resurgence of religion is a cause of concern, precisely because it transgresses the division between the religious and the secular; it threatens the settled secular character of some dominant political formations (the democratic nation–state, in particular, and also international relations institutions such as the United Nations). As we shall see, the Parliament is a forum that sees itself as confronting these issues, and indeed sometimes challenging the assumptions behind these paradigms. Nevertheless, my argument will be that the positioning apparent in dialogues over political violence demonstrates the complexity of the power relations at stake; however, the identification of processes of inclusion and exclusion can provide some perspective on these relations.

PARLIAMENTARY LANGUAGE

The 2004 Parliament took place over six days and was attended by nearly 9000 delegates from all over the world 'representing', as the Parliament's website has it, 'the vast diversity of the world's religious, spiritual and cultural traditions'.[9] The Parliament was certainly a major feat of organisation. Each day began with about 20 concurrent religious observances, and then proceeded with about sixty different panels, divided into three sessions across the day. These panels were punctuated by a series of performances, exhibitions, and symposia. Proceedings were rounded off in the evening with a plenary session that focused on a different theme each day. High ceremony was a feature of the event. The opening day saw a procession to the 'Tree of Peace', planted by Chief Jake Swamp of the Mohawk Nation, and the lighting of the World Peace Flame, a 'universal symbol of hope'. The ensuing opening plenary was due to be addressed by two Nobel Peace Laureates, the Iranian human rights activist and lawyer Shirin Ebadi, and his Holiness the fourteenth Dalai Lama (although the latter was, in the end, unable to attend). The plenary sessions included a 'Sacred Music concert' at one of the most recognisable landmarks of modern Barcelona, the Sagrada Familia church, which was broadcast live throughout Spain. This was also a well-heeled event, with partner and sponsorship deals with such major companies as Toyota, Coca-Cola, and Discovery Communications, enabling, amongst other things, the production of a glossy and very thorough guidebook to the Parliament, which was made available to all delegates.[10] It was also an integral part of a broader event held in Barcelona throughout the summer of 2004, the UNESCO-sponsored Universal Forum of Cultures 2004.[11]

The Parliament of the World's Religions, then, was a global event. It repeatedly symbolised this global status through ritual performances such as the Sagrada Familia concert ('An evening of music, movement, meditation, and chant inspired by religious and spiritual traditions from around the world'[12]). It was framed by a major exhibition that billed itself as 'an expression of the cultural heritage of humanity'.[13] It was reported in newspapers across the world in precisely these terms, under headlines such as 'Nobel Laureate Shirin Abadi helps inaugurate world religious conference', 'A World Gathering', and 'Gujarat rights activist to address world meet'.[14] There were also delegates at the Parliament from across the world, representing a plethora of linguistic groups. But the character of this global image was to some extent indicated by the fact that although there were three official languages—English, Spanish, and Catalan—it was English that emerged as the quite definite lingua franca at the Parliament, both in terms of institutional performance and informal networking. This is of course because in a contemporary context, English is a global language. But it also reflects the fact that despite this gathering taking place in Catalonia, the Parliament organisation is overwhelmingly American in terms of its conception, its institutional base, its officers, and its funding. This point was reinforced by the fact that a substantial proportion of delegates to the Parliament were indeed from the United States.[15]

This is clearly relevant when we talk about power and representation in a contemporary context. More specifically, it gives us an indication of the trajectory of the dominant discourse of religion at the Parliament. The history of the Parliament is strongly related to the United States, in the sense that the first Parliament in 1893 was held in Chicago as part of the Columbian Exposition, a grand exhibition nominally held as a celebration of the 400th anniversary of the voyages of Columbus. As mentioned earlier, the

second Parliament, in 1993, was also held in Chicago as a centennial celebration of the first. To an extent, then, the discourse of religion extant at
the Parliament has been fashioned within a specifically American environment, and I want to return to this point later in this chapter. More broadly,
we may be able to point to the dominance of English at the Parliament as
an indication of what has been termed 'linguistic imperialism',[16] part of
the network of powerful cultural markers through which globalisation is
perceived to be homogenising global culture on a Western model. To what
extent is this argument supported by the way in which religion is understood and articulated at the Parliament of Religions?

Some scholars of religion have in recent years argued that because of its
specific history, 'religion' is inevitably a concept that is tightly bound into a
system of dominance and oppression related to capitalist/imperialist development.[17] Moreover, it has been argued that using this concept to represent
the ideas and practices of those at the sharp end of such development is
tantamount to acquiescing, if not actively engaging, in this dominance and
oppression. Arguments that identify 'Hinduism' as a colonial construction
are good examples of this; as Robert Frykenberg said, 'a continued and
blind acceptance of this concept [Hinduism] . . . is not only erroneous, but,
I would argue, it is dangerous'.[18] Against this position, some other scholars
have argued for a reflexive usage of the concept, as an analytical tool that
has representational value in a multidimensional and complex world.[19] It is
interesting to place this debate up against similar debates in anthropology
over recent years. The issue of dominance and its impact on subjected cultural formations is one that has concerned anthropologists for some time.
Talal Asad has reviewed this concern specifically in the context of a focus
on religion in the introduction to his volume, *Genealogies of Religion*. He
notes the trend in recent years to insist on cultural autonomy and independent, creative agency in the history and cultural development of colonised and otherwise dominated regions of the world. To demonstrate this
point, Asad cites Marshall Sahlins' argument that colonial encounters were
'guided by the cultural logic of the local people concerned'[20]—that is, there
was a critical local authorship, a cultural autonomy that framed colonial
encounters, ensuring that in the end local peoples remained the authors of
their own history, reinventing, and sometimes subverting the products of
colonial domination through frameworks of indigenous culture.

Asad goes on to problematise this notion of authorship by questioning
the validity of the notion of cultural autonomy. He points to figures such
as James Clifford as having identified the emergence of a fractured, fluid
world in which it is difficult to identify any form of cultural authenticity. According to Asad, for Clifford, cultural identity is, 'mixed, relational,
inventive'.[21] The idea of autonomy has no salience in an environment such
as this because everyone is precisely *dis*located in the context of the modern world—this is, as Clifford would have it, the predicament of culture.
Asad however, is not satisfied with this answer to the problem of autonomy,

largely because it re-presents fluidity as an inherently invigorating force. Clifford's predicament of culture, Asad complains, is inexorably cheerful, an affirmation of 'libidinal energies and creative human agencies'.[22] Asad, as ever, is concerned with the operation of power in this dynamic. It is, he says, precisely 'by means of geographical and psychological movement'— that is, the kind of cultural fluidity that Clifford highlights—'that modern power inserts itself into pre-existing structures'.[23] He develops this point in the following way:

> When a project is translated from one site to another, from one agent to another, versions of power are produced. As with translation of a text, one does not simply get a reproduction of identity. The acquisition of new forms of language from the modern west—whether by forcible imposition, insidious insertion, or voluntary borrowing—is part of what makes for new possibilities of action in non-Western societies. Yet although the outcome of these possibilities is never fully predictable, the language in which the possibilities are formulated is increasingly shared by Western and non-Western societies. And so, too, the specific forms of power and subjection.[24]

Languages and concepts ('projects') can be shared in different ways, then, but the sharing in itself also implies the sharing of 'specific forms of power and subjection'. This point is reminiscent of the one drawn from Foucault about power being exercised 'from innumerable points' and 'in the interplay of nonegalitarian and mobile relations'. On the basis of this understanding, Asad demonstrated the ways in which networks of power infiltrate and impinge upon the appearance of religion in a variety of social contexts. I want to explore the idea that the articulation of religion at the Parliament is marked by this kind of dynamic. This was an international forum in which the manifestation of difference, sourced from around the globe, was vigorously celebrated. But how far does the 'sharing' of the language of religion imply also the sharing of 'specific forms of power and subjection'?

A NARRATIVE OF VIOLENCE

I attended the Parliament with the intention of exploring the idea of Hinduism and the way it is articulated in this environment. I wanted to see how Hindu groups operated, and what values they promoted as Hindu values in this paradigmatic context of religious pluralism. As I attended, however, I became frustrated by my inability to pick out a distinctive Hindu approach to the Parliament and its concerns. The succession of sessions and plenaries I attended were marked by some persistent patterns of narrative, which were articulated in quite uniform ways. It was as if everyone was speaking the same language. In saying this I am not exactly referring to the dominance of English noted earlier, but rather to the replication of ideas and approaches: no matter who you conversed with or listened to, the same points about religion and its place in the world recurred. In the focused space of the Parliament, the narratives that articulate a specific discourse of religion were beginning to reveal themselves.

I began to follow a particular narrative strand—a strand that, as indicated earlier, was quite dominant at the Parliament. This was a strand concerned with religion and violence. Frequent references can be found in the Parliament Guide to religiously motivated violence, and more specifically to the 9/11 and 3/11 incidents in the United States and Madrid.[25] In relation to these acts, the Parliament's *Program Book* noted that 'religion has been emphasised in a negative light'. The Parliament presented the opportunity to challenge this, to demonstrate the 'positive role and healing power of religious and interreligious responses'.[26] The Chair of the Council for the Parliament of the World's Religions, Rev. Dr William Lesher, also noted in his welcoming statement that the Parliament would provide a forum for fostering 'the kind of understanding, mutual respect and goodwill that can be the basis for shared work of seeking peace, justice and sustainability'. This, he continued, constitutes 'second tier diplomacy', a 'person-to-person and community-to-community approach (which) establishes the trust and the will to seek the practical solutions that make for peace'.[27] The Parliament, then, constituted an opportunity for inter-faith dialogue that would in some way counter the escalation of violence. Indeed, the Parliament had the overall theme of 'pathways to peace', and in the wake of the session the Parliament website gives a high profile to the 'thousands of commitments to address religious violence' that apparently emanated from its deliberations.[28]

With a remarkable degree of consistency, discussions over what to do about violence apparently inspired by religious identity and conflicts between different forms of such identity were framed by a mutual understanding that such action was not true religion. Rather, this violence was perceived as politically motivated, a manipulation of religion that was not representative of religious views of the world. This is not to say that differences between religious world views were not recognised or accommodated—indeed, as noted earlier, they were vigorously celebrated—but this was difference within certain parameters. To return to Asad, the language in which the possibilities of difference were formulated was shared amongst participants. We still need to investigate to what extent this also meant sharing 'specific forms of power and subjection', as Asad claims.

Some examples of dialogue at the Parliament may be useful in pursuing this line of enquiry. One panel I attended was entitled 'Responding in Solidarity to Acts of Communal Violence'. The panel included a range of speakers who had direct experience of conflict in such areas of the world as Rwanda, India, and Israel/Palestine. The objective of the panel was stated as to 'discuss ways in which communities can not only respond in solidarity to acts of communal violence, but also harness and sustain this emergent interreligious camaraderie, so that these acts of violence will not have the intended effect of sowing fear and distrust, but rather serve as a catalyst for sustainable inter-religious cooperation'.[29] The panel began to follow a particular pattern: the speakers gave accounts of a variety of situations of communal violence, and then explained how acts of individual 'cross-community' heroism or generosity took place within these situations—acts that often led to the preservation of life. The implication, made explicit in the ensuing discussion, was that 'true' religion was to be located in those acts of heroism and generosity, and that the violence which had preceded them was created by a range of other social pressures, through which religion was manipulated and distorted. As one panellist exclaimed (perhaps rather rashly), 'there has never been a riot over a question of theology', going on to explain that riots and violence were products of issues such as poverty and the denial of social justice or education.

An interesting development in this panel was the observation that violence ultimately strengthened inter-religious dialogue, as it led to a concentration of efforts to bring together the 'representatives' of different communities in Interfaith Councils and other such forums. Indeed, this process is hinted at in the introduction to the panel noted above. Of course, in one sense this response is an expression of defiance against the perceived objective of such acts of violence to splinter existing social relations. However, by viewing religion as a dynamic discourse it is also possible to identify violence as having an active role in the contemporary identification of the religious. As Stuart Hall notes in a discussion of identity formation, this is a process that 'entails discursive work, the binding and marking of symbolic boundaries, the production of "frontier effects". It requires what is left outside, its constitutive outside, to consolidate the process'.[30] The relationship between interfaith dialogue and religious violence may be read here as a relationship between religion and its 'constitutive outside'. This suggests that violence plays an active role in the consolidation of the contemporary discourse of religion as articulated at the Parliament.

Another panel I attended was entitled 'Finding the Brother in the Other: Overcoming Negative Images of Other Faiths As We Build Our Religious Identities and Seek Common Ground'. This panel sought to confront the issue of difference and 'negative attitudes toward other religions . . . by drawing on their own religious resources'.[31] The speakers on this panel were all male Americans, although they clearly gained their legitimacy from their representation of a range of different religious traditions: the panel consisted of two Jews, two Christians (one a Presbyterian, one a Catholic), one Hindu, and one Muslim. Despite this representative inflection, the panel members were keen to express a kind of humanistic particularism, in which the individual's sense of religious identity was perceived as a product of individual choice—neither more nor less significant than the choice of the next man ('man', of course, being the operative word in the context of this panel). A New York rabbi, for example, explained that his Jewish identity was part of a multilayered self, part of his hyphenated individual existence. We all, he said, 'live in the particular'. The Muslim, who was also from New York, confirmed that we are not 'mono-dimensional', and that he could speak for no 'other person on this earth than me'. The overall idea was expressed quite succinctly by the panel chair as 'epistemological humility'. He further explained how we must be humble about our own structures of knowing and acknowledge the value of others' structures of knowing.[32] Armed with such a sense of epistemological humility, it may be more possible to discover the brother in the other. The idea was dramatically illustrated by a spontaneous and heartfelt embrace between the New York rabbi and a Muslim Rwandan mufti who had contributed a speech from the floor, an embrace augmented by the cheers and applause of attending delegates.

At the same time as it demonstrates the idea of particularism and respect for the other as an individual, this act was replete with a specific representative connotation: the two protagonists effectively performed a Muslim–Jewish rapprochement. A rapprochement, that is, which is particularly poignant not because it represented resolution of any outstanding conflict between America and Rwanda, but precisely because this was a Jew and a Muslim. The act was made meaningful for the attending delegates by a conflict in West Asia that articulates Muslims and Jews as antagonistic. From the particularity of the self, then, there is a radical reframing of participant identity in this panel, projecting them as representative of global communities, World Religions: in this case, the communities of Jews and Muslims. This is a kind of fabulation that dramatically dislocates religious identity from its contextual construction. In this dislocation, the 'stuff' of context is left behind, a welter of social, political, and economic issues, which as in the previous example, are subsequently identified as the source of violence and conflict. Religion emerges as an identity that is constructed through a common language of respect, love, harmony, and peace. The point is reiterated by the host website of the Parliament: 'the leaders of more than 100 faiths showed that, in spite of all their differences, everybody has a fundamental principle that unites them: universal peace and mutual respect'.[33] In the end, then, as people of religion, we all speak the same shared language—a language configured by some 'fundamental principles' of 'religion', amongst them 'universal peace and mutual respect'.

In the Parliamentary space, these radical swings from the identity of the individual to the identity of vast, imagined communities are commonplace. The very idea of the Parliament, with its qualitatively insubstantial connotation of representation, invokes this process. It provides an apparatus for the legitimation of community identity on the basis of a discourse of religion, which disengages this identity from the networks of contexts within which it is constructed. What, though, can the identification of such an apparatus tell us about the 'specific forms of power and subjection' at work at the Parliament? Examining the history of the organisation can throw some light on this issue.

POWER AND SUBJECTION FROM
CHICAGO TO BARCELONA

As noted earlier, the first and most famous Parliament was that of 1893 in Chicago. Interesting work has been done on the 1893 Parliament by James Ketalaar.[34] He highlights the case of Pung Kwang Yu, a representative of the Chinese Imperial Court who was invited to the Parliament by the chair of the organising committee, the Chicago Presbyterian minister John Henry Barrows (1847–1902). In the manner of all the other non-Christian delegates, Pung was asked to present 'Chinese religion' to the delegates by focusing briefly on six topics chosen by Barrows: God, man, the relation of man to God, the role of woman, education, and social morality. This, Ketalaar remarks, set the parameters of what was to be considered religion at the Parliament; a strategy, he says, which 'could only result in all religions appearing to be concerned with the same issues and appearing to be different only as to particular terminology'.[35] It is interesting to note these pressures exerted on Pung in the light of Tarocco's account in this volume of the development of Chinese religion around the same time. One of the features of this development was the identification of Buddhism by Christian missionaries as having 'prepared the way to Christianity' in China,[36] and by a variety of Chinese cultural and political activists as a potential 'national religion' for the emerging Chinese nation. Buddhism, then, may be perceived as a key factor in the emergence of *zongjiao*. Buddhist representatives were in fact quite prominent at the Parliament (though they were predominantly Sri Lankan and Japanese, rather than Chinese), often presenting Buddhism as an alternative to Christianity, competing in the common discursive space articulated by Barrows.[37] As a representative of the Imperial Court, Pung did not engage in this fashion. He responded to Barrows' request with a not very brief (35,000 word) exposition on Confucianism, in which he resisted the suggested categories. Pung stated that he wanted primarily to provide 'an outline of the political and educational principles of China that have stood the test of six thousand years'; in the wake of this outline in seven chapters, he then added two supplementary chapters that 'touched upon some of the questions proposed for discussion in the sessions of the Parliament', as well as taking 'the liberty to criticise the methods of conducting missionary work in China'.[38] In the introduction to his discourse Pung discussed the problems he encountered in translating some of the concerns of Barrows into Chinese, and commented on God that 'Confucianists have never indulged in speculations of this nature'.[39] More generally, his approach to religion by no means follows the guidelines laid down by Barrows: in China, he said, 'religion has never been a desirable thing for the people to know and for the government to sanction'.[40]

However, despite this quite forthright resistance Ketalaar demonstrates how Pung's presentation at the Parliament was crucially mediated. Using evidence from the contemporary press, Ketalaar argued that 'Pung was only *heard* . . . to say that Confucianism was a form of proto-humanism and that humankind is "the heart of heaven and earth. Humanity is his natural faculty and love his controlling emotion"'.[41] This Ketalaar interpreted as an example of the 'staging of the other' at the Parliament. 'Even the clearest opposition,' he said, was translated into 'harmonious utterance', articulating Confucianism as 'a promising but lesser developed Chinese-styled precursor to the Christian message'. The Parliament, he continued, 'succeeded in providing the "Orient" not only with a voice but also with the language and ideas with which to animate that voice'.[42] In this context, then, the 'shared' language of religion can be seen struggling to marginalise the resistant epistemology represented by Pung. It is a language that seeks to instantiate 'specific forms of power and subjection' precisely by insisting on a particular idea of what constitutes 'religion'.

This brief reference to the 1893 session gives us some perspective on the operation of religion and power at the 2004 Parliament. Here, religion is articulated without challenge as a universal type that signifies a specific set of key values—values that are indeed very reminiscent of those promoted by Barrows at the 1893 Parliament. The various religions represented at the Barcelona Parliament (by 'the leaders of more than 100 faiths') are all examples of this type, and fundamentally express these values as a marker of their belonging. In this context the Parliament can be construed, I suggest, as a kind of 'technology of faith'. I am adapting this term from a usage by Penny Harvey of the Foucauldian notion of social or human technologies—that is, 'hybrid assemblages of knowledges, instruments, persons, systems of judgement, buildings and spaces, underpinned at the programmatic level by certain presuppositions about, and objectives for, human beings'.[43] Harvey explains these assemblages as engaging 'in processes of naturalisation which render constitutive social relations and interests inaccessible or invisible'.[44] From this starting point, she develops the idea of 'technologies of nationhood' as a tool for analysing Expo '92, the Universal Exhibition held in Seville in 1992. For Harvey, technologies of nationhood are the 'processes of standardisation . . . through which social forms [i.e. nations and national cultures] are rendered equivalent through the display of particular, apparently defining, component elements'. Through such processes, she says, 'the unpredictablility of social relations' is effectively 'sidestepped'.[45]

This approach, and its location in the context of the Universal Exhibition environment of Expo '92, provides a useful analytical model for an examination of approaches to religion and violence at the Parliament of

Religions. Here, 'religions' as social phenomena are standardised by reference to defining, component elements such as the insistence on respect,
love, and harmony. This insistence marginalises the 'unpredictability' of
religiously-inspired ideas and actions—in this context, ideas and actions
associated with violence in the contemporary world. Such ideas and actions
are represented as not really religious, and are therefore not a feature of
the colourful diversity of contemporary social formations signified by the
'100 faiths', and produced time and again in the context of the Parliament.
Indeed, their very outsideness contributes to the integrity of religious diversity as a series of complimentary units drawing on a common reservoir
of normative ethics. This then, again indicates the 'frontier effect' being
established at the Parliament around the relationship between religion and
violence; it governs a critical process of inclusion and exclusion through
which the role that religious ideologies may play in the articulation of political violence is erased. This whole process is framed by the construction of
religion as a universal type, in which there are a number of recognisable
units: the World's religions, the 100 faiths, and so on—tropes that derive
their efficacy from the dominant World Religions model.

The proliferation of religions as represented at the Parliament by this
invocation of '100 faiths' is reminiscent of the emergence of multiculturalism as a key facet of the modern representation of nations as composite
cultural forms. It has been argued by a variety of commentators that paradoxically the multiculturalism of nation–states reinforces the homogeneity
of the nation because, as Segal and Handler state, people 'differ from one
another in uniform and acceptable ways'.[46] The moment one steps outside these uniform and acceptable ways, the idea of cultural difference is
marginalised and condemned, as happened to many Muslims during the
Salman Rushdie affair in the United Kingdom in the late 1980s. The same
kind of uniform and acceptable proliferation of difference is apparent at the
Parliament, accompanied by a process of marginalisation. The relationship
that may exist between political violence and religiosity—be it based on
resistance or domination—is externalised. The 'technology of faith' operates in multiform ways to reinforce the 'specific forms of power and subjection' that identify those outside—that is, those engaged in violence—as
flawed, atavistic, un-modern, and un-religious.

CONCLUSION

The argument in this chapter, then, is about understanding how 'religion'
is developing in an environment in which ideas of 'fundamentalism' and
'religious extremism' are identified as major sources of political violence.
This form of violence has been characterised by some commentators as
indicative of a critical shift towards culture or 'civilisation' as the key force
for political motivation in the post-Cold War period.[47] 'Religion' in various

guises, most of them unpredictable and/or rather bloodthirsty, confronts the civilisational moderation of a somewhat nonspecific Western secularism. More generally, religion has been identified as a resurgent force in world politics, and violence perpetrated by 'fundamentalists' is perceived as a feature of this resurgence. Examining the 'technology of faith' apparent at the Parliament of the World's Religions enables us to see the way in which a key discursive process is developing, specifically excluding this kind of political violence from being understood as motivated by religion. Both ideas—the identification of religiously-inspired violence as a new development in world politics, and the denial of this violence as religiously-inspired—are to my mind based upon a similar assumption that 'religion' constitutes an identifiable category of human experience, characterised by some key characteristics that are apparent in a series of ontologically equivalent forms; that is, the World Religions, systems of belief and practice that operate on the basis of qualitatively different principles to those understood as secular.[48] The premise of this essay is that these influential ideas need to be understood as component elements in the developing discourse of religion; a discourse with a quite specific history that is bound up with developing power relations in the modern world. In understanding the way in which this discourse has and does operate—and in particular, identifying the critical boundaries, the frontier effects being established through the discourse—we may understand more about how notions such as 'fundamentalism' and 'religious extremism' are being constructed as key features of modern global politics.

NOTES

1. For a review of this perceived trend, see J. Haynes, "Religion and International Relations After 9/11", paper presented at the European Consortium for Political Research General Conference, Budapest, 2005.
2. S. Hall, "The Work of Representation", in S. Hall (ed.), *Representation: Cultural Representations and Signifying Practices* (London: Sage, 1997), p. 44.
3. Cited in Hall (1997), p. 70.
4. For discussion of the idea of religion as discourse, see T. Asad, *Genealogies of Religion: Discipline and Reasons of Power in Christianity and Islam* (Baltimore: John Hopkins University Press, 1993); J. Carrette, *Foucault and Religion: Spiritual Corporality and Political Spirituality* (London: Routledge, 2000); R. King, *Orientalism and Religion: Postcolonial Theory, India and "The Mystic East"* (London: Routledge, 1999); and the introduction to this volume.
5. M. Foucault, *History of Sexuality* (vol. 1; 1976), cited in Carrette (2000), p. 148.
6. It is also apparent in this volume in Searle-Chatterjee's account of the uses of the word 'Hindu' by different social groups in colonial and postcolonial India, and in Christmann's identification of 'mysticism' as an indication of the 'ecstatic, fanatic, unrestrained, and irrational' in the context of mid-eighteenth century European Enlightenment discourse.

7. See the introduction to this volume and J. Suthren Hirst & J. Zavos, "Riding a Tiger? South Asia and the Problem of 'Religion'", *Contemporary South Asia* 14, 1 (2005).

8. For an elaboration of this idea, see T. Fitzgerald, *The Ideology of Religious Studies* (Oxford: Oxford University Press, 2000). See also Christmann in this volume, where it is demonstrated that European Orientalist scholars in the nineteenth century increasingly perceived mysticism as 'the quintessence of religious experience', a realm 'outside the political, commercial, military, administrative, and bureaucratic spheres'.

9. www.cpwr.org/2004Parliament/ (accessed 18/7/05).

10. *Program Book—Pathways to Peace: The Wisdom of Listening, The Power of Commitment* (Parliament of the World's Religions, 2004), hereafter *Program Book*.

11. For information on the Forum, see www.barcelona2004.org.

12. http://www.cpwr.org/2004Parliament/ parliament/sessions.htm (accessed 19/7/05).

13. http://www.barcelona2004.org/eng/quees/agenda.htm (accessed 19/7/05).

14. Respectively *Associated Press*, New York 7/7/04; *Pioneer Press*, Chicago 3/7/04; *Times of India*, New Delhi 7/7/04; all cited at http://www.cpwr.org/2004Parliament/ news/articles.htm (accessed 19/7/05).

15. The Council for the Parliament of the World Religions' (CPWR) own estimate was that the nationality of delegates was divided roughly equally between Spain, the United States, and the rest of the world; personal communication from Dirk Ficca, Executive Director of CPWR.

16. R. Phillipson, *Linguistic Imperialism* (Oxford: Oxford University Press, 1992).

17. See especially Fitzgerald (2000).

18. R. Frykenberg, "The Emergence of Modern 'Hinduism' as a Concept and as an Institution: A Reappraisal With Special Reference to South India", in G. Sontheimer & H. Kulke (eds.), *Hinduism Reconsidered* (Delhi, India: Manohar, 1989), p. 29.

19. W. Sweetman, *Mapping Hinduism: 'Hinduism' and the Study of Indian Religions 1600–1776* (Halle, Germany: Franckesche Stiftungen zu Halle, 2003), p. 51.

20. Asad (1993), p. 3.

21. Asad (1993), p. 10.

22. Asad (1993), p. 10.

23. Asad (1993), p. 11.

24. Asad (1993), p. 13.

25. See for example *Program Book*, pp. 11, 58.

26. *Program Book*, p. 58.

27. *Program Book*, pp. 9–10.

28. www.cpwr.org/2004Parliament (accessed 20/7/05).

29. *Program Book*, p. 192.

30. S. Hall, "Introduction: Who Needs Identity?", in S. Hall & P. du Gay (eds.), *Questions of Cultural Identity* (London: Sage, 1996), p. 3.

31. *Program Book*, p. 184. For further comment on this panel, see J. Zavos, "Bin Laden is one of us! Representations of Religious identity at the Parliament of the World's Religions," Culture and Religion 9, 1 (forthcoming, 2008).

32. Interestingly, I have seen a similar phrase ('epistemological uncertainty') attributed to former President Bill Clinton in the wake of the 9/11 attacks, in a speech at Georgetown University, 8 November 2001. Clinton contrasted this uncertainty, 'part of the limitation imposed on us by God', with the certainty of the terrorists: 'They believe they got it'. See http://www.uexpress.com/maggiegallagher/?uc_full_date=20011112 (accessed 11/7/05).

33. Forum 2004 Dialogue Synthesis IV: Parliament of the World's Religions, see http://www.barcelona2004.org/eng/banco_del_conocimiento/documentos/ficha.cfm?IdDoc=1304 (accessed 11/7/05).
34. J. Ketalaar, "The Reconvening of Babel: Eastern Buddhism and the 1893 World's Parliament of Religions", in E. Ziolkowski (ed.), *A Museum of Faiths: Histories and Legacies of the 1893 World's Parliament of Religions* (Atlanta, GA: Scholars Press, 1993).
35. Ketalaar (1993), p. 271.
36. This phrase was used by the missionary James Dyer Ball in a lecture delivered at the Young Men's Christian Association of Hong Kong. On Ball, see also Francesca Tarocco's essay in this volume.
37. Ketalaar (1993), p. 255.
38. J. H. Barrows, *The World's Parliament of Religions: An Illustrated and Popular Story of the World's First Parliament of Religions, Held in Chicago in Connection With the Columbian Exposition of 1893* (Chicago: Parliament Publishing Company, 1893), p. 387.
39. Barrows (1893), p. 375.
40. Ketalaar (1993), p. 271.
41. Ketalaar (1993), p. 271. Ketalaar's citation is from *Chicago Daily Times* 14th September 1893.
42. Ketalaar (1993), pp. 271–272.
43. N. Rose, "Identity, Genealogy, History", in Hall & du Gay (1996), p. 132.
44. P. Harvey, *Hybrids of Modernity: Anthropology, the Nation State and the Universal Exhibition* (London: Routledge, 1996), p. 53.
45. Harvey (1996), p. 54.
46. Cited in Harvey (1996), p. 70.
47. See especially S. Huntington, "The Clash of Civilizations", *Foreign Affairs* 72, 3 (1993).
48. For a development of these ideas about the discourse of religion and the World Religious Paradigm, see Zavos (2008).

2   The Making of 'Religion' in Modern China[1]

Francesca Tarocco

The Chinese are emphatically not a religious people, though they are very superstitious.

—H. A. Giles, *The Civilisation of China*, 1911

I have found that the Buddhists considered the Taoists superstitious; the Confucians considered the Buddhists superstitious; the Christians considered them all superstitious and were considered superstitious themselves by the Confucians and the Communists.

—H. Welch, *The Buddhist Revival in China*, 1968

The historical myth that diversity in social relations and religious belief undermines the strength of the regime continues to inform Communist Party policy.

—P. B. Potter, *Belief in Control: Regulation of Religion in China*, 2003

INTRODUCTION

Research on religion in modern China has been constantly growing during the last decade. Scholars have been particularly concerned with assessing the impact of legislation upon religious practice and, to a lesser extent, with looking at how practitioners have accommodated themselves to the changing cultural and political environment.[2] While such studies have done much to illuminate several aspects of the Chinese religious world in the twentieth century, this essay takes one step back and begins to look at the emergence of a novel conception of 'religion' between the last decades of the nineteenth century and the first decades of the twentieth, a notion that was at considerable variance with the ideas and practices of earlier periods. In particular, I look at how notions surrounding *zongjiao*—the term used to translate the English term 'religion' in modern Chinese—emerged out of several processes of cross-cultural translation and linguistic accommodation that involved primarily, but not exclusively, China and Europe, the beginnings of which can be dated back to the seventeenth century. In fact, premodern China lacked both a lexical equivalent of the English term religion and the current notion of 'religion' as a discrete feature of culture and matter of individual belief.[3] The following comments will hopefully reveal something of the processes that took place both with respect to some of the attempts at representing the Chinese indigenous worldview along lines similar to those of Christianity and to the slow but progressive assimilation of a modern version of Chinese Buddhism into the new religious order.[4]

BEFORE *ZONGJIAO*

In his seminal work *Genealogies of Religion*, Talal Asad convincingly demonstrated that any definition of religion is itself the 'historical product of discursive processes'. Thus, in the context of nineteenth-century Western evolutionary discourse, 'religion' came to be regarded as an earlier stage of the human condition from which modern law, modern science, and modern politics had emerged, and from which they should be detached.[5] No longer a set of practical rules attached to specific processes, 'religion' became something with an increasingly abstract nature. The sheer scale of the Christian missionary enterprise that followed in the wake of European high imperialism contributed to the widespread diffusion of this notion beyond Europe and North America.[6]

The idea of 'religion' as operating in a realm separate from that of the state, the family, and the community, and as a matter of individual belief, must have been alien to the experience of any lettered or indeed illiterate person born in late imperial China. Law was promulgated by the emperor, who was also the supreme judge and guarantor of harmony under heaven (*tian*), and was administered by a bureaucracy of scholars–officials. Moreover, it was the sincere (*cheng*) performance and participation in rituals (*li*) that mattered the most to late-imperial Chinese.[7] As Stephen Feuchtwang and others pointed out, the terminology determining Chinese questions of authority and of identification with that authority revolved around the terms 'orthodox' (*zheng*) and 'heretical' (*xie*), 'order' (*anping*) and 'chaos' (*luan*), which were crucial to any activity, and to ritual activity in particular.[8] Beside the officially sanctioned rituals for the ordering of the universe and for death rituals, the state traditionally patronised and controlled, members of the Buddhist and Daoist orders (for instance, by issuing ordination certificates) while local cults continued to thrive in local societies, generally resisting most attempts at official control.

This fluid situation was reflected by the lack of an umbrella term subsuming all religious beliefs and practices. Yet regardless of its manifestly complex genealogy, the introduction of *zongjiao* to the modern Chinese intellectual vocabulary to 'translate' the term 'religion' has up till now been understood as a relatively transparent process. *Zongjiao* is generally as a borrowing from Japan, where it was supposedly used in the context of the rapid modernisation and Westernisation of the country in the second half of the nineteenth century. For instance, in his important study of the expansion of the Chinese lexicon in the nineteenth century, Federico Masini described it merely as a 'graphic loan' from Japanese and dated its first occurrence in Chinese to around 1890.[9] This view, still current among China scholars, is only just beginning to be challenged.[10]

The two terms forming the disyllabic compound *zongjiao* have a long history as separate elements. They both figure in some of the earliest Chinese written sources, including the *Shijing* (*The Book of Songs*) and *Shujing* (*The Book of Documents*), datable to the Eastern Zhou period (*c.* 1000 BCE and *c.* 600 BCE), and in the equally early *Shuowen jiezi*, the first comprehensive dictionary of Chinese characters ever to be compiled. But crucially they are also found in premodern Buddhist texts in some form of relation to each other. *Jiao* can be glossed as to 'teach', 'instruct', and 'set an example'. The second element, *zong* is slightly more complex. Its original meaning refers to the main ancestral line, and in more abstract terms, it is often translated as 'principle'. It was not used exclusively in Confucian contexts but was also appropriated by Buddhists.[11] As noted by T. H. Barrett, even before the arrival of Christianity definitions surrounding *jiao* were highly ideological.[12] In the sixth century, 'teaching' featured as a key term in imposing Buddhist norms. Centuries later, in nineteenth-century Yunnan, the term took on a broad cultural meaning in which Islam was the norm.[13] Interestingly, the first *Dictionary of the Chinese Language* in English, compiled in the early nineteenth century by the British missionary Robert Morrison, who based his work on existing Chinese dictionaries, contains the following entry:

> Superiors giving inferiors something to imitate, viz. a precept; a rule; a law; to teach; to instruct; that which is taught; a system of opinion or a religion; to command; to order; *keaou men* [i.e. *jiaomen*] commonly denotes the Mohammedans, but it also means Religion or Sect generally.[14]

In fact, *jiao* has been used to designate Buddhism, as in *fojiao* or 'the teaching of the Buddha', and Christianity, as in *tianzhujiao* or 'the teaching of the lord of heaven' in seventeenth-century Jesuit Chinese parlance. But there was also *xiejiao* or 'heretical teachings', a rather elusive category inclusive of everything the regime regarded as threatening to social security and state authority, regardless of its specific religious identity, from millenarian Buddhist groups to local sorcerers and Chinese Christians. Indeed, one of the enduring legacies of the late imperial rulers to modern Chinese nation makers was that of the battle conducted against such loosely defined *xiejiao*. Indeed, the Chinese state's anxiety toward all forms of religious affiliation that exist outside its ritual and ideological boundaries, and its fear of religiously inspired political uprisings is not simply a twentieth century invention.[15] Similarly, *zongjiao* was not invented *ex novo* in a short time either. On the contrary, its roots are to be found in Chinese Buddhist terminology dating back to medieval times. Its modern incarnation emerged first in nineteenth century China rather than Japan over the course of a couple of generations of linguistic instability. In 1838, for instance, the missionary and prolific Chinese-language writer Karl Friedrich August Gützlaff (1803–1851), eager to interest his audiences in various aspects of the life and thought of Western countries, described the unusual status of the Papal State in the Italy of his day as constituting a *jiao-zong* state.[16] As T. H. Barrett and the present author recently pointed out, the meaning of *zongjiao* for Chinese language speakers was from its inception fatally skewed in the direction of the beliefs and practices of the relatively few religious professionals, clerical groups representing such religions as Buddhism and Christianity, and so failed to 'translate' many realities of the Chinese religious world.[17]

Echoes of earlier semantic and semiotic negotiations still resound in today's Chinese language. While the semantic range of the majority of compounds with *zong* is linked with indigenous religious practices, *zongjiao* on the other hand is the only word with a wide range of cross-cultural and modern meanings. There are, for example, terms like 'religious psychology' and 'the policy on religion'. Moreover, *zongjiao* is often associated with Buddhism and Christianity, and conveys a sense of an organised institution of beliefs and textual authority. In a sense, this reflects the fact that 'religion' was established in China through the concurrent effort of Buddhists and Christians and to the exclusion of the daily practices of the many.

WHAT IS 'CHINESE RELIGION'?

As the first two quotations at the beginning of this chapter show (there are scores of similar statements), descriptions of China's religious world by outsiders have been largely negative. To a large extent, observers' representations, including scholarly ones, failed to account for its utter dynamism, its shifting patterns of development, and its underlying principles. In order to understand how some of these misrepresentations came about, one has to turn to the work of Jesuit missionaries in seventeenth-century China.[18]

In the view of European Jesuits, the Chinese had had an early belief in a transcendent, presumably male, deity, which over the course of time degenerated into the then, widespread 'idolatry' of the populace. The Jesuits described the existence of 'three teachings' (*san jiao*), understood as discrete entities and separable from the body of religious practice in general. Yet the historical record shows that in Daoism, for instance, self-perceptions and self-representations were shaped through rituals whose cosmological meanings and boundaries were negotiated with, and against, Buddhist and popular religious practices. Clear-cut divisions between Buddhism and Daoism were mostly true only in the case of religious professionals and their scriptural materials, whereas 'community rituals . . . were themselves not exclusive; indeed they readily accommodated the different private understandings of the participants'.[19]

The talented Matteo Ricci (1552–1610) was for years engaged in multiple, cross-cultural translations. In China, he translated 'Western books' (*xishu*)—this was also the name by which Chinese scholars traditionally referred to Buddhist books—and told the Chinese court and literati about the culture of another 'West' (*Daxiguo*, literally the 'great western country'), which lay to the west of China's traditional 'West', India (*Shendu*).[20] In Europe, his description of China's religion for centuries proved the most influential. Ricci wrote his *Della entrata della Compagnia di Giesù e Christianità nella Cina* ('On the Entry of the Company of Jesus and Christianity to China') while living in Beijing. From its idiosyncratic central Italian vernacular with Spanish and Portuguese influences, in 1615 the text was eventually revised and translated into Latin by Nicolas Trigaut. It was this later version, thanks also to the incorporation of large extracts in the *China Illustrata* (1667) of the Jesuit polymath Athanasius Kircher, and its subsequent translations into French (1616), German (1617), Spanish (1621), and eventually English, that became an important source of first-hand knowledge about China until well into the nineteenth century. A section of the book is devoted to the 'various sects that surround religion in China' (*varie sette che nella Cina sono intorno alla religione*). Of 'all the tribes known to Europe', wrote Ricci, no people made 'fewer mistakes' than the ancient Chinese who worshiped one 'ultimate deity' (*suppremo nume*) called the 'lord of heaven' (*re del cielo*). However, over the course of time they came to believe in the existence of not one but three teachings—'three laws' (*tre leggi*) in Ricci's parlance—and to worship idols everywhere and not just in temples. Of the three laws, he chose to describe two as idolatrous, but made a favourable portrait of the teaching of the literati, which was represented as mostly devoid of religious elements.[21]

Ricci described what we now call Buddhism as having a huge following, if only among 'women, eunuchs and rude people' (*donne, eunuchi e gente rude*). What he or his interlocutors perceived as similarities between his teachings and those of the Buddhists he tried to explain away as intellectual theft. The Chinese must have somehow 'heard about the fame of the holy Gospel and sought it in the West'. However, by 'mistake or malice', instead of Christianity their emissaries brought back the 'fake doctrine' of Buddhism. Buddhism's creators (*autori di questa dottrina*), he wrote, must have known about 'our philosophers' (*nostri philosophi*) and about 'Christian things' (*cose della christianità*). How is it otherwise possible to explain the fact that they believe in the trinity (*trinità*), promise alternatively rebirth in paradise (*paradiso*) or eternal damnation in hell (*inferno*), teach about repentance (*penitentia*), and lead a celibate life (*la vita del celibato*)?[22] Yet Jesuit missionaries showed comparatively little interest towards many aspects of China's 'idolatry', and focused their attention instead on specific issues that were in line with the preoccupations of their interlocutors of choice, the elite literati. If initially the Jesuits donned the robes of Buddhist monks, they soon decided it was more politically expedient to align themselves to the mores of the Confucian literati, rather than those of the people with whom they shared some more or less profound similarities. In time, Ricci came to see a sort of preparation for Christ in the classical texts of the Confucian tradition which he carefully studied.[23]

In his writings in Chinese, Ricci was polemical towards Buddhism. This attitude, as Jacques Gernet pointed out, may well have been one of the reasons behind the initial success of Christianity among some members of the Chinese ruling classes, since their anti-Buddhist feelings were growing vis-à-vis the widespread diffusion of Buddhist-inspired practices among all strata of the population. In the treatise *Tianzhu shiyi* ('True Meaning of the Lord of Heaven'), printed in Beijing in 1603, after condemning the 'mistake' made by those who brought back to China the teachings of Buddha instead of the 'true teachings' of Christianity, Ricci offered arguments against transmigration and criticisms of abstention from meat. The latter was clearly not a distinctively Christian preoccupation, but a crucial marker of Buddhist-inspired religious identities in the Chinese context. While offering a rationale for Christian celibate life, he made no mention of similar Buddhist monastic attitudes.[24] For their part, Buddhist clerics did not remain silent at Ricci's criticisms and launched several campaigns aimed at confuting and ridiculing Christian doctrines. The love–hate relationship between Christianity and Buddhism in China, and their battle over a comparatively small number of otherwise politically influential souls, had started in earnest.[25]

In some important ways, the representations of China's religion by Victorian Protestant missionaries echoed those of Matteo Ricci.[26] Yet much had also changed, for Europe had been rife with religious controversies. As Susan Rosa pointed out, the formalized credos issued by the competing Christian denominations in the wake of the Reformation had encouraged the development of the notion of religion as 'adherence to a set of propositions'. The creation of such 'propositional religion' in turn enabled the emergence of a 'discussion of the merits of other "religions" conceived to similarly exist as sets of beliefs.' In this way, 'true religion' became 'a body of certain knowledge'.[27] To a certain extent, as C. John Sommerville argued in *The Secularization of Early Modern England*, it became 'something one thinks about rather than something one does'.[28]

The writings on China of Protestant missionaries, who often doubled as scholars and journalists, reflected a variety of intellectual, political, and religious agendas. But there were some underlying presuppositions. One of their primary quests was that of forming a new Chinese language of religion.[29] In the eyes of Griffith John (1831–1912), the Chinese were 'irreligious', so much so that they did not even have a word for religion. In his *China Her Claim and Call*, he observed that religion . . . as realised by the Chinese in their inward experience, is not worthy of the name, and it is a remarkable fact that they have not in their language a generic term for it. The Chinese are as immoral as they are irreligious'.[30]

Yet earlier he had proclaimed in a missionary journal 'our indebtedness to Buddhism for the use of many of our religious terms, as well as for the existence of many religious ideas at the present time among the Chinese. Without it they would have been materialists and unbelievers in a future state'.[31] Others presented Buddhism as a *preparatio evangelica* of sorts. It has 'not been without its use', we read elsewhere, for it has 'enlarged the vocabulary of mercy in the Chinese language'.[32] In *The Celestial and His Religions, or the Religious Aspect in China*, originally a series of lectures delivered at the Young Men's Christian Association of Hong Kong, Dyer Ball (1847–1919) stated that Buddhism

> has prepared the way to Christianity in China; for the Indian Buddhists introduced different terms into the Chinese language, and [to] some of these terms Christianity is indebted in conveying its truths . . . So we are indebted to Buddhism for the terms for heaven, hell and devil, as well as saviour'.[33]

However, this was far from being a discussion of technical terms. New battles were fought with tools both old and new. Walter Medhurst (1796–1857), founder of the first Christian printing press in Shanghai, commented in his *China, Its State and Prospects*, that Buddhism was 'despised by the learned' and that its practices were highly reminiscent of those of the 'Popists'. Buddhism is '*in decadence* and can only be regarded as a spent force'. Buddhist temples are 'manifestly the centres of a worship which is both polytheistic and idolatrous'. Similarly, Buddhist 'priests' may well wear their 'priestly robe', sport 'clean-shaven heads' and carry the rosary, but 'their lives are lazy' and the 'prayers that they daily repeat before their images are a jumble of now meaningless sounds, which even they themselves do not understand'.[34] In the *North China Herald*, the English-language periodical published in Shanghai, Joseph Edkins (1823–1905) of the London Missionary Society wrote that 'after so many centuries of successful domination over the Oriental mind' Buddhism had 'lost its proselytising power'.[35] In fact, for all their calculated anti-Buddhist rhetoric, the missionaries' representations once again echoed certain strands of Chinese elite opinion of the time. As Vincent Goossaert pointed out, 'unreconstructed Confucian scholars', now finding work in the emerging modern periodicals, were more 'anti-clerical' than 'anti-religious'. Thus, one of the important forces in the making of China's modernity, the periodical press, was initially marked by a certain anticlericalism, which both Christian and Buddhists addressed forcefully.[36]

THE MODERN CHINESE LANGUAGE OF 'RELIGION'

From the time of the publication of Morrison's dictionary in the early nineteenth century onwards, the Chinese language underwent a significant lexical expansion for within less than a hundred years it absorbed the nomenclatures of the most diverse branches of Western knowledge and thought. Highly-ideological labelling in the religious field on the part of observers, and ad hoc strategies of self-representation of (mainly Christian and Buddhist) Chinese practitioners, became especially relevant during the last decades of the nineteenth and the first decades of the twentieth century, a time of great social and political unrest and of heightened intercultural exchange. By the late 1890s, the discourse about 'religion' was of increasing interest as any search of the Chinese-language press, or of other non-Chinese-language periodicals produced in China, would reveal.[37] The missionary and amateur linguist Ada Even Mateer (1847–1936) culled Chinese-language periodicals for years in her search for new lexical items, especially with reference to religion. One of her studies contained the translation of a compelling article taken from such a Chinese-language periodical. The anonymous author (maybe Liang Qichao, to be discussed below) advocated the unification of China's now infamous 'three religions' into a single 'new religion'.

> The Buddhist religion came from India, the Protestant, Catholic, Christian and Mahommedan from Eastern and Western Europe. Our nation has originally no 'state teaching' (*guo jiao*). . . . Is it only in matters of religion (*zongjiao*) that we are not to have reform (*gaige*) and progress? China has from of old the Confucian religion; but since men only recognize that as a religion which holds some theology, Confucianism, which makes no mention of theology, cannot claim to be a perfect religion. But setting aside the question as to whether or not Confucianism is a religion, as well as the question of the origins of each religion, and speaking only of adaptation to changing conditions, there is advance in civilization, there is enlargement in physical science, there is revolution in government, and religion also cannot but adapt itself to circumstances and change with the rest. Then again, speaking only of the three religions (*san jiao*) held by the majority of the nation, from the ordinances and codes of these three religions, by combination and adaptation, a new religion (*zongjiao*) should be formed, called the Great Union New Buddhist religion.[38]

The possible connection between 'national progress' and 'religion' was not lost on a number of late nineteenth-century Chinese cultural and political activists in search of an overarching meta-narrative of national salvation. The secretary of the Christian Literature Society of China, Timothy Richard (1845–1919), worked for years to provide books and pamphlets in Chinese that showed 'the bearing of educational and religious development in industries and trade and in every department of national progress'.[39] He told 'all the followers of the non-Christian religions' that they should not 'take alarm, because we bring them new religious ideas', because 'the new is so much better than the old'. Those resisting change in religion, he added, 'are to-day in danger of retarding progress, as Roman Catholicism and Islam do in all countries under their sway. They bring on inevitable national death . . . hence the prosperity of all Protestant countries. . . . In religion, we must not be behind'.[40]

The highly influential journalist Liang Qichao (1873–1929), who had for a time been in close contact with Timothy Richard, was one of the first propagators of the modern Chinese discourse of religion.[41] In his essays from the early 1900s, Liang described religion (*zongjiao*) as 'the root of Western civilization' and actively sought for a Chinese alternative to Christianity. In the essay 'On Religious Reform in China' (*Zhina zongjiao gaige huanshuo*), he argued that the West succeeded in 'reforming its ancient schools thereby giving the people what they needed in terms of consciousness and spine to renew itself.'[42] He advocated a similar kind of restoration of the Chinese 'ancient teachings' of Buddhism and Confucianism. In his 'On the Relationship Between Buddhism and Social Order' (*Lun Fojiao yu qunzhi zhi guanxi*), he lamented the fact that China, differently from Europe or America, did not have a 'national religion', and asked, 'Will progress in governing China be attained using faith or not? . . . The root of faith is religion. . . . Some say that education can take the place of religion, but I dare not accept this statement'. He then listed several reasons for which Buddhism should be the ideal choice as the 'Chinese national religion', as it is a 'rational belief' (*zhe xin*) and not a 'superstition' (*mixin*). Buddhism trusts in one's strength and not in the strength of others, has faith in universal goodness and not in individual goodness, and teaches equality rather than discrimination because all sentient beings possess 'Buddha nature'.[43] Similarly, Yang Wenhui (1837–1911), one of the most influential Buddhists of modern times, was convinced that Buddhism could certainly stand up to each and every 'teaching of the West' (*xi yang ge jiao*) and become the first religion (*zongjiao*) of the world.[44]

Such an ambitious project was not to be realised. And yet, an attempt to recontextualise their cultural heritage vis-à-vis the prevalent secularism of both Nationalist and Communist nation makers, a new generation of Chinese religious activists, many of whom were close to Buddhism, became acquainted with the language of religious modernity. Many sought to negotiate a legitimate place for Buddhist practice in the context of the modernist and secularising debates about which aspects of the existing Chinese religious landscape could, and indeed should, be placed in the novel category of 'religion' as opposed to the concurrently emerging Christian-inspired category of 'superstition' (*mixin*).[45]

In 1918 the Chung Hwa Book Company printed the *Modern Dictionary of English Language* (with Anglo-Chinese explanations), based on

Webster's New International Dictionary. This dictionary, whose compilers were all Chinese, registered the definitive move towards standardising the modern Chinese lexicon and, as the preface states, 'technical and scientific terms relating to the most modern developments'. The gloss for religion reads thus:

> 1. The outward act or form by which man indicate recognition of a god or gods to whom obedience and honour are due; the feeling or expression of human love, fear or awe of some superhuman or over-ruling power; a system of faith and worship; a manifestation of piety
> 2. Specif. Christian faith and practice.[46]

Since the late Qing and the Republic, the Chinese state has conducted several attempts to frame the indigenous worldview along lines similar to those of the post-Reformation conception of religion, which in many important ways equates 'religion' with 'church'. The modern Chinese language situation underwent a significant shift in order to take into account and accommodate novel ideas about 'religion' and 'superstition'. But while those in power in China have until now largely failed to create uncontroversial and universally acceptable taxonomies of the religious field, the state has succeeded to an extent in imposing novel rules on the public practice of religion.

CONCLUSION

As Kenneth Dean pointed out, 'local Chinese religion resists definition'. As, indeed, any definition derived from Western critical traditions that revolve around doctrine, institutionalisation, and priesthood, is not very useful for describing local communal religion.[47] In today's Hong Kong, Taiwan, and various sites of the Chinese diaspora, people frequently organise temple festivals to celebrate the birthdays of their patron deities. They regularly visit shrines and temples seeking the blessings of a large pantheon of deities, both local and translocal, when facing difficulties, financial or sentimental concerns, or health problems. In order to come into contact with the gods and solicit their positive response, believers perform their own private rituals in temples, at countless ritual sites, or in front of domestic altars. In China however, the lack of a positive definition for many local and community-based practices is still problematic. Whatever is not 'religion' (*zongjiao*), in fact, may be 'superstition' (*mixin*) and must, according to China's law, be suppressed. Today's Chinese constitution officially grants the freedom of religious 'belief' (*xinjiao ziyou*), but many aspects of religious practice, including proselytising, are not contemplated. Generally speaking, the authorities seem to be most concerned with all things outside the realm of the officially registered sites and the five institutional 'religions' that is Buddhism, Daoism, Islam, Catholicism, and Protestantism.[48] Indeed, *zongjiao*, a by-product of several different things, including the Chinese imperial state's anxieties towards religiously inspired political uprisings, Christian missionaries' evangelising strategies, elite Buddhist modernisers' struggles for legitimacy, and Nationalist and Communist nation-makers' secularising attitudes, remains a problematic category. Beside being used in a positive sense to grant 'freedom of religion', for a number of citizens of the People's Republic of China, including members of the officially sanctioned Protestant and Buddhist communities, its adoption has ended up relegating several ordinary and traditionally widespread religious activities to the realm of superstitions.

Among cosmopolitan Chinese especially, a process of convergence with a conception of religion that had initially emerged outside China was clearly part of the shift to accommodate the new generic term for 'religion'. In order to fully understand these processes, one should take into account emerging notions of 'superstition', and consider more extensively the language used to represent the identities of the various religious traditions present in nineteenth- and twentieth-century China. However, even the present cursory examination of available sources reveals some of what took place. Remarkably, along with the great difficulties inherent to the many attempts at reconfiguring the Chinese indigenous worldview along lines similar to those of Christianity, some parts of 'Chinese religion', namely what we now call Buddhism, came to be regarded as commensurate to Christianity and so, ultimately, as 'religion'.

NOTES

1. I gratefully acknowledge the Leverhulme Trust for awarding me a fellowship (ECF/2005/0186) that allowed me to carry out the background research for this chapter. I am indebted to T. H. Barrett, Jeremy Gregory, John Zavos, Nile Green, and an anonymous reader for their insightful comments on previous drafts of this essay.
2. For a recent volume of studies on Chinese religion see D. Overmyer (ed.), 'Religion in China Today' (Special Issue), *The China Quarterly* 174 (2003); see also A. Anagnost, "The Politics of Ritual Displacement", in C. F. Keyes, L. Kendall, & H. Hardacre (eds.), *Asian Visions of Authority: Religions and the Modern States of East and Southeast Asia* (Honolulu: University of Hawaii Press, 1994), pp. 221–254; K. Dean, "Ritual and Space: Civil Society or Popular Religion?", in T. Brook & B. M. Frolic (eds.), *Civil Society in China* (Armonk, NY: Sharpe, 1997), pp. 172–192.
3. Cf. U. Bianchi (ed.), *The Notion of 'Religion' in Comparative Research: Selected Proceedings of the XVIth Congress of the International Association of the History of Religions* (Rome: L'Erma di Bretschneider, 1994); J. Paper, *The Spirits Are Drunk: Comparative Approaches to Chinese Religion* (Albany: State University of New York Press, 1995).
4. For some further comments on Buddhists' view of their own tradition, see F. Tarocco, *The Cultural Practices of Modern Chinese Buddhists* (London: Routledge, 2007).

5. See T. Asad, *Genealogies of Religion: Discipline and Reasons of Power in Christianity and Islam* (Baltimore: John Hopkins University Press, 1993), pp. 27 & 29.

6. See the primary sources and studies underlying T. D. Dubois, "Hegemony, Imperialism, and the Construction of Religion in East and South East Asia", *History and Theory* 44 (December 2005), pp. 126–131.

7. For a thorough examination of ritual, orthopraxy, belief, and state standardisation among other issues in late imperial China, see the essays in the special issue of *Modern China* 33, 1 (2007).

8. S. Feuchtwang, *Popular Religion in China, The Imperial Metaphor* (London: Curzon, 2001), p. 10.

9. See F. Masini, *The Formation of Modern Chinese Lexicon and Its Evolution Toward a National Language: The Period From 1848 to 1898* (Berkeley: University of California, Berkeley, Project on Linguistic Analysis, 1993), p. 223.

10. For the moment, see T. H. Barrett & F. Tarocco, "East Asian Religion Unmasked: A New Genealogy", *Dangdai zongjiao yanjiu* 4 (2006), pp. 37–43.

11. For the shift of other terms of kinship to indicate more abstract religious or intellectual phenomena, see M. Csikszentmihàlyi & M. Nylan, "Constructing Lineages and Inventing Traditions Through Exemplary Figures in Early China", *T'oung-pao* 89 (2003), pp. 59–99 and T. H. Barrett, "'Kill the Patriarchs!'", in T. Skorupski (ed.), *The Buddhist Forum*, I (London: School of Oriental and African Studies, 1990), pp. 87–97.

12. T. H. Barrett, personal communication (30 January, 2006).

13. For Buddhism: see M. Levering, "Scripture and Its Reception: A Buddhist Case" in M. Levering (ed.), *Rethinking Scripture: Essays From a Comparative Perspective* (Albany: State University of New York Press, 1989), p. 64; for Islam: see D. G. Atwill, *The Chinese Sultanate: Islam, Ethnicity and the Panthay Rebellion in Southwest China, 1856–1873* (Stanford, CA: Stanford University Press, 2006), pp. 158–159. I am grateful to T. H. Barrett for bringing these works to my attention.

14. R. Morrison, *A Dictionary of the Chinese Language in Three Parts* (Macao: East India Company Press, 1815–1823), p. 533.

15. For a study of state-sponsored actions against Christians, see L. Laaman, "Anti-Christian Agitation As an Example of Late Imperial Anticlericalism", *Extreme-Orient Extreme Occident* 24 (2002), pp. 47–63. For the late imperial state relationship with popular religious networks, see B. ter Haar, *The White Lotus Teachings in Chinese Religious History* (Leiden, The Netherlands: Brill, 1992).

16. Aihanzhe (ed.), *Dong-Xiyang kao meiyue tongjizhuan* 3 (1984), p. 48 (as reprinted in Beijing: Zhonghua shuju, 1997, p. 342). For a brief introduction to this figure and his publishing ventures in China, see J. Lutz, "Karl F. A. Gützlaff, Missionary Entrepreneur", in J. K. Fairbank & S. Wilson Barnett (eds.), *Christianity in China: Early Protestant Writings* (Cambridge, MA: Harvard University Press, 1985), pp. 61–87.

17. See T. H. Barrett & F. Tarocco, "East Asian Religion Unmasked: A New Genealogy", *Dangdai zongjiao yanjiu* 4 (2006), pp. 37–43.

18. For a critique of the academic representation of the Chinese religious world see Paper (1995). For the genealogy of 'religion' in the West, see Asad (1993).

19. S. Naquin & Chün-fang Yü (eds.), *Pilgrims and Sacred Sites in China* (Berkeley: University of California Press, 1992), p. 10. On the formation of Daoist rituals and cosmologies see for instance the studies in L. Kohn & D. Roth

(eds.), *Daoist Identity: Cosmology, Lineage and Ritual* (Honolulu: Hawaii University Press, 2001).

20. Note that in the mid-nineteenth century, Chinese scholars were still using the term 'Western books' (*xishu*) to indicate Buddhist books thus clear differentiation with Christian texts is quite slow (T. H. Barrett, personal communication 30 January 2006).

21. On Matteo Ricci, see J. Spence, *The Memory Palace of Matteo Ricci* (London: Faber & Faber, 1984). For an examination of the relationship between Jesuit writings and the origins of Sinology, see D. E. Mungello, *Curius Land: Jesuit Accommodation and the Origins of Sinology* (Honolulu: University of Hawaii Press, 1989). The text of the *Storia* is reprinted in P. M. D'Elia, *Storia dell'introduzione del cristianesimo in Cina*, in *Fonti Ricciane: documenti originali concernenti Matteo Ricci e la storia delle prime relazioni fra l'Europa e la Cina* (Roma: La Libreria dello Stato, 1942–1949), vol. 1, pp. 108–126; See also J. Gernet, "Della entrata della Compagnia di Giesù e Christianità nella Cina de Matteo Ricci (1609) et les remaniements de sa traduction latine (1615)", *Académie des Inscriptions et Belles-Lettres: Comptes rendus des séances de l'année 2003, janvier-mars* (Paris: Diffusion de Boccard, 2003), pp. 61–84; L. Fezzi, "Osservazioni sul De Christiana expeditione apud Sinas suscepta ab Societate Iesu di Nicolas Trigault", *Rivista di Storia e Letteratura Religiosa* 2 (2000), pp. 541–566.

22. See P. M. D'Elia, ibid., p. 126.

23. See J. Gernet, *China and the Christian Impact: A Conflict of Cultures*, trans. J. Lloyd (Cambridge: Cambridge University Press, 1985). For a fuller account of Ricci's views on Chinese religion see D. Porter, *Ideographia: The Chinese Cipher in Early Modern Europe* (Stanford, CA: Stanford University Press, 2002), especially pp. 90–108.

24. The original text is found in the database of the Ricci Institute for Chinese–Western Cultural History http://www.usfca.edu/ricci/resources/library/tianxue_chuhan_vol1/tianxue_chuhan359.htm (accessed October 2005). For a study of missionary attitudes with regard to vegetarianism, see E. Reinders, "Blessed Are the Meat Eaters: Christian Antivegetarianism and the Missionary Encounter With Buddhism", *Positions: East Asia Cultures Critique* 12, 2 (2004), pp. 509–537. For Buddhism and religious life in late imperial Beijing, see S. Naquin, *Peking: Temples and City Life, 1400–1900* (Berkeley: University of California Press, 2000).

25. See Jiang Wu, "The Revival of Yogâcâra Studies in Seventeenth-Century China and the Use of Buddhist Syllogism in Anti-Christian Polemics", *Studies in Yogâcâra Buddhism, A Seminar of the American Academy of Religion, Yogâcâra in East Asia, 2001:* http://www.uncwil.edu/p&r/yogacara/eastasia/ (accessed February 2003).

26. See T. H. Barrett's insightful comments about the enduring legacy among British sinologists of Ricci's views as represented by Trigault's version of Ricci's text in T. H. Barrett, "Chinese Religion in English Guise: The History of an Illusion", *Modern Asian Studies* 39, 3 (2005), pp. 509–533.

27. Susan Rosa's study of the text *Dialogues Among a Lutheran Theologian, a Jesuit, and a Chinese Philosopher* contains an engaging history of the rise of new attitudes toward religion in post-Reformation Europe; see S. Rosa, "Seventeenth-Century Catholic Polemic and the Rise of Cultural Rationalism: An Example From the Empire", *Journal of the History of Ideas* 57, 1 (1996), pp. 87–107; (the quotation is on p. 88). For a revealing study of Christianity in Europe before the eighteenth century, see J. Bossy, *Christianity in the West, 1400–1700* (Oxford: Oxford University Press, 1985). I am grateful to Jeremy Gregory for pointing me to the latter study.

28. See C. J. Sommerville, *The Secularization of Early Modern England: From Religious Culture to Religious Faith* (Oxford: Oxford University Press, 1992), p. 9.

29. For a study of the famous 'terms question' that consisted in finding a suitable Chinese translation for the words god, holy spirit, baptism, and so forth; see I. Eber, "The Interminable Term Question", in I. Eber, Wan Sze-kar, & W. Knut (eds.), *The Bible in Modern China: The Literary and Intellectual Impact* (Sankt Agustin, Germany: Institut Monumenta Serica, 1999), pp. 135–161.

30. See "Report of the Missionary Conference Held in Shanghai, May 10th–24th, 1877," China's Millions, 1877, pp. 105–106. John's Statement is found at p. 106.

31. G. John (1877), p. 106.

32. *Christianity and the Religions of China: A Brief Essay in Comparative Religions* published and distributed by the London Missionary Society, n.d. (The Library, School of Oriental and African Studies, London, Council for World Mission Archive Collection, Q222) .

33. D. J. Ball, *The Celestial and His Religions or the Religious Aspect in China* (Hong Kong: Kelly & Walsh, 1906), p. 115. For a discussion of the Victorian world's encounter with Buddhism, see P. C. Almond, *The British Discovery of Buddhism* (Cambridge: Cambridge University Press, 1988) and the review article by J. A. Silk who critiques and integrates some of Almond's views in *Journal of Indian Philosophy* 22 (1994), pp. 171–196.

34. See W. Medhurts, *China: Its State and Prospects: With Special Reference to the Spread of the Gospel Containing Allusions to the Antiquity, Extent, Population, Civilization, Literature, and Religion of the Chinese* (London: John Snow, 1840), p. 217. Medhurst referred specifically to 'the celibacy, tonsure, professed poverty, secluded abodes, peculiar dress of the priests: the use of the rosary, candles, incense, holy water, bells, images, and relics, in their worship; their belief in purgatory, with the possibility of praying souls out of its fires; the offering up of prayers in a strange language, with their incessant repetition; the pretension to miracles; the similarity of their altar pieces'.

35. *North China Herald*, 29 April 1854. Apart from his contributions to the popular knowledge of Buddhism, Edkins also authored scholarly works, including *Chinese Buddhism* (1880). Another member of the London Missionary Society who was active as a scholar was Ernest Eitel, author of the *Hand-Book for the Student of Chinese Buddhism* (1870).

36. See V. Goossaert, "Anatomie d'un discours anticlérical: le *Shenbao*, 1872–1878", *Extrême-Orient, Extrême- Occident* 24 (2002), p. 127. For Buddhist reformist views, see G. Müller, *Buddhism und Moderne* (Stuttgart, Germany: Franz Steiner Verlag, 1993); R. Birnbaum, "Buddhist China at the Century's Turn", in Overmyer (2003), pp. 122–144.

37. A search of the very influential *Shenbao* for the years 1872 to 1895 reveals that some two hundred items were published in the newspaper that dealt with religious issues, ranging from spirit mediums to the morals of Buddhist monks and Chinese converts to Christianity. See the *Electronic Index to the Early Shenbao (1872–1889)* at http://www.sino.uni-heidelberg.de/database/shenbao/manual.htm.

38. Adapted from A. H. Mateer, *New Terms for New Ideas: A Study of the Chinese Newspaper* (Shanghai, China: Presbyterian Mission Press, 1917), pp. 49–50.

39. T. Richard, *Forty-Five Years in China* (London: T. Fisher Unwin, 1916). See especially pp. 159, 218–219, 222, 231.

40. W. E. Soothill, *Timothy Richard of China: Seer, Statesman, Missionary and the Most Disinterested Adviser the Chinese Ever Had* (London: Seeley, Service & Co., 1924), p. 210.
41. For a study of Liang Qichao and other modern Chinese intellectuals' involvement with Buddhism see, Chan Sin-wai, *Buddhism in Late Ch'ing Political Thought* (Hong Kong: Chinese University Press, 1985).
42. Liang Qichao, "Zhina zongjiao gaige huanshuo", in *Yinbingshi wenji* (Shanghai, China: Guangzhi shuju, n.d.), vol. 5, pp. 33–36.
43. Liang Qichao, "Lun Fojiao yu qunzhi zhi guanxi" (On the Relationship Between Buddhism and Social Order) in Shi Jun et al. (eds.), *Zhongguo fojiao sixiang ziliao xuanbian* (Selected Materials on Chinese Buddhist Thought) (Beijing, China: Zhonghua shuju, 1990), pp. 49–56.
44. Yang Wenhui, "Zhina Fojiao zhanxing ce yi, er", reprinted in S. Jun et al. (1990), pp. 12–13.
45. On the problematic use of the term 'superstition' in Republican-period and communist China, see P. Duara, *Rescuing History From the Nation: Questioning Narratives of Modern China* (Chicago: University of Chicago, 1995). On religious persecution in 1920s China, see M. Bastide-Bruguière, "La campagne antireligieuse de 1922", *Extreme-Orient Extreme Occident* 24 (2002), pp. 77–93.
46. See the *Modern Dictionary of English Language* (n.p.: Chung Hwa Book Company, 1918), p. 813. Every sentence in English is followed by a sentence in Chinese, which is omitted here.
47. See K. Dean, "Local Communal Religion in Contemporary Southeast Asia", in Overmyer (2003), pp. 32–52.
48. For state control over religious practice in contemporary China, see P. B. Potter, "Belief in Control: Regulation of Religion in China", in Overmyer (2003), pp. 11–31.

3 Reclaiming Mysticism

Anti-Orientalism and the Construction of 'Islamic Sufism' in Postcolonial Egypt

Andreas Christmann

INTRODUCTION

In his recent criticism of the different constructs of the 'Mystic East', Richard King avoided the common reflex to put the blame entirely upon Western Orientalists. He showed that native Indians were not passive recipients of Western Orientalist discourses but in fact were actively involved in discursive and nondiscursive processes that led to the rise of definitions that homogenised 'Hindu Mysticism' or 'Buddhist Mysticism' and that served as powerful ideological and explanatory constructs in the political context of modern India. Using theoretical concepts such as 'bricolage', 'hybridity', and 'intercultural mimesis' from postcolonialist theory, King was able to demonstrate how India's intellectual elite had subtly appropriated the Orientalist discourse about homogenized Hinduism (both for colonial and anticolonial ends), and how this has disproved the simplistic and exclusive 'Saidian' association of Orientalism with Western colonial aspirations.[1]

So far, most of the critical work on 'Eastern Mysticism' as a form of 'reversed colonial ideology' has focused on the Indian subcontinent.[2] Much less attention has been paid to the Middle East and to the ways in which Orientalist discourses on Sufism and Islam have led Arab intellectuals to contribute to such constructs as an 'Islamic Mysticism'. Although some research has explored the effects of the colonial encounter with Islamic reformism leading to the initiation of hostile anti-Sufism, much less of this critical gaze has been placed on exploring the postcolonial period.[3] Little attention has been given, for example, to the sudden revival of Sufism after the gain of national independence in many countries of the Arab–Muslim world, which occurred in spite of the initial hostility from religious reformists and secular nationalists. In their desire to create a counterbalance to the increasing threat of political Islamism, nationalist governments in the Middle East often promoted a form of Sufism that they regarded as compatible with their political and cultural agendas.[4] Furthermore, oppressive authoritarianism, economic instability, and mounting state bureaucracy inspired a search for alternative moral values and role models, which a re-defined Sufism possibly seemed to provide.[5] Given the political context of this revival, it is important to explore to what extent the different constructs of an 'Islamic Sufism' by Arab–Muslim writers in fact perpetuated some of the Orientalist notions of 'mysticism' and 'Sufism' in spite of the often rampant anti-Orientalist tone that was officially the norm, and whether such constructs ideologically confirmed or undermined the official versions of a state-promoted Sufi-religiosity.

MYSTICISM, SUFISM, AND ORIENTALISM

In order to understand why and how European studies of Sufism became the subject of 'decolonising' efforts one has to recall the history of the concept 'mysticism' and of 'Sufism', prior to the middle of the twentieth century, and how both concepts were then transmitted into Egyptian intel-lectual and academic circles. As Leigh Schmidt showed in her study of the term 'mysticism', it first came into the English language in the mid-eigh-teenth century together with a critique of religious enthusiasm by advocates of the European Enlightenment.[6] In a discourse that stressed the virtues of the liberal, reasonable, rational, and social; 'mysticism' was created as a term that denoted the exact opposite: the ecstatic, fanatic, extravagant, unrestrained, and irrational. For Christian theologians, such as Ephraim Chambers (d.1740) or Henry Coventry (d.1752), who began to reify Chris-tianity according to new enlightened notions of 'reasonable religion', mysti-cism came to mean those dark sides of religion that were not acceptable any longer as 'true religion'. Carved out from religion, mysticism developed a note of sectarianism, as a result of which 'mystics' came to mean just one more sect in contrast to more acceptable forms of established Christianity. However, at the same time there was an intellectual stream within Euro-pean history that worked against the thrust of Enlightenment thinking, emerging as early as in the eighteenth century (e.g., T. Hartley, W. Law, J. Fletcher, F. Okely, and E. Stiles), but in particular in the nineteenth century (e.g., R. A. Vaughan, J. Heinroth, and S. Johnson). Rather than excluding mysticism from religion, these thinkers put mysticism on top of it by refor-mulating mysticism as the fountainhead of all genuine spirituality and by praising mystics as the guardians in all ages of 'true' religion. In this roman-ticised image of religion, which undermined the Enlightenment mood of rationalism, soberness, scientific spirit, and civility; mysticism reclaimed a positive connotation of 'religious enthusiasm' because it was then under-stood as intuitive insight, inward purity, ascetic piety, and spiritual eman-cipation. And yet in spite of their turn against the Enlightenment, writers who tried to absolve mysticism from its 'darker meanings', could only do so by following the Enlightenment paradigm of separating mysticism from the 'rude and unenlightened' forms of spiritual life, creating a mysticism that was stripped of lavish rituals, elaborate material symbols, sacramental hosts, and bleeding bodies. Moreover, such distinctions, moreover, became the norm when from the mid-1840s onwards transcendentalist circles in Europe and North America formulated a Perennialist philosophy, in which 'mysticism' developed into a form of eternal, universal spirituality beyond the limits of any specific religion or time period. Such a primordial divine tradition was also sought and found outside the European context, and the new discipline of Comparative Religion supported such efforts by publishing studies of common concepts, mutual influences, chronologies of formations, alterations, and degenerations. Mysticism became the connecting thread of a universal religion, while the search for its essence revealed innumerable subspecies—historical, geographical, and national: Oriental mysticism, Neo-Platonic mysticism, Greek mysticism, German mysticism, Spanish mysticism, French mysticism, and others.

With the 'psychological turn' in Western studies (W. James, E. Underhill, R. Jones, N. Söderblom, C.G. Jung, et al.), by the end of the nineteenth and the first half of the twentieth centuries mysticism was predominantly reduced to a universal and timeless religious experience, a solitary subjectivity without any distinct practices that could possess cultural particularities. In addition, as turned into 'a psychology', mysticism covered a wide range of experiences that were by and large not strictly religious: from the narcotic, neurotic, and hysterical to the sublimely artistic, creative, and inspirational. However, what linked the psychological studies of the twentieth century with the romantics of the eighteenth century was that mysticism served nicely as a conceptual foil against which one could project antipositivist and antimaterialist sentiments: 'It offered an intellectual shield against untrammelled naturalism, the fierce onward current of purely scientific thought.'[7] Moreover, defined as the quintessence of *religious* experience, mysticism still conveyed the post-Enlightenment tendency to relegate the religious out of the secular: Genuine mysticism could only be found outside the political, commercial, military, administrative, and bureaucratic spheres.[8] Mysticism found inside those areas was labelled as corrupted, degenerated, polluted, or simply false. By the end of this conceptual process, the focus of spiritual life, as it was perceived by European scholars, had moved away from the centre of the religious community to the heart of the individual believer, whereby the term mysticism more and more defined only the individual quest for the Divine rather than the socio-religious and political realities of everyday society.[9]

Inevitably, the Western study of Sufism could not escape the influence of these intellectual streams. Firstly, there was the liberalist/Protestant perception of Sufism as a sectarian cult of superstition, talismanic magic, witchcraft, and saint worship, which violated the higher ideals of 'universal' religiosity. Such perceptions of a dangerous sect with only very nebulous, vague relations to Islam 'proper'—often dichotomised through labels such as 'Dervishism' or 'Fakirism' in contrast to orthodox 'Mohammedanism'—were fuelled by encounters between colonial administrators and Sufi orders that had fiercely resisted European powers in the nineteenth and early twentieth centuries.[10] Such resistance to colonial premises could only be interpreted as Sufism's innate hostility to 'progress', as an expression of its 'irrationality' and 'blind fanaticism'. Particularly troublesome for colonial administrators was the structural fluidity of the Sufi orders, which fostered theories about their supposedly subversive and conspiratorial character. Writing home from Madras in India, for example, the reverend Canon Sell reported the following anxieties:

> Since the beginning of the nineteenth century, this same movement has grown with great rapidity. Under various pretexts, innumerable agents of the Religious Orders have gone throughout the Muslim world. They have adopted many disguises. Sometimes they are students, preachers, doctors; sometimes artisans, beggars, quacks; but they are everywhere received by the people and protected by them when they are suspected by the ruling [colonial] powers.[11]

Fear of unpredictable 'secret societies'[12] inspired colonial administrators to actively support and then institutionalise a form of a more controllable Islamic orthodoxy, which was based on *ulama*-scholarship and their focus on law and scripture, while Sufi practices and political militancy were defined as outside of the Shari'a, and then branded as heterodox. As a result, the construction of Sufism as either a heterodox subsect of Islam or as a separate movement, entirely detached from the roots of Islamic orthodoxy was a very virulent perception until only very recently.[13]

Secondly, there was the romanticised projection of Sufism as the free-thinking, poetical, spiritual, and intuitive source of 'original' religiosity in opposition to Islam's ossified, legalist-scripturalist orthodoxy. Within this stream of thought, Sufism was not identified with secretive, marauding mystical brotherhoods but with the abstract world of poetry and mystical metaphysics. Unlike European studies of Islam's authoritative texts of the Qur'an, Hadith, and Islamic Law, which were first of all based on Arabic sources from the Middle East, the study of Sufism started in South Asia with a particular focus on Indian and Persian manuscripts. Such interest in non-Arabic literary mysticism by pioneering Orientalists (such as W. Jones, W. Graham, F. A. Tholuck, E. H. Palmer, et al.) led to the discovery of a distinctly pantheistic and theosophical 'character' of Sufi doctrines, which was explained by historical-philological links to Hindu and Buddhist influences from South Asia. 'Pantheism' (belief in an ontological unity between the divine and humans) and 'theosophy' (the attainment of meaning through contact with the divine knowledge) thus became the fundamental classificatory yardsticks for the definition of what constituted Sufism, and since pantheism in particular had been fiercely rejected by what was perceived as Islam's (Arab) scripturalist elite, Sufism was once more placed outside

Islamic orthodoxy. For some Orientalists, Sufi-religiosity embodied the literary and ideological expression of an 'Aryan' rebellion against a conquering 'Semitic' mindset, but even without such ethnic/racial underpinnings (typical for nineteenth-century comparative philosophy), Sufism—defined through the prism of love poetry and mystical cosmologies—remained conceptualised as what Islam's orthodox zealotism was not: high spirited, liberal, genuine, and above all as opposed to ritualism, literalism, and dry scholasticism. Among liberal-Protestant academic circles in Europe in the twentieth century, it became established doctrine to introduce Sufism as the alternative of genuine religiosity as contrasted with the dominance of a formalistic, legalistic, and scholastic Islamic tradition.

Thirdly, Sufism became a 'religious philosophy' whose spiritual underpinnings were, within a Perennialist framework, compatible with the essence of 'universal' mysticism. Orientalists had produced a large quantity of translations of Persian, Turkish, and Arabic Sufi manuscripts, which European writers on 'comparative mysticism' could then use in their exploration of a primordial mystical paradigm. Encouraged by William James, who had already included Sufism in his account of an 'everlasting and triumphant mystical tradition',[14] authors such as Evelyn Underhill began to compare and contrast Sufi poets such as Rumi, Hafiz, Sa'adi, Jami', and Ghazzali with such Christian mystics as Ruysbroeck, Suso, Eckhart, Boehme, and others, albeit very often with the result of preferring the latter to the former.[15] Next to other 'expressions' of mysticism such as, 'Nature-Mysticism'; 'Christo-Mysticism', 'Nature-Mysticism', 'Soul-Mysticism', and 'Theodosis: The Deification of the Creature'; F. C. Happold's anthology of mystical texts contained an entire chapter on 'The Sufi Path of Love' in which he discussed Persian mystics as they were translated by their Orientalist 'discoverers' (R. A. Nicholson, A. J. Arberry, E. H. Whinfield, E. Fitzgerald, W. H. T. Gardner, and E. J. W. Gibb). His verdict on Sufism exemplifies the by then typical thinking of Perennialist writers who, driven by the impulse to locate mysticism in all possible cultural contexts, drew a sharp line between Sufism and Islam:

> The emergence of a rich mystical tradition in the heart of Islam, the most transcendental of all the higher religions, may seem at first sight surprising. That it should emerge suggests that mystical experience is the fundamental stuff of religion, that it is bound to burst out and be given expression, however alien to it the theological tenets in which a particular religious belief is expressed may seem to be.[16]

By and large by the middle of the twentieth century, Perennialist writers, inspired by the works of A. Huxley, R. Guénon, and F. Schuoon; by the neo-spiritualism of New Age literature; and in particular by the universalism of Hazrat Inayat Khan's neo-Sufism, had resolutely reified Sufism as an integral part of a 'universal' religion whose spiritual essence they underlined by referring exclusively to a neatly defined body of classical Sufi texts. [17] Such a one-sided and virtually decontextualized perception of Sufism, stripped of its practical and ritual, (i.e. prosaic) manifestations, fitted very well into a comparative phenomenology of the 'divine' core, by which the many different expressions of mysticism were rendered as essentially secondary to their attempt to demonstrate similarly the nature of the Absolute.

As a result of connecting Sufism to the universal concept of a socially and politically abstract 'mysticism', many aspects of Sufism's past and present that did not fit the ideal picture were cleared out. Concrete ritual and political performances in Sufi orders that struck the observer as odd or strange were perceived as degenerated forms of 'true' or 'high' Sufism—'no man of education would speak in their favour'.[18] Observations of existing Sufi practices that fell short of the 'devotional introspection' and 'cultivated interiority' of the classical poets and cosmologists could only be described as 'corruptions to which a purely subjective mysticism is liable [as] cankers' of a once blossoming rose.[19] Pantheism, Orientalists argued, once sublimely expressed in noble metaphysics, had degenerated and was now vulgarly understood by the ignorant masses as antinomianism and libertinism. Such pantheism led to the 'rotten' contemporary Sufi practices: Because a theory of the divinity in men and of the divine emanation in the world can only guide mystics to the removal of the discrimination between good and evil; to the rejection of civil law, to moral laxity, other-worldliness, quietism; and even worse to fatalism, passivity, and helplessness.[20] George Swan, the then Secretary of the General Mission in Egypt, summarised a widely shared view about the perceived decay of Sufism:

> In their beginnings often very attractive, they produced some noble lives and they inspired much of the very best of Islamic poetry; but undoubtedly their full fruit is to be found in the debasing ideas of the Moslem masses of to-day. They may use the dervish prayers, some of which are beautiful, and also the *zikr*, or repetition of special phrases designed for the purification of the soul's diseases, wholly with the idea of piling up merit; they may attend the public performances of *zikr* only because of the pleasurable emotions there stimulated; their minds may be wholly uneducated and densely ignorant; yet it will be found that the really formative influences that mould their lives are to be found in the mysticism which has degenerated into dervishism.[21]

To sum up, in most colonial and Orientalist discourses, 'Sufism' signified heterodox, universal, philosophical, and spiritual sides of 'Islam', which were thought to have been absorbed from 'foreign' sources outside the Arabic–Semitic tradition, but which had relapsed into the old forms of orthodoxy's rigid legalism and the 'soul-destroying' exteriority of political activism. Only a minority of Western scholars was sceptical about the non-Islamic influences on Sufism and highlighted instead its Semitic and

Islamic origins. It was German scholarship in particular that suggested as early as the nineteenth century that Sufism was not just an Aryan response to a Semitic religiosity but had first emerged from the widespread Arab tendency to asceticism within the Arabian Peninsula. In 1821, F. D. Tholuck claimed that 'Sufi doctrine was generated from Muhammad's own mysticism and must be illustrated out of it'.[22] In 1868, A. von Kremer also based Sufism on Arab asceticism and saw the nineteenth century as the transition period from asceticism to pantheistic 'enthusiasm' ('Religionsschwärmerei'), which marked the beginning of anti-Islamic tendencies.[23] Ignaz Goldziher, slightly modifying von Kremer's theory, isolated two distinct currents of Sufism (pure asceticism, closely related to the orthodox doctrine of Islam) and speculative theosophy (received from outside the Islamic tradition and derived from Greek Neo-Platonism and Buddhist doctrines).[24] Other scholars shared such an interest in Islam's early period of asceticism as the prerunner of Sufism, but still maintained that early Muslim ascetics were influenced by non-Islamic elements. For example, Richard Hartmann claimed that al-Bistami's quietism ultimately reflected a genuine Indian ideal, which his teacher 'Abu Ali al-Sindi taught him.[25] Max Horten was similarly convinced that such early mystics such as Bistami (d. 875) and al-Junayd (d. 910) were already thoroughly permeated with Indian thoughts; he also called al-Hallaj (d. 922) a 'Brahmanist thinker of the clearest water'.[26] Meanwhile Margaret Smith traced early Islamic asceticism back to the influence of Christian monasticism.[27] In 1906, R. A. Nicholson was the first British scholar to claim that 'Sufism of the ascetic and quietistic type . . . owes comparatively little either to Christianity or to any foreign source', which led him to conclude that 'this type of mysticism was—or at least might have been—the native product of Islam itself'.[28] Moreover, he not only declared asceticism a prestage of Sufism but regarded it as an integral part of 'Islamic mysticism', a historical phenomenon that had witnessed several historical and intellectual transformations. Later Louis Massignon was the first to grant al-Hallaj the status of an Islamic mystic who showed no foreign influence at all—something that Nicholson had only conceded to the ascetics of the seventh and eighth centuries (i.e., Ibrahim Ibn Adham, Ma'ruf al-Karkhi, Fudayl Ibn 'Iyyad, Shaqiq al-Balkhi, etc.). Massignon's conclusion, written in 1922, contained the then novel and astonishing formulation that

> it is from the Qur'an, constantly recited, meditated and practised, that Islamic mysticism proceeds—in its origin and in its development. Islamic mysticism derived its distinctive characteristics from the frequent re-reading and recitation of a text that is considered as sacred.[29]

These thoughts, which were later dubbed 'Massignon's Islamic theory', have rooted Sufism firmly within Islamic orthodoxy and for the first time described Sufism as a fundamental part of divine revelation. In addition, both Massignon and Nicholson acquitted early Sufism of the influence of philosophical pantheism, which they saw emerging only much later in the work of Ibn al-'Arabi (d. 1240).

EGYPT AND ORIENTALISM IN THE TWENTIETH CENTURY

Egyptian intellectuals came into contact with the thrust of Western studies on Sufism and mysticism mainly through three channels of transmission. The first channel was created by educational institutions that were set up in Egypt by colonial administrators for the spread of what were called 'modern European ideals of teaching and learning'. A second channel was established when in the 1920s and 1930s more and more Egyptian graduates replaced their Orientalist teachers and thus became the main transmitters of their masters' methodologies. Some of them followed their professors back to Europe in order to do their doctorates at European universities before they took up their teaching positions in Egypt. They were then involved in the creation of a third channel of communication in the 1940s and 1950s: translations of Orientalist literature into Arabic. By then, almost all European Orientalists had been replaced by indigenous Egyptian staff; while the newly created state universities (such as Cairo University; 'Ain Shams University, and Alexandria University) experienced a dramatic increase in student numbers and therefore needed mass teachable textbooks. In order to cope with the demand, Orientalist standard works on Sufism were translated from European languages into Arabic, in particular the above mentioned works of Nicholson, Massignon, Kremer, and Goldziher. [30]

Paradoxically, the sudden explosion of interest in Orientalist ideas of Sufism after World War II coincided with the decline of traditional Sufism in Egyptian society. Since the end of the nineteenth century, traditional Sufism, organised in the form of state-protected but doctrinally and ritually autonomous brotherhoods, had experienced a number of serious drawbacks. Anti-Sufi attacks by the Islamic reform movement created a climate in which traditionally-run Sufi orders lost their appeal to the younger generation of Muslims. However, against all expectation of a complete disappearance of mystical Islam, organised Sufism witnessed a remarkable revival after the Egyptian revolution in 1952, paradoxically under the secular and socialist regime of Jamal 'Abd al-Nasir (1952–1970). The number of new brotherhoods increased, new institutes for the study of Sufism were established, Sufi teachings were officially mediated and public rituals were organised jointly by Sufi orders and national political parties, such as by the Arab Socialist Union. This development continued under Nasir's successor, Anwar al-Sadat (1970–1981), under whose presidency an official parliamentary law (1976) and even a presidential decree (1978) were issued that formally sanctioned the significance and legitimacy of mystical Islam.[31] With the rise of the Islamist political opposition in the 1980s and 1990s, such ties between the regime and official Sufi orders were tightened under the presidency of Husni al-Mubarak (1981-present), who has been seen as trying to counterbalance the influence of radical Islamic groups by mobilising shaykhs of Sufi orders against them.[32]

It is within this decline of traditional Sufism and a subsequent emergence of a new interest in a reformed mystical Islam, in particular during the period of 1952 to 1981, that we need to locate the appearance of the *al-Tasawwuf al-Islami* ('Islamic Sufism') literature. This literature was part of a wider intellectual campaign to critically re-examine the entire output of Western Orientalism (*al-istishraq*). The campaign had started before the Second World War, almost immediately after the first Egyptian intellectuals began to use Orientalist methods and research strategies in their own work, but it intensified after Egypt had gained full political sovereignty in 1936 and independence as a Republic in 1953, which brought a new self-confidence that the country's intellectual elite wanted to translate into cultural and ideological autonomy from the West. Critics of Western Orientalism blamed the inherent ethnocentrism in Western studies of Islam as the main obstacle to accepting the research results of Orientalists. They also maintained that in spite of its pretence of advocating scientific universality, Western Orientalism was biased 'outsider science' that followed the ideals, norms, and prescriptions of secular ideologies that were deemed incompatible with the Muslim quest for 'truth'. Furthermore, they accused Orientalists of having monopolized access to the texts of their *own* heritage after they had 'stolen' Arabic manuscripts from Middle Eastern libraries and archives, which they then used to manipulate the public's knowledge about Islam and its history. After having established such antagonist positions, they maintained that every single proposition by a Western Orientalist needed to be contradicted by a critical revision from a genuine Islamic point of view.

In contradiction to this total rejection of Orientalism, some other voices called for a more nuanced view on Orientalism. They argued that there were 'upright' Orientalists (*al-munsifun*) and 'biased' Orientalists (*mujhifun*), and that the atrocities of the latter did not cancel out the achievements of the former.[33] Authors who followed this more moderate and benevolent position distinguished between different types of Orientalism and tried to avoid a complete rejection of European scholarship by highlighting the instrumental usage Orientalism could have for the propagation of Islam. With such a dual position of selective rejection and constructive insertion of Orientalist research it became possible to argue for a widespread circulation of Orientalist literature in Egypt, which in fact took place as described above through constant translations of European texts on Islam into the Arabic language. Such ambivalence towards Western Orientalism certainly explains the re-occurrence of some paradigms of Sufism that European authors helped to create in Arabic publications on the topic of 'Islamic Sufism'.

CONSTRUCTING AN 'ISLAMIC SUFISM' IN EGYPT

The term '*al-Tasawwuf al-Islami* literature' is defined here as the entire corpus of written material published for the purpose of demonstrating the *Islamic* nature or essence of Sufism. It refers to a public debate in response to the above mentioned twentieth-century influx of Orientalist ideas that had questioned the Islamic roots of Sufism. It also spoke against anti-Sufi writings by authors who were either inspired by Wahhabism or secular modernism.[34] The beginning of this debate in the mid-1940s coincided with the Arabic translations of texts by Orientalist authors who had argued for the Islamic origins of Sufism, such as Massignon and Nicholson,[35] and continued until the 1980s and 1990s in response to publications on 'Islamic Mysticism' written by the next generations of Orientalist writers (A. Arberry, H. Corbin, A. Schimmel, W. Stoddart, T. Burckhardt, L. Gardet, et al.).[36]

The point of departure for all participants in the debate was to disprove the Orientalists' descriptive notion of Sufism and to replace it with a prescriptive and normative category of 'authentic' *al-Tasawwuf al-Islami*. With the impact of Orientalist comparative studies of mysticism, phenomenological, or psychological studies of religion and Perennialist philosophies, Egyptian authors had been confronted with a huge variety of different mysticisms. Writers on *Islamic Sufism* felt that 'mysticism' (translated as 'al-tasawwuf' in Arabic translations) had become too wide a category. They drew sharp boundaries between 'pure' and 'impure' forms of mysticism; they wanted nothing to do with occultists, psychopaths, neurotics, charlatans, and magicians. The scholar 'Abd al-Wahid Yahya mourned that the 'psychological trend' (*al-ittijah al-nafsi*) in Western mysticism had emptied 'al-tasawwuf' of any association with *Shari'a*-based religiosity, against which he proposed an *Islamic Sufism* in order to correct such trends.[37] Mahmud Abu'l-Fayd al-Manufi's book title 'Unadulterated Islamic Sufism' already indicated that he believed in the existence of an opposite type of Sufism that had been adulterated by improper notions of mysticism. For him, *Islamic Sufism* is the opposite of 'nihilistic mysticism' (*al-tasawwuf al-salbi*) that he associated with Buddhist and Hindu mysticism, and of 'philosophical mysticism' (*al-tasawwuf al-falsafi*) that he linked with mystical doctrines permeated by Greek Gnosticism and Christian Neo-Platonism.[38] Similarly, Mustafa Ghalush wanted to purify Sufism from all external mysticisms that had crept into *Islamic Sufism*, elements that he called 'extraneous Sufism' (*al-tasawwuf al-dakhil*) or 'mysticist Sufism' (*al-tasawwuf al-tasawwufi*) and that were incompatible with proper 'Sunni Sufism' or 'Salafi Sufism'—both synonyms for Islamically normative mysticism.[39] Other authors equally dismissed 'inferior types' of mysticism;

mysterious voices, strange sights, spiritualist séances, body piercing, and fleshly mortifications were seen as primitive, naïve subcategories compared to 'authentic Sufism' (*al-tasawwuf al-haqiqi*), which is embodied by a spiritual aristocracy (*al-aristuqratiya al-ruhiya*) that demands an abstracted experience of divine union, an immediate consciousness of God's presence, or a contemplative intuition of the Absolute.[40] Writers on *Islamic Sufism* responded to the challenge that whether in historical-critical, phenomenological, comparative-religion, philosophical, or spiritual-esoteric studies; the category 'al-tasawwuf' had attained connotations that violated their sense of what should be included in *Islamic Sufism*. For them, these categories were either too wide because they included phenomena that should be excluded (e.g., unorthodox Sufi orders, 'foreign' sources, pantheism, miracle-performances, esoteric séances, antinomianism, etc.) or too narrow because they excluded notions that should be included (e.g., *Shari'a*-based piety, asceticism, social ethics, and spiritual morality). That is the reason why the adjective 'Islamic' was added to 'Sufism', which opened up the possibility for its advocates to objectify what constitutes *Islamic Sufism* in contradistinction to other, non-Islamic variants of mysticism.

The remaining sections of this chapter survey the variety of discursive strategies with which authors of *Islamic Sufism* have argued against the grain of colonialist and Orientalist writings and their 'intellectual crusade against the Islamic world', while the ramifications of this discourse within the context of Egyptian national and religious policies will also be considered.[41]

A major task of *Islamic Sufism* writers was to dissociate Sufi religiosity from militarily active mystical brotherhoods, a connection that as we have seen had captivated the colonial imagination throughout the nineteenth century. In order to avoid such associations, authors excluded specific references to the social and political history of Sufi orders and instead documented mystical spirituality entirely from its 'classical' literary canon. *Islamic Sufism* exclusively entailed mystical prose and poetry devoid of any explicit political connotations. Authors primarily located *Islamic Sufism* within the periods of Islamic history *before* the emergence of Sufi orders, that is the thirteenth century and thus favoured the internal, immanent (*batin*) and transhistorical esoteric side of Sufism over its exoteric, outward (*zahir*) manifestations in the form of brotherhoods, ritual performances, and worldly affairs—a move that authors, ironically, very often legitimised by referring to European theories on mysticism and their nonhistorical and similarly purely psychological approach to 'religious experiences'. Their historical accounts almost always exclude Sufism's collective and institutionalised forms, that is, the orders (*turuq*) and lodges (*zawaya* and *rabitat*, etc.). *Islamic Sufism* is instead embodied by individual masters, spiritual heroes, ascetics, poets, and scholars who personally 'incarnate' Sufism, not as public political actors but as moral icons that exclusively symbolise the accomplishment of spiritual transformation and not worldly concerns.

If Sufi orders were mentioned at all in the literature then it was primarily through portraits of individual law-abiding, nonecstatic and predominantly quietist Sheikhs whose description of their mystical path excluded any possibility for readers to identify them politically, socially, and sometimes even geographically.[42] Curiously, writers on *Islamic Sufism* turned to the romantic move in the European construct of 'mysticism' and were thus able to present a sanitised picture of Sufism that was abstracted from the nastiness of ritual aberrations or political entanglements that did not fit the picture.

Such definitions, of course, tried to circumvent colonialist paradigms as well as reformist polemics in which Sufism was attacked primarily with reference to the all-too-worldly aspirations of Sufi Shaikhs who had supposedly transformed their brotherhoods into networks of wealth, prestige, and power.[43] Moreover, to portray *Islamic Sufis* without political aspirations was evidently a reflection of the current impoverished status of Sufi orders in Egypt, and it found the enthusiastic approval of state authorities.[44] If widely circulated in the official media, a nonpolitical conception of Sufi religiosity would undoubtedly counter-balance and contradict the nonquietist stance conception of Sufi-religiosity, of the Islamist movement, in particular the influential *Jama'at al-Ikhwan al-Muslimin* (Muslim Brotherhood), which in spite of its later anti-Sufi rhetoric had ironically preserved for itself much of the organisational and hierarchical structures of traditional Sufi orders.[45] In case of public conflict, when the revolutionary, political, and all-too-worldly potential of Islam was invigorated, nonpolitical versions of *Islamic Sufism* were mobilised to combat 'dangerous', 'marauding' Islamist groups.[46] An *Islamic Sufism* without (the necessity of having) Sufi orders also de-legitimised calls for the existence of external religious institutions, which in the case of unruly brotherhoods, for example, could be reformed, temporarily closed or completely dissolved at will—all with reference to the violated norms of *Islamic Sufism*.[47] Notions of an individual and personal Sufism that transcends the social boundaries of a Sufi order invariably attracted the newly educated, urbanised, and not yet affiliated members of the middle class, and it was no surprise that new Sufi circles based on principles of *Islamic Sufism* have been established in Egypt since the 1960s, often replacing the old-type brotherhoods.[48] Such developments show to what extent definitions of what constitutes *Islamic Sufism* were thoroughly permeated by the political interests of all parties involved and how deeply political a supposedly nonpolitical concept of Sufism can become.

A second discursive move was to dissociate Sufism from 'foreign influences', that is from its Christian, Greek, Persian, or Indian roots. Reversing the early Orientalist paradigm that Sufism blossomed as an Aryan resistance against Semitic religiosity, authors of *Islamic Sufism* restricted the boundaries of 'authentic' Sufism to the period *before* so-called non-Islamic ideas had crept into Sufism from Persia and India in the sixth and seventh centuries. Foreign influences that were thought to have slipped into Islam from Greek Gnosticism and Christian Monasticism during the first four centuries of Islamic history were deemed to have been faithfully eradicated by 'orthodox' Sufis by the end of the eleventh century. In spite of their often rampant anti-Orientalist rhetoric, most authors used Massignon as the main witness for their view that in contrast to the common belief Arabic sources were the true origins of Islamic mysticism. Almost all publications contained sections that repeat Massignon's etymological exercise of tracing Sufi mystical vocabulary back to the Qur'an and the Prophetical Sunna, while displaying its further developments in other 'purely' Arabic academic disciplines, such as grammar, jurisprudence, and theology. In fact, they claim that Sufism, defined as an Arabic 'religious philosophy', developed from the prophetical tradition as a sphere of scholarship in its own right, alongside such other legitimate scholarly disciplines as *fiqh, falsafa,* and *kalam.*[49] Specialists in Islamic and pre-Islamic poetry, such as 'Abd al-Hakim Hassan and Muhammad Yasir Sharaf, furthermore 'proved' the indebtedness of mystical love poetry to profane Arabic poetry rather than to Persian love poetry as had for too long had been the standard explanation.[50] One strategy of authors was to restrict their chronology of *Islamic Sufism* to the period between the seventh and ninth centuries, thereby emphasising the 'genuine' Arab asceticism as the indispensable prestage of Islamic mysticism. Knowing from their readings of Orientalist texts that those ascetics were the decisive link between the period of the *Sahaba* (contemporaries/companions of the Prophet) and the mystical schools of the ninth/tenth centuries, authors delved into portraying ascetic practices of *zuhd* (renunciation), *wara'* (piety), *tawakkul* (God-centeredness), *dhikr* (God-remembrance), *hubb* (love of God), and so forth, as *the* ultimate precondition of 'authentic' mystical states.[51] The calculated effect of such emphasis was the impression that the subsequent mystical states (*ahwal*) and stations (*maqamat*), including the controversial states of annihilation (*fana'*) and union (*ittihad*), had to be read and understood in light of the ethical and spiritual ideals of Arab asceticism and not from the perspective of the (not yet encountered) Buddhist or Hindu pantheisms (*pace* Nicholson's legacy). Such definitions tacitly adopted Orientalists' 'back to the Ur-text' approach and used their (not uncontested) theory of an Islamic origin to establish the root (*asl*) of Sufism within the authoritative texts of Qur'an and Sunna, thereby exempting Sufism from the accusation of being an illegitimate novelty (*bid'a khadi'a*).[52]

More controversial, however, was the attempt to exclude the philosophies of pantheism from the canon of *Islamic Sufism*. Authors differed considerably in their treatment of early mystical eponyms such as Muhy al-din Ibn al-'Arabi (d. 1240), Ibn Sabi'in (d. 1268), Jalal al-din al-Rumi (d. 1273)), Ibn al-Farid (d. 1235), al-'Attar (d. circa 1220), or al-Suhrawardi (d. 1192) who previously were all subsumed under the rubric of advocating pantheism. The debate split Egyptian writers into two groups. The first group consisted of authors who uncompromisingly rejected the entire tradition of philosophical Sufism and who categorised mystical poets as heretics if their texts allowed even a hint of pantheistic interpretation.[53] A second group permitted a more nuanced reading of these texts, applying Nicholson's distinction on the one hand between mystical texts that in spite of their pantheistic impressions in fact referred to psychological states of the mystics' mind, not philosophical theories (e.g., by al-Bistami, al-Hallaj, al-Rumi, al-Farid) and, on the other hand, texts that were indeed intended to be understood as theories of philosophical pantheism (by Ibn al-'Arabi, al-Suhrawardi, Ibn Sabi'in, etc.).[54] Authors of this group were keen to propagate Nicholson's attempt to exempt Sufism of the first five centuries of Islam from any pantheistic influences, but they were also at pains to exclude pantheistic authors from the canon of *Islamic Sufism*, something that Nicholson had in fact not intended.[55]

A particular reason why writers on *Islamic Sufism* aimed to purify Sufism from the influence of pantheism was the mystical concept of *wahdat al-wujud* 'unity of [divine and human] existence', which they believed contradicts the theological doctrine of *tauhid Allah* 'God's [singularity and] unity' and by doing so attempt to harmonise Sufism with other Islamic sciences (*'ulum*) deemed 'orthodox'. One central hermeneutical operation in their description of the *unio mystica* with Allah was to interpret the mystics' ecstatic utterances of union not as sober exposés about ontological realities but as impulsive reflections of their (often confusing) psychological experiences, whose apparent pantheistic connotations they afterwards denied when asked in a sober, nonecstatic state of mind. The concept of *wahdat al-wujud* was as a result re-read as *wahdat al-shuhud*, that is as a unity of divine and human existence that was only mentally witnessed but not ontologically proved. The ecstatic mystics were then, by the rules of *fiqh*, exempted from the accusation of (wilful, deliberate) *kufr*, that is wrongful belief stated with a sober state of mind.[56] Remarkable in this respect is a renaissance of references to Abu Hamid al-Ghazzali (1058–1111), whose reputation as a 'harmoniser of Sufism with Islamic orthodoxy', attributed to him by Orientalists, was eagerly popularised among *Islamic Sufism* authors.[57] Similarly striking is how frequently writers mentioned Ibn Taymiyya's (1263–1328) and Ibn al-Jauzi's (1114–1201) Hanbali legal positions toward Sufism, whose strong criticism of Ibn al-'Arabi's pantheistic metaphysics was put next to their general approval of an ascetic, Salafi type of Sufism, a distinction they wanted to reappraise.[58] However, this created a sharp division between Islamically proper and improper Sufism and helped to advance a public disapproval of the Ibn al-'Arabi tradition, culminating in an (unsuccessful) attempt in 1981 to officially declare Ibn al-'Arabi's work as heretical.[59]

Thirdly, one of the most rigorous manoeuvres by the authors of *Islamic Sufism* works was to associate Sufi religiosity with the Golden Age period of Islam and thereby portray Sufism as *the* spiritual precondition for inner-worldly success, contradicting the reformists' claim that with the arrival of Sufism moral and political decline had set in. Central to this manoeuvre was the projection of contemporary ideological battles with secularism, materialism, liberalism, and Marxism back into the time of early Islam and the claim that the existence of *Islamic Sufism* secured Islam's triumph over its ancient rival antagonists (paganism, Hellenism, rationalism, sectarianism, etc.). Such historical analogy allowed writers to postulate what contemporary Muslims currently lacked to overcome their social, political, and moral crises: 'genuine spirituality' or a 'spiritual philosophy of life' that aims towards moral growth of the human soul.[60] Against the current grip of a 'tyrannical materialism' they claimed to advance Sufism as a 'spiritual revolution' (*thaura ruhiya*) that would eventually lead to a comprehensive cultural reform of Egyptian society.[61] Against 'soulless' Western philosophies based on rationalism, humanism, and positivism, they advocated Sufism as a 'life philosophy' (*falsafa hayat*) that aims not just at rational enlightenment but also spiritual happiness, and that is—according to Abu'l-Wafa' al-Taftazani—realised by a 'mystical annihilation into a higher reality where gnosis is achieved through non-rational experiences (*dhauqan la 'aqlan*)'.[62] And in contrast to empiricist, human-centred Western psychology they depicted Sufism as a superior form of psychology that combines the analytical skills of Western diagnostics with the moral teachings of the early Islamic mystics, thus offering a form of 'spiritual medicine' (*al-tibb al-ruhani*) as 'Abd al-Latif Muhammad al-'Abd had put it.[63]

Beneath all such definitions of Sufism was a strong dissatisfaction with the Western episteme that authors feared was now about to conquer the East. They felt that Western universities and Western society, with Orientalism as their academic mouthpiece, were dominated by positivism, relativism, and secularism. However, they conceived human existence as being founded on sacred realities of the ontologically different unseen world, but the predominance of social sciences and historicism in Orientalist academia and Western society had eroded the possibility of relating philosophies meaningfully to such sacred spheres. *Islamic Sufism* was an attempt to restore lost spirituality, and was equally an explicit critique of secular modernity, which ironically resembled the views and writings of such Western neo-conservative writers as Rudolf Otto, Friedrich Heiler, Mircea Eliade, René Guenon, and Henry Corbin, who were intensely studied by the Egyptian writers.[64]

With the exclusion of pantheism from *Islamic Sufism* and its portrayal as quintessentially 'spiritual ethics', writers achieved an important goal: the exclusion of antinomianism from any association with Sufism. Accusing Orientalists of having artificially created boundaries between Sufic religiosity and *Shari'a*-based Islam, the Egyptian writers maintained that Sufism's concept of knowledge (*ma'rifa*) combines instead both exoteric intellection (*'ilm*) for the understanding of Shari'a-law and esoteric gnosis (*ma'rifa*) for grasping mystical matters. 'Abd al-Halim Mahmud even went as far as to claim that mystics were the better jurists (*fuqaha*) because of their closeness to Allah and their taste of the divine reality (*al-haqq*) behind the letters of law.[65] And Rashid Naji al-Hasan exemplarily wrote, 'Who only rationally argues but has no mystical insight, has sinned (*tafassaqa*); who only mystically acts but does not argue rationally, is an atheist (*tazandaqa*); however, who combines the mystical and the rational has truly received the truth (*tahaqqaqa*).'[66] By quoting traditional authorities of *fiqh* who spoke in favour of Sufism[67] and by reiterating the views of the so-called 'sober Sufis', such as al-Junayd, al-Qushairi and al-Hujwiri, who had emphasised the central role of the *Shari'a* for Sufi practice, authors of *Islamic Sufism* stressed (once more) the natural symbiosis between Sufism and Islamic law, coining terms such as 'lawful Sufism' (*al-tasawwuf al-mashru'*) in order to bring their point home.[68]

Central to their argument was to state that the mystical phase of annihilation (*fana'*) is not a reflection of an antinomian attitude of escapism but an exceptional state of superior spiritual perception of reality (*haqiqa*) that is both the product and precondition of a *Shari'a*-centred daily life. These mystical states are, writers claimed, not alternative ways of religiosity against a *Shari'a*-led scripturalism but the mystic's typical path towards a more sublime way of living according to the Divine law. Such passionate appeals for synchrony between spirituality and *Shari'a* law clearly went against everything that had been said about Sufism by Western writers. They particularly questioned the validity of a universal concept of 'mysticism', although Egyptian authors did not negate the possibility of other, albeit inferior, forms of mysticism. They did, however, aim at a normative evaluation of mystical phenomena in the light of prescriptive norms by Islam's textual tradition in a critical response to a supposedly historical or scientific phenomenology of 'mysticism' that still permeated Christian/ Western concepts of what constitutes 'religion'.

Within the public debate in Egypt, such 'Islamised' definitions of Sufism worked in two ways. On the one hand, they forced Sufis to rethink their commitment to Islamic law, leading to a constant revision of their doctrinal and ritual resources in light of the legal prescriptions of Islam's textual tradition. On the other hand, they were a forceful reminder of the fact that the Islamists' demand for the immediate implementation of *Shari'a* law in Egypt must be accompanied by an equally important spiritual renewal if it was to meet those ideals of traditional religiosity. In both cases, as the officially accepted version of Sufism, *Islamic Sufism* was employed by the Egyptian authorities as a disciplinary tool to regulate the internal practices of Sufi orders and as an ideological weapon to undermine the radical claims of Islamist movements, in particular in the 1980s and 1990s. However, *Islamic Sufism* also produced a sudden convergence of Sufi and non-Sufi reformist positions, a shared legal and ritual universe that downplayed the formerly sharp divisions between the two, and which has over time has integrated *Salafi* positions into Egyptian mainstream thinking. Given the fact that Egyptian public discourse has seen a gradual Islamisation in rhetorical and symbolic ways of communication, in particular since the late 1980s, one might even regard *Islamic Sufism* as a concept of religiosity that has spiritualised the Islamist discourse as much as it has Islamised the spiritual discourse, leading to the paradoxical effect of both enriching as well as neutralising each other.

CONCLUSION

In this chapter, I demonstrated the remarkable similarities in the modern construct of 'mysticism' by European and American authors and Egyptian writers on 'Islamic Sufism', in particular in their common quest for spirituality in an age of modern secular philosophies, but also in their attempt to formulate a higher form of sublime religiosity in contradistinction to the dark and seamy side of traditional religion. As it was crafted by Egyptian academics and intellectuals in post World War II Egypt, *Islamic Sufism* was a pious construct made by scholars for other scholars or their students. It represented an objectified form of Sufism that emerged parallel and in contrast to actual Sufi-teachings practised in Egyptian lodges and mosques; a fact that undoubtedly prevented a wider recognition of this literature among Egypt's literate population. However, it was a remarkable achievement in both appropriating and rejecting Orientalist writings on Islam and Sufism, in as much as it both absorbed and resisted anti-Sufi polemics by reformist and secularist circles. This essay has shown that unlike Western constructs of 'mysticism' *Islamic Sufism* was both product and facilitator of religious politics during the second half of the twentieth century. It was nourished by waves of Islamic neo-conservatism and disillusionment with existing political regimes. It has been argued that antimodernisms in the texts of *Islamic Sufism* gained force the more emphatically post World War II failures of Egyptian nationalist (and at times socialist) regimes that led Egyptian Muslims to question the legitimacy of secular ideologies. The political and military disaster of the June War in 1967, the economic hardship during the *infitah* policy in the 1970s under Sadat, and the political stalemate due to the authoritarian rule of the Mubarak regime since the 1980s, led to a revival of religion and a desire to return to 'divine roots' of human existence and subsequently increased the popularity of such resacralised concepts of 'being' and 'authentic life' as *Islamic Sufism*. As a predominately quietist concept of Islamic religiosity it canalised general dissatisfaction into peaceful channels of resistance and attracted the support of political authorities in its capacity as an alternative to more radical opposition.

And yet, in spite of several occasions when *Islamic Sufism* was exploited as a rhetorical/ideological tool of disciplinary religious policy, it can be argued that it also contained a subversive element of dissent and opposition to the bureaucratic domination of the Egyptian state. This is because the saintly mystic of *Islamic Sufism*, even if he/she lived way back in the past, represented the ideal antitype to the menacing, corrupt, and greedy politician or bureaucrat who had achieved his power through ruthless plotting and rivalry. The charisma of the saintly mystic—and his attainment of autonomy from external considerations—is depicted as resulting from his moral battle for generosity, love, self-denial, and spiritual strength. In other words, *Islamic Sufism* as a tool of criticism of radical Islamism and its all-too-worldly obsession with political power was also used in an emotional discourse for resisting 'cold' and 'technical' bureaucracy, which put state authorities under greater pressure to 'perform' more ethically and spiritually according to the models of *Islamic Sufism*. Amongst religious constructs of Islam in the twentieth century, the construct of *Islamic Sufism* in postindependence Egypt is unique in that it attained authority both for suppressing/excluding specific types of Sufi-religiosity and for emancipating other forms of religiosity that empowered their agents in their opposition against authoritarian rule.

NOTES

1. R. King, *Orientalism and Religion: Postcolonial Theory, India and 'The Mystic East'* (London: Routledge, 1999), in particular chapters 5–7; also see King's bibliography for references to the relevant postcolonial literature.
2. e.g., P. van der Veer, *Imperial Encounters: Religion and Modernity in India and Britain* (Oxford: Oxford University Press, 1990), chapters 3 and 5; C. A. Breckenridge & P. van der Veer (eds.), *Orientalism and the Postcolonial Predicament: Perspectives on South Asia* (Philadelphia: University of Pennsylvania Press, 1993), in particular the contributions by N. Dirks (pp. 279–313) & D. Lelyveld (pp. 189–214).
3. For Syria: see D. Commins, *Islamic Reform: Politics and Social Reform in Late Ottoman Syria* (Oxford: Oxford University Press, 1990); for Egypt: see J. Johansen, *Sufism and Islamic Reform in Egypt: The Battle for Islamic Tradition* (Oxford: Clarendon Press, 1996).
4. A. Christmann, "An Invented Piety? Subduing Ramadan in Syrian State Media", in A. Salvatore (ed.), *Muslim Traditions and Modern Techniques of Power, Yearbook of the Sociology of Islam 3* (Hamburg, Germany: Lit Verlag, New Brunswick, NJ and London: Transaction Publishers, 2001), 243–263.
5. A. Christmann, "Ascetic Passivity in times of Extreme Activism: The Theme of Seclusion in a Biography by al-Buti," in P. Alexander et al. (eds.), *Festschrift for the Journal of Semitic Studies* (Oxford: Oxford University Press, 2005), 279–303.
6. L. E. Schmidt, "The Making of Modern 'Mysticism'," *Journal of the American Academy of Religion* 71, 2 (2003), 273–302. The following section follows very closely the excellent account of Schmidt. A similar 'late' entry into English vocabulary is reported for the term 'spirituality', which was not used until the seventeenth century. See J. R. Carrette & U. King, *Selling Spirituality: The Silent Takeover of Religion* (London: Routledge, 2005), p. 37.
7. Schmidt (2003), p. 288.
8. For a criticism of such an oversimplified understanding of mysticism that ignores the political aspirations of Christian mystics, see G. Jantzen, *Power,*

Gender and Christian Mysticism (Cambridge: Cambridge University Press, 1995), in particular pp. 1–11; 305–307.

9. For a similar trajectory of the concept 'spirituality' see Carrette & King (2005), U. King, "Spirituality in a Post-Modern Age," in U. King (ed.), *Faith and Praxises in a Postmodern Age* (London: Cassel, 1998), 94–112; P. Heelas, "The Spiritual Revolution: From Religion to Spirituality," in L. Woodhead et al. (eds.), *Religions in the Modern World* (London: Routledge, 2002), 357–377.

10. See a summary of existing studies about such encounters in A. Knysh, "Sufism As an Explanatory Paradigm: The Issue of the Motivations of Sufi Resistance Movements in Western and Russian Scholarship", *Die Welt des Islams* 42, 2 (2002), 139–173.

11. C. Sell, *The Religious Orders of Islam* (Wilmington, DE: Scholarly Resources, 1976; Originally published 1908), p. 3.

12. Sell (1976), p. 5.

13. For a discussion see C. W. Ernst, *The Shambhala Guide to Sufism* (London: Shambala, 1997), chapter 1: "What is Sufism?," 1–31.

14. W. James, *The Varieties of Religious Experience* (London: Routledge, 1982), p. 419.

15. "Now without prejudice to individual beliefs and without offering an opinion as to the exclusive truth of any one religious system or revelation—for here we are concerned neither with controversy nor with apologetics—we are bound to allow as a historical fact that mysticism, so far, has found its best map in Christianity." E. Underhill, *Mysticism* (London: Methuen, 1911, 4th ed., 1912), p. 125. See also R. King's analysis of Otto's biased comparison between Meister Eckhart and Śankara's Vedānta system, King (1999), pp. 125–128.

16. F. C. Happold, *Mysticism: A Study and an Anthology* (Harmondsworth, England: Penguin, 1963, rev. ed. 1970), p. 248.

17. For the latter, see J. Figl, *Die Mitte der Religionen: Idee und Praxis Universalreligiöser Berwegungen* [The unifying centre of religion: beliefs and practices of universalistic religious movements] (Darmstadt: Germany, 1993), in particular pp. 89–140.

18. A. J. Arberry, *Sufism: An Account of the Mystics of Islam* (London: Mandala Books, 1950), p. 122.

19. R. A. Nicholson, *The Mystics of Islam* (London: Bells, 1914), p. 95.

20. With the psychological turn in the study of mysticism, pantheism as a philosophical notion had lost much of its appeal because of its perceived 'dangerous' psychological implications. See, e.g., 'Unless safeguarded by limiting dogmas, the theory of Immanence, taken alone, is notoriously apt to degenerate into pantheism; and into those extravagant perversions of the doctrine of "deification" in which the mystic holds his transfigured self to be identical with the Indwelling God.' Underhill (1912), p. 119.

21. G. Swan, "The Mystical Life in Modern Islam," in J. R. Mott (ed.), *The Moslem World of To-Day* (London: Hodder and Stoughton, 1925), pp. 291–301.

22. F. A. D. Tholuck, *Ssufismus, sive theosphia Persarum pantheistica* [Sufism, or: the Persians' pantheistic theosophy] (Berlin: Dümmler, 1821), p. 71.

23. A. von Kremer, *Geschichte der herrschenden Ideen des Islams. Der Gottesbegriff, die Prophetie und Staatsidee* [The history of Islamic thought: God, prophethood and the concept of state] (Leipzig, Germany: Brockhaus, 1868), pp. 69ff.

24. I. Goldziher, *Mohammed and Islam* (*Vorlesungen über den Islam*, 1910) trans. K. C. Seelye (New Haven: Yale University Press, 1917), pp. 162ff.

25. R. Hartmann, "Zur Frage nach der Herkunft und den Anfängen des Sûfitums" [About the origins and early history of Sufism], *Der Islam* 6 (1916), 31–70.

26. M. Horten, "Indische Strömungen in der islamischen Mystik" [The influences of India in Islamic mysticism], *Materialien zur Kunde des Buddhismus* (1927/1928), p. 5.

27. M. Smith, *Studies in Early Mysticism in The Near and Middle East* (London: Sheldon Press, 1931).
28. R. A. Nicholson, "Historical Enquiry Concerning the Origin and Development of Súfism, With a List of Definitions of the Term 'Ṣúfí' and 'Taṣawwuf', Arranged Chronologically," *Journal of the Royal Asiatic Society* (1906), pp. 303–348.
29. L. Massignon, *Essai sur les origines du lexique technique de la mystique musulmane* [A study of technical terms in Islamic mysticism] (Paris: Librarie Philosophique, 1922), p. 35.
30. R. A. Nicholson, *Fi'l-Taṣawwuf al-islāmī wa-ta'rīkhihi* [History of Islamic mysticism], trans. and explained by Abū'l-A'lā 'Afīfī (Cairo, Egypt: Lajnat al-Ta'līf wa'l-Nashr, 1947, 2nd ed. 1956); R. A. Nicholson, *Al-Ṣūfīya fi'l-islām* [Mystics of Islam], trans. Nūr al-Dīn al-Sharīf (Cairo, Egypt: Maktabat al-Khānjī, 1951); R. A. Nicholson, 'Abd al-Raḥmān Badawī, *Shakhṣīyāt qaliqa fi'l-islām* [Restless Personalities in Islam], (Cairo, Egypt: Maṭba'at Muṣṭafā al-Bābā al-Ḥalabī, 1947, 3rd ed. 1964) contains translations of L. Massignon about al-Ḥallāj and also of H. Corbin about Suhrawardī. See also Massignon's collection of several articles on Ibn Sina in Arabic: L. Massignon et al., *Dhikrā Ibn Sīnā: ba'ḍ mabāḥith* [Studies in memory of Ibn Sina] (Cairo, Egypt: Maṭba'at al-Ma'had al-'Ilmī al-Firanjī, 1954); A. von Kremer, *Al-Ḥaḍāra al-islāmīya wa-maddā ta'ththurihihā bi'l-mu'athirāt al-ajnabīya* [The Islamic civilization and the extent to which it has been influenced by foreign ideas], trans. Muṣṭafā Ṭaha Badr (Cairo, Egypt: Maṭba'at al-I'timād, 1947); I. Goldziher, *al-Madhāhib al-Islāmīya fi'l-tafsīr al-Qur'ān* [Islamic schools of qur'anic exegesis] (Cairo, Egypt: Maktabat al-Khānjī, 1947) one section on Sufi *tafsīr* and I. Goldziher, *Al-'Aqīda wa'l-sharī'a fi'l-Islām: Ta'rīkh al-taṭawwur al-'aqdī wa'l-tashrī' fi'l-diyāna al-islāmīya* [English title: Introduction to Islamic theology and law, 1981], trans. and explained by M. Yūsuf Mūsā, 'Abd al-'Azīz 'Abd al-Ḥaqq and 'Alī Ḥasan 'Abd al-Qādir (Cairo, Egypt: Dār al-Kitāb al-Miṣrī, 1946).
31. No other Arab-Muslim country created legal and administrative regulations for both recognizing and controlling the Sufi orders, see J.-P. Luizard, "Le Soufisme Egyptien Contemporain," [Contemporary Egyptian Sufism], *Egypte/Monde Arabe* 2 (1990), 35–94.
32. F. De Jong, "Aspects of the Political Involvement of Sufi Orders in Twentieth Century Egypt (1907–1970)—An Exploratory Stock-Taking" in G. R. Warburg & U. M. Kupferschmidt (eds.), *Islam, Nationalism, and Radicalism in Egypt and the Sudan* (New York: Praeger, 1983), 183–212; and F. De Jong, "Die mystischen Bruderschaften und der Volksislam" [Mystical Brotherhoods and Popular Islam], in U. Steinbach & W. Ende (eds.), *Der Islam in der Gegenwart* (München, Germany: Beck, 1996), 646–662.
33. M. al-Bahī, *Al-Fikr al-islāmī al-ḥadīth wa-ṣilatuhu bi'l-isti'mār al-gharbī* [Modern Islamic Thought and Its Connection With Western Colonialism] (Cairo, Egypt: n.p., 1957, 8th ed, 1975), p. 299; this article is an Arabic translation of an article in English that first appeared in *Muslim World* 53 (1963).
34. Exemplary for anti-Sufi polemics whose main aim is to prove that "Sufism and Islam are incompatible" ("al-taṣawwuf laisa min al-islām") is the work by 'A. al-Karīm al-Khaṭīb, *al-Taṣawwuf wa'l-mutaṣawwifa fī muwājihat al-islām* [Sufis and Sufism vis-à-vis Islam] ,(Cairo, Egypt: Dār al-Fikr al-'Arabī, 1980), his summary pp. 260–271.
35. The noun and adjective term is a predominately modern phenomenon that was widely put in circulation after it occurred in Abū'l-A'lā 'Afīfī's Arabic introduction to the work of R. A. Nicholson, *Fi'l-Taṣawwuf al-islāmī wa-ta'rīkhihi* [History of Islamic mysticism], (Cairo, Egypt: Lajnat al-Ta'līf wa'l-Nashr, 1947), and was immediately adopted by I. Aḥmad Nūr al-Dīn's study

of the Egyptian Sufi-Sheikh Aḥmad al-Badawī in *Ḥayāt al-Sayyid al-Badawī: Baḥth fi'l-ta'rīkh wa'l-taṣawwuf al-islāmī* [Studies on the history of Islamic mysticism], (Ṭanṭā: al-Maṭbaʿa al-Yūsufīya, 1948) and then popularised by Ṭāha ʿAbd al-Bāqir Surūr's study of al-Shaʿrānī in *al-Taṣawwuf al-islāmī wa'l-imām al-Shaʿrānī* [Imam al-Shaʿrānī on Islamic Sufism], (Cairo, Egypt: Dar Naḥdat Miṣr, 1950). In contrast to the proliferation of books with the term "al-taṣawwuf al-islāmī" in their titles since the 1950s, there are only two publications before the World War II that contain this term; both talk about Sufism from a purely ethical perspective: ʿAbd al-Laṭīf al-Ṭībāwī, *al-Taṣawwuf al-islāmī al-ʿarabī* [Arab-Islamic Sufism], (Cairo, Egypt: Dār al-ʿUṣūr li'l-Ṭabʿ wa'l-Nashr, 1928) and Zakī Mubārak, *al-Taṣawwuf al-islāmī fi'l-adab wa'l-akhlāq* [Moral practice and ethics in Islamic Sufism], (Cairo, Egypt: Maṭbaʿat al-Risāla, 1938).

36. M. ʿAbdallāh al-Sharqāwī, *al-Ittijāhāt al-ḥadītha fī dirāsa al-taṣawwuf al-islāmī: muṣādiruhu wa-āthāruhu—taḥlīl wa-naqd* [Modern theories in the study of Islamic Sufism: an analysis and critique of its origins and its impact] (Cairo, Egypt: Dār al-Fikr al-ʿArabī, 1993), p. 8, criticised in his book the previous fixation of Egyptian authors on early Orientalists such as Nicholson and Massignon and demanded his colleagues to be aware of more recent Orientalist research on Sufism.

37. In ʿA. al-Ḥalīm Maḥmūd, *Qaḍīyat al-taṣawwuf—al-Munqidh min al-ḍalāl* [The matter of Sufism—The deliverer from error] (Cairo, Egypt: Dār al-Maʿārif, 5th ed. 1981), pp. 133–137.

38. M. Abū'l-Fayḍ al-Manūfī, *al-Taṣawwuf al-islāmī al-khāliṣ* [Unadultered Islamic Sufism], (Cairo, Egypt: Dār Naḥdat Miṣr, 1969), pp. 178ff. Similarly arguing is M. K. I. Jaʿfar, *al-Taṣawwuf: ṭarīqan wa-tajribatan wa-madhhaban* [Sufism: a path, an experience, and a school], (Cairo, Egypt: Dār al-Kutub al-Jāmiʿīya, 1970), pp. 220–255.

39. M. Ghalūsh, *al-Taṣawwuf fi'l-mīzān* [A balanced study of Sufism], (Cairo, Egypt: n.d.), p. 13.

40. ʿA. Maʿbud Firghalī, *al-Taṣawwuf bayn muʿayyadīn wa-muʿāriḍ* [Sufism in the eyes of its supporters and its opponents], (Cairo, Egypt: Dār al-Ṭibāʿa al-Muḥammadīya, 1988), pp. 34–35; ʿA. al-Ḥalīm Maḥmūd *Qaḍīyat al-taṣawwuf—al-Munqidh min al-ḍalāl* [The matter of Sufism—The deliverer from error], (Cairo, Egypt: Dār al-Maʿārif, 1981), pp. 256–259.

41. S. al-Dīn al-Sayyid Ṣāliḥ, *Mushkilāt al-taṣawwuf al-muʿāṣir* [The problems of Modern Sufism], (Cairo, Egypt: Dār al-Maʿārif, 1993), p. 63.

42. Exemplary publications in this respect are for example Ṣalāḥ ʿIzzām, *Aqṭāb al-taṣawwuf al-thalātha* [Three leading figures of Sufism], (Cairo, Egypt: Dār al-Shaʿb, 1968/69); M. ʿAbduh al-Ḥijājī, *Shakṣīyāt ṣūfīya fī saʿīd Miṣr fi'l-ʿaṣr al-islāmī* [Sufi personalities in Upper Egypt during the Islamic Era] (Cairo, Egypt: n.p., 1971); M. ʿAbduh al-Ḥijājī, *Shakhṣiyāt islāmīya* [Islamic personalities], (Cairo, Egypt: Dār al-Shaʿb, 1977); S. ʿAbd al-Fattāḥ al-Ṣayyād al-Rifāʿī, *al-Taṣawwuf: ʿAqīda wa-Sulūk—wa-Shaikh al-imām Aḥmad al-Rifāʿī (r)* [Imam Ahmad Rifāʿī and Sufism—doctrine and practice], (Cairo, Egypt: n.p., 1984). With a stronger historical and chronological focus but still without any social and political analysis, see M. ʿAbd al-Munʿim Khifājī, *al-Turāth al-rūḥī li'l-taṣawwuf al-islāmī fī Miṣr: Qiṣṣat al-taṣawwuf wa-ṭabaqāt al-ṣūfiya fī Miṣr al-islāmīya mundhu 'l-fataḥ al-islāmī ilā'l-yaum* [The spiritual heritage of Islamic Sufism in Egypt: the history of Sufis and Sufism in Islamic Egypt since the Islamic conquest until today], (Cairo, Egypt: Dār al-ʿAhd al-Jadīd, n.d. [c.1957]).

43. Such apologetic literature often included printed interviews in which Sufi shaykhs were directly confronted with accusations that undermined their

credibility and charismatic authority, see M. Barakāt, *al-Sayyid Aḥmad al-Badawī wa-ḥiwār ḥaul al-taṣawwuf* [al-Sayyid Aḥmad al-Badawī talks about Sufism], (Cairo, Egypt: Dār al-Madīna al-Munawwara, 1991).

44. Some publications were jointly edited by academics and state officials or were prefaced by notes of support and approval by representatives of the Egyptian government; see for example the preface by the former Egyptian minister for trade and commerce Ḥasan ʿAbbās Zakī in ʿA. al-ʿAzīz Aḥmad Manṣūr, *al-Taṣawwuf al-islāmī al-ṣaḥīḥ* [The authentic Islamic Sufism], (Cairo, Egypt: 1996).

45. R. Mitchell, *The Society of the Muslim Brothers* (Oxford: Oxford University Press, 1993, originally published 1969), pp. 163–195. A similar observation can be found in I. Weismann, "The Politics of Popular Religion: Sufis, Salafis, and Muslim Brothers in 20th-Century Hama," *Journal of Middle Easter Studies* 37 (2005), 39–58.

46. De Jong (1996), pp. 661–662.

47. De Jong (1983), p. 200 gives examples of brotherhoods (e.g., the particularly spectacular case of the al-Burhaniyya al-Dusiqiya al-Shadhiliya order) that were destroyed, always on grounds of doctrinal aberrations, if they had ceased to fit into official government policies.

48. DeJong (1996), pp. 658–660; M. Gilsenan, *Saint and Sufi in Modern Egypt. An Essay in the Sociology of Religion* (Oxford: Oxford University Press, 1973), pp. 188–207.

49. e.g., M. Jalāl Sharaf, *al-Taṣawwuf al-islāmī: madārisuhu wa-naẓariyātihu* [Islamic Sufism: its schools and thoughts], (Beirut, Lebanon: Dār al-ʿUlūm al-ʿArabīya, 1990), p. 8.

50. ʿA. al-Ḥakīm Ḥassān, *al-Taṣawwuf fīʾl-shiʿr al-ʿarabī: nashʾatuhu wa-taṭawwuruhu ḥatā ākhar ʾl-qarn al-thālith al-hijrī* [Sufism in Arabic poetry: its emergence and development until the end of the third century], (Cairo, Egypt: Maktabat al-Anglo al-Miṣriya, 1954), M. Y. Sharaf, *Ḥarakat al-taṣawwuf al-islāmī* [The movement of Islamic Sufism], (Cairo, Egypt: al-Hayʾat al-ʿĀmma liʾl-Kitāb, 1986).

51. I. Basyūnī, *Nashʾat al-taṣawwuf al-islāmī* [The emergence of Islamic Sufism], (Cairo, Egypt: Dār al-Maʿārif, 1969).

52. See the criticism by J. Baldick, *Mystical Islam* (London: Tauris, 1989), pp. 47–48. Even Massignon himself, towards the end of his life, seemed to have lost confidence in the credibility of his 'Islamic theory'; see A. J. Arberry's remarks in his *An Introduction to the History of Sufism* (London: Longmans, 1942), pp. 46–52.

53. The following writers belong to this group: M. al-Sayyid al-Jalaynad, *Min qaḍāyā ʾl-taṣawwuf fī ḍauʾ ʾl-kitāb waʾl-sunna* [The problems of Sufism in the light of the Qurʾan and the Sunna], (Cairo, Egypt: Maṭbaʿat al-Taqaddum, 1985); M. Jalāl Sharaf, *Dirāsāt fīʾl-taṣawwuf al-islāmī: shakhṣiyāt wa-madhāhib* [The movement of Islamic Sufism], (Beirut, Lebanon: Dār al-Nahḍa al-ʿArabīya, 1980).

54. There is a third, minority position that includes wholeheartedly the philosophical Akbarian tradition of Ibn al-ʿArabi into the canon of Sufi-orthodoxy, for example F. ʿAun, *al-Taṣawwuf al-islāmī: al-ṭarīq waʾl-rijāl* [Islamic Sufism: the path and the men], (Cairo, Egypt: Maktabat Saʿīd Raʾfat, 1983) and Ḥ. ʿĀṣī, *al-Taṣawwuf al-islāmī: mafhūmuhu; taṭawwuruhu wa-makānatuhu min al-dīn waʾl-ḥayāt* [Islamic Sufism: its concept, its delvepment, and its place in religion and life], (Beirut, Lebanon: ʿIzz al-Dīn, 1994).

55. See the exemplary ʿA. al-Raḥmān Badawī, *Taʾrīkh al-taṣawwuf al-islāmī—min al-bidāya ḥatā nihāyat al-qarn al-thānī* [The history of Islamic Sufism—from its beginning to the end of the second century], (Kuwait: Wikālat al-Maṭbūʿāt, 1975); M. al-Bahlī al-Naiyāl, *al-Ḥaqīqa al-taʾrīkhīya liʾl-taṣawwuf al-islāmī*

[The historical reality of Islamic Sufism], (Tunis, Tunisia: Maktabat al-Najāh, 1965).

56. 'A. al-Ḥalīm Maḥmūd, *Qaḍīyat al-taṣawwuf—al-Munqidh min al-ḍalāl* [The matter of Sufism—The deliverer from error], (Cairo, Egypt: 1981), pp. 154–163.

57. Publications in which al-Ghazzālī's positions are central in defining *Islamic Sufism* are for example M. al-Sayyid al-Jalaynad, *Min qaḍāyā 'l-taṣawwuf fī ḍau' 'l-kitāb wa'l-sunna* [The problems of Sufism in the light of the Qur'an and the Sunna], (Cairo, Egypt: 1985), M. Ghalūsh, *al-Taṣawwuf fi'l-mīzān* [A balanced study of Sufism], (Cairo, Egypt: n.d.), 'A. al-Ḥalīm Maḥmūd, *Qaḍīyat al-taṣawwuf—al-Munqidh min al-ḍalāl* [The problems of modern Sufism], (Cairo, Egypt: 1981).

58. Exemplary are: 'A. Ma'bud Firghalī, *al-Taṣawwuf bayn mu'ayyadīn wa-mu'āriḍ* (Cairo, Egypt: Dār al-Ṭibā'a al-Muḥammadīya, 1988); 'A. al-Laṭīf M. al-'Abd, *al-Taṣawwuf fi'l-islām wa-ahamm al-i'tirāḍāt al-wārida 'alaihi* (Cairo, Egypt: Dār al-Thaqāfa al-'Arabīya, 1986); S. al-Dīn al-Sayyid Ṣāliḥ, *Mushkilāt al-taṣawwuf al-mu'āṣir* (Cairo, Egypt: Dār al-Ma'ārif, 1993).

59. In 1981 the National Assembly (Majlis al-Sha'b) called for the confiscation of Ibn al-'Arabī's *Al-Futūḥāt al-Makkīya* on the basis of atheism (*zandaqa*), but appeals were rejected by courts of law; see M. Stagh, *The Limits of Freedom of Speech: Prose Literature and Prose Writers in Egypt Under Nasser and Sadat* (Stockholm, Sweden: Almqvist & Wiksell, 1993), pp. 141–142.

60. A. al-Ghanīmī al-Taftāzānī, *Madkhal ilā 'l-taṣawwuf al-islāmī* [Introduction to Islamic Sufism], (Cairo, Egypt: Dār al-Thaqāfa, 1974), p. 10.

61. A. al-'Afīfi, *al-Taṣawwuf: al-thaura al-rūḥīya fi'l-islām* [Sufism: the spiritual revolution in Islam], (Alexandria, Egypt: 1963); Yusuf (1987); see also A. Taufīq 'Iyād, *al-Taṣawwuf al-islāmī: ta'rīkhuhu wa-madārisuhu wa-ṭabī'atuhu wa-athruhu* [Islamic Sufism: its history, its schools, its nature and its impact], (Cairo, Egypt: Maktabat al-Anjilū al-Miṣrīya, 1970), who defined Sufism as 'one of the most powerful spiritual movements' (*min aqwā 'l-ḥarakāt al-rūḥīya*) in history (p. 9).

62. Al-Taftazānī (1974), p. 10.

63. 'A. al-Laṭīf M. al-'Abd, *Iṣlāḥ al-nafs: bain al-Rāzī fi'l-ṭibb al-rūḥānī wa'l-Kirmānī fi'l-Aqwāl al-Dhahabiyya* [The healing of the soul: from al-Razi's *Spiritual Medicine* to al-Kirmani's *Golden States*], (Cairo, Egypt: 1986).

64. The 'phenomenology of religion' school (Otto, Heiler, Eliade) was popularised mainly through academics from Cairo University, while the ideas of Guenon and Corbin came into Egyptian circles primarily through the work of the Azhar scholar 'Abd al-Ḥalīm Maḥmūd; see 'A. al-Ḥalīm Maḥmūd, *Al-Failasūf al-Muslim René Geunon aw 'Abd al-Wāhid Yaḥyā* [The Muslim philosopher René Guenon, alas 'Abd al-Wāhid Yaḥyā], (Cairo, Egypt: Maṭba'at al-Lajna li-Bayān al-'Arabī, 1954).

65. 'Abd al-Ḥalīm Maḥmūd (1981), chapter 2.

66. R. Nājī al-Ḥasan, *Hādhā huwa al-taṣawwuf* [This is Sufism], (Homs, Libya: Maṭba'at al-Yamāma, 1996), pp. 9–10.

67. M. 'Abd al-Mun'im Khifajī even considers Muḥammad Idrīs al-Shāfi'ī (767–820) as equally important for the emergence of Sufism in Egypt as his contemporary famous mystic Dhū al-Nūn al-Miṣrī (796–859), *al-Turāth al-rūḥī li'l-taṣawwuf al-islāmī fī Miṣr* [The spiritual heritage of Islamic Sufism in Egypt], pp. 34ff. For a passionate defence of the symbiosis between Sufism and Shari'a, see also 'A. al-Fatāḥ Aḥmad al-Fāwī, *al-Taṣawwuf: 'aqīdatan wa-sulūkan* [Sufism: as doctrine and practice], (Cairo, Egypt: Dār Shams al-Ma'rifa, 1992).

68. A. Maḥmūd al-Jazzār, *al-Imām al-mujaddid Ibn Bādis wa'l-taṣawwuf* [The renewer Imam Ibn Bādis on Sufism], (Cairo, Egypt: Dār al-Wazzān, 1988), p. 9.

Part II

Execrating and Excluding the Other

4   Insider/Outsider Labelling and the Struggle for Power in Early Judaism

Philip S. Alexander

VOCABULARIES OF ORTHODOXY

How does language function within religious communities to gain power, to project power, and to subvert power? I explore this question by examining its use by three distinctive groups in early Judaism—the Rabbinic movement, the Descenders to the Chariot (the *Yoredei Merkabah*), and the community of the Dead Sea Scrolls. I focus on the attempt by each of these groups to exploit a 'vocabulary of orthodoxy', to apply to themselves terms that assert that their views are normative and those of their opponents deviant. The basic scenario I envisage has three fundamental elements:

1. Two parties in competition, already well defined with their own distinctive ideologies.
2. An audience observing the competition: It is this audience made up of the wider society to which the parties belong that they have to address and persuade.
3. A power-play: this can take place on a variety of levels. Physical violence and coercion may be applied, but this does not concern me here. Rather I am interested in the contest at the linguistic level. This fundamentally involves each party trying to appropriate society's core values by claiming the right to certain epithets which express those values, while at the same time labelling its opponents in ways that stigmatise them as deviant.

This scenario has been exhaustively analysed by sociologists of deviance, some of whom have stressed the important role labelling plays in this process.[1] My analysis intersects with theirs only tangentially because my interest is not so much strictly sociological as sociolinguistic. The sociologists' approach has tended to be asymmetrical in that it has concentrated on how a dominant group labels a less powerful, marginal group and on how such labelling constructs the marginal group as deviant. I am not concerned in the first instance with the actual power relationships between my parties but more with the power to which they aspire as expressed by the labels they use. I am also concerned with language, and at this level the situation is always binary: that is to say, we should not simply study the labels party A gives to party B, but also the labels party B gives to party A, and the labels that both parties apply to themselves. Sociologists of deviance have not analysed in depth exactly how the labels operate *linguistically* to achieve their purpose.

The three short case studies that follow raise some interesting general questions that need to be tested against data drawn from other cultures and other religious traditions. Among these I would highlight the following:-

1. Does the use of a vocabulary of orthodoxy of the sort I document here only pertain to a particular type of religion and if so what type is it? Is a key feature that it correlates closely with a type that puts a high premium on belief and on divine revelation, in other words a prophetic religion?

2. Is it the case that a vocabulary of orthodoxy always presupposes a high level of commonality between the 'orthodox' and the 'heterodox'—shared symbols, beliefs, and traditions to which both parties lay claim, but which one denies that the other truly owns. To put this another way: does a vocabulary of orthodoxy arise only within concentrated and compact as opposed to diffuse religious traditions, and even more precisely in situations of inter-sectarian struggle within such traditions?

3. What precise linguistic strategies are employed to claim orthodoxy? I have suggested that insider/outsider labelling plays a key role but such labelling is not linguistically straightforward. There is a fundamental problem of reference. It might seem obvious for insiders to apply to themselves common terms such as 'true, good, righteous', and 'false, bad, wicked' to their opponents. There is undoubtedly an attempt to appropriate such generic language by religious parties bidding for power, in order to lay claim to society's core values, but on its own this strategy suffers from a fundamental weakness. For the audience (i.e., society at large, uncommitted to either party) the referent of these terms may not be self-evident. A third party will not automatically associate 'the good' with a particular 'orthodox' group and 'the bad' with the 'heterodox' whom it opposes. Moreover, it seems to be important, as part of the psychological struggle between the groups, that opponents should feel the force of the insiders' disapproval, but 'deviants' will not necessarily recognise themselves as the target of attack if they are addressed only by generically negative labels. Few will readily accept that the terms 'wicked' or 'false' or 'bad' on their own could apply to them.

How is this problem solved? What sometimes happens is that peculiar linguistic usages are developed for purposes of labelling. These usages are recognisably part of the labelling group's religious idiolect, that is to say, only members of this particular group will use this precise terminology and by using it will be recognised by others, both insiders and outsiders, as members of this group, but at the same time the terms are sufficiently transparent to convey to opponents and uncommitted third parties approval or disapproval. For example, instead of speaking very generically of 'those who are truthful' and 'those who are false', a group may refer more precisely to 'the men of truth' (themselves) and 'the men of falsehood' (their opponents). Or instead of talking about 'the righteous' and the 'wicked' they will talk of 'the righteous of the way' (themselves) and the 'perverted of the way' (their opponents). The linguistic act involved here is complex: It establishes an identity; it excludes others from that identity; the referents of the labels are reasonably clear and they are sufficiently transparent to opponents and third parties for them to be able to determine whether or not the labels convey approval or disapproval.

4. Another set of questions relates to the crucial role of transparency that plays a crucial role in this type of labelling. Some idiolects are meant to be opaque: They are constructed to *exclude* comprehension except in the case of insiders 'in the know'. This seems to be the function of the idiolects deployed by many subcultures, such as various forms of youth culture today. But transparency seems to be important when there is a bid for power that involves influencing uncommitted third parties. The 'orthodox' will only win the day if they can persuade a majority of their constituency that they and not their opponents are right. This provokes a number of questions. Does this linguistic strategy apply only to situations where one party is not in the position physically to coerce the other? This is certainly the case with my Jewish groups: they did not have the political clout to impose their views and so had to rely on persuasion. Does this rhetoric of persuasion vanish when naked power can be deployed? Or does power, however naked and absolute, still need to dress itself up in the rhetoric of persuasion? If even the most absolute and ruthless of tyrants still feels a need for propaganda, what do we deduce from this?

5. What are the precise socio-psychological mechanisms involved in this kind of labelling? The most obvious one as I have indicated is to associate one's own group with universally recognised virtues ('goodness, truth, righteousness') and one's opponents with the opposite. Most people have an instinctive desire to be on the side of the angels and so will feel drawn to identify with the 'goodies' and reject the 'baddies'. But there is another mechanism that is often built into labelling though it can exist in its own right, namely ridicule. Ridicule is a powerful rhetorical device that pressurises people to disassociate themselves from those subjected to it and to identify with the speaker: it challenges audiences to take sides. No one wants to be the butt of jokes. An example of this is the way in which some of

my groups in humorous ways deform terms that are characteristic of their opponents' discourse and used by them positively or terms that refer to objects or individuals to which the opponents attach high value. Thus the Dead Sea sect refers to its antagonists (in this case probably the Pharisees) as 'expounders of smooth things' (*doreshei halaqot*), probably a deformation of 'expounders of religious laws' (*doreshei halakhot*).[2] Or take the Rabbinic deformation of *euangelion*, in the sense of the Christian Gospels, into *'aven gilayon'* or *'avon gilayon'*, a kind of nonsense phrase but suggesting something like 'falsehood/perversion of blank parchment.'[3] The deformation is a witty put-down that not only expresses disapproval and devalues what the opponent holds dear but invites the hearer to disassociate himself from the butt of this humour.[4]

6. All the groups that I mention in this short study are what might be called logocentric. That is to say they have a profound reverence for the word, and a strong belief in the power of speech. This belief in the power of speech is deeply rooted in Judaism: God created the world through speech (Genesis 1) and a work like the *Sefer Yetzirah* believes that by exploiting speech we too can to a degree imitate God's creative act.[5] Part of Adam's role in creating was the naming of species and that naming in some sense determined their essence (Genesis 2:19–20). Labelling is important. One of our groups, the Dead Sea sect, spent a great deal of time cursing its opponents and blessing itself. It had such faith in the performative power of incantation that one of its secret weapons in the eschatological war was a series of incantations hurled at the foe by its priests as well as 'magical' formulae inscribed on its weapons that were clearly intended to enhance their power.[6] The question arises whether irrespective of general sociolinguistic mechanisms that may be at work there may also be specific cultural factors to be taken into account related to the particular philosophy of language held by the society in view.[7] To put this at its most universal: Is there any evidence that language as a weapon for gaining and exercising power correlates particularly with logocentric societies and groups or is it such a fundamental aspect of human speech that it must apply to any human society?

7. My final question is this: Language is clearly a weapon for asserting, gaining, and maintaining power. It is also by the same token a means of subverting power. But are the linguistic mechanisms the same in both cases? I have stated that unlike sociologists of deviance I am not primarily concerned with the *actual* power relations between the parties but these cannot in the end be ignored since they may have a significant impact on the linguistic strategies employed. Will the underdogs in a power-play simply turn back on their oppressors the weapons that their oppressors use against them ('Despite what *you* say, *we* are the righteous not *you*!') or do their linguistic strategies

subtly shift? One feels they ought to. For one thing, once the imbalance in power between the parties reaches a certain level the underdogs may give up any hope of influencing their oppressors or society at large. Their linguistic strategies may focus more on preserving their own morale, identity, and loyalty. One effect of this may be that their idiolect becomes more opaque: it is intended to speak to insiders rather than outsiders. I also wonder if ridicule, parody, caricature, and vilification will tend to feature more prominently in this situation on the principle that satire is the last defence of the powerless. Another strategy, which my evidence suggests marks powerless groups, is what I would call 'appropriation' or what political journalists might call 'stealing your opponents' clothes'. This is the case where the underdogs borrow language from their oppressors and use it in such a way as to challenge their hegemony. I analyse a possible example of this below in the Descenders to the Chariot's reference to the angels as 'the celestial family'. To put this question very simply: do the *actual* power relationships between competing groups affect the linguistic strategies they use to maintain or subvert power?

THE RABBINIC MOVEMENT

The first and historically most important group that I want to consider is the Rabbinic movement. Emerging out of the Pharisaic party of Second Temple times, the Rabbis made a concerted bid for power after the destruction of the Temple in 70 CE.[8] They were ultimately to triumph within Judaism and their worldview came to form the basis of normative Orthodox Judaism right down to the present day, but in the immediate aftermath of the destruction their triumph was by no means assured. At this point in time the field seems to have been more or less level for all the competing parties, with no single group holding a decisive advantage. Everything was to play for: there was a broad constituency to be worked upon and won over to Rabbinism. In this situation it is not surprising that although the Rabbis developed a distinctive Rabbinic religious idiolect, it had high levels of transparency and on the whole would have communicated readily to outsiders. The Rabbis' broad strategy was to assert that they were the obvious and natural heirs of pre 70 Judaism, and one effect of this was that they claimed generic-value terms for themselves: those who followed their teachings were self-evidently the righteous, the good, and the pious.

Rabbinic discourse is remarkably weak on distinctive self-designations and this may be precisely because the Rabbis were attempting to claim the centre ground. It is interesting that they seldom use the name of 'Pharisee'. This does occur in some old polemical traditions for example in opposition to 'Sadducee' but in general Rabbinic discourse it is noticeable by its absence and when it does occur it can carry negative connotations of asceticism, a form of spirituality of which the Rabbis tended to disapprove.[9] The absence of the term 'Pharisee' in Rabbinic literature is a long-standing puzzle. It may be because it was a derogatory name applied to the movement by others (in the pre-70 period it occurs only in non-Pharisaic sources), but there are plenty of examples of groups proudly appropriating to themselves names that originated among outsiders.[10] It is possible the Rabbis avoided the term 'Pharisee' because it had a sectarian ring to it (it means literally 'those who separate themselves') and the last thing the Rabbinic movement wanted to suggest after 70 CE was that it was a sect: rather it was the establishment!

Conversely, the Rabbinic movement did develop a range of terms in the second century for its opponents, the precise purpose of which was to label them as 'heretical' and by implication the Rabbis as 'orthodox'.[11] The most widely used of these is *min*. This is usually translated 'heretic' and that is clearly its basic sense but by etymology it is a common Hebrew word meaning 'kind' or 'type'.[12] Hebrew lexicographers have been at a loss how to explain the semantic evolution from 'kind' to 'heretic.' Though the semantic development is puzzling, the means by which the term achieves its purpose of marginalising and rejecting the groups to whom it applies (i.e., all those Jews who reject Rabbinic authority and who are deemed sectarian) is reasonably clear. The term in the sense of 'sectarian/heretic', was, I would suggest, a linguistic usage peculiar to Rabbinic Jews. It belonged to their religious idiolect: only Rabbinical Jews used this perfectly ordinary nondescript Hebrew word in this sense. This may explain an oddity in the use of the term in one of the benedictions of the standard synagogue prayer known as the *ᶜAmida*. This benediction, introduced into the prayer by the Rabbis, curses 'the heretics' (*minim*).[13] But what is the point of cursing 'heretics'? It would surely always be possible for anyone in the congregation to say 'Amen' when the prayer-leader pronounced this benediction on the grounds that *he* was certainly not a 'heretic', whoever else was. Nobody readily believes that *they* are heretics. The word *min*, however, was a give-away since only Rabbinical Jews employed it to denote those who did not accept Rabbinical authority. Consequently a non-Rabbinical Jew in the congregation would be in no doubt that the prayer was getting at him and 'Amen' would have stuck in his throat.

There is possibly another linguistic way in which the term *min* fulfils its purpose of putting people down. It is remarkably bland and unspecific as to its linguistic content: 'he's a type'—'he's a heretic' denies the person so labelled any individuality and hence any respect or dignity. He's 'a whatsit' or 'a thingummyjig' or 'a so-and-so.' This use of language can be attested elsewhere. The Hebrew word *aher* ('another') can function in a similarly pejorative way. The arch-heretic in Talmudic literature was a Rabbi called Elisha ben Abuyah. Everybody knew his name, but he was usually not referred to by it but by the sobriquet *Aher* (A.N. Other).[14] It is possible *min* functions linguistically in the same sort of way.

A second distinctive Rabbinic term for 'heretic' is *meshummad* (usually translated as 'apostate').[15] Again lexicographers have scratched their heads over the semantic development of this word. The basic verbal root is well-attested in Classical Hebrew in the sense of 'destroy, annihilate, exterminate' and the form *meshummad* is clearly a *pucal* participle of the root (meaning 'someone destroyed'). The active *picel* form of the verb can apparently sometimes be used in the sense of 'force someone to apostasise from Judaism', so it has been suggested that *meshummad* means specifically someone who has apostasised under duress but actual usage does not seem to bear out this subtle distinction: in most cases apostasy under duress does not seem to be in view but wilful abandonment of Judaism. Hence the traditional explanation that *meshummad* indicates that a Jew who has abandoned his faith has 'destroyed himself' has to my mind much to commend it. The term may effectively mean something like 'as good as dead' or 'as good as annihilated', with a hint that the person so named is destined for 'the eternal bonfire' and will definitely miss out on the resurrection. If this is roughly correct, then the pejorative connotations are clearly built in to the word. But again this term belongs to the Rabbinic idiolect and I know of no evidence that it would have been used in this sense by anyone who was not a Rabbinical Jew.

Two other Rabbinic terms for heretic—*Epiqoros* and *Tzeduqi*—involve generalising the titles of two identifiable and specific non-Rabbinic groups to cover *all* opponents of Rabbinism. *Epiqoros* clearly in origin means Epicurean, that is follower of the Greek philosopher Epicurus.[16] The term, however, does not seem to be at all used in this restricted etymological sense but denotes any kind of heretic. There is a pejorative double-whammy here: first to see anyone as a follower of Greek philosophy was suspect in the Jewish world but, second, Epicureans specifically had (unfairly) a bad name for loose morals even within the Greek world, a slander probably put around by those earnest, law-abiding Stoics. One might linguistically compare the loose and extended use of 'Commie', 'Nazi' or 'Fascist' today to denigrate political opponents. *Tzeduqi* is a term from within Jewish culture. It means literally 'Sadducee', but like *Epiqoros* is seldom used in its strict historical sense.[17] There is little evidence that an organized Sadducean party survived the destruction of the Temple for long.[18] For this term to work as a general designation for 'heretic' it is necessary, I think, to suppose that 'Sadducee' had for some reason come to carry negative connotations in society at large.

The emergence of this vocabulary of orthodoxy marks a decisive bid for power by the Rabbinic movement. The linguistic character of the terms employed (*min, meshumad*, etc.) is interesting in three ways. First, they are distinctive of Rabbinic speech, part of the Rabbinic religious idiolect: They are peculiar usages intended to express disapproval of non-Rabbinic groups. Second, they seem to involve a put-down of some kind though the precise nature of this is now a bit obscure. Third, there is a highly significant asymmetry between insider and outsider labelling by the Rabbinic movement. Insider labelling tends to use generic terms, whereas outsider labels are idiosyncratic. This is probably the most effective linguistic strategy the Rabbis could have adopted. If both insider and outsider labels are generic then their power to differentiate is limited. The same is true if both are idiosyncratic, with the added problem that the insiders effectively brand themselves as sectarian. The compromise of generic insider labelling and idiosyncratic outsider labelling serves well the purpose of establishing the insiders as holding the centre ground, as being the true faith, and marginalizing the outsiders as the deviants.

The emergence of this vocabulary of orthodox within Rabbinic Judaism seems to take place in the second half of the second century CE. It coincides with a parallel phenomenon within Christianity at the same period—the growth of a concept of Christian orthodoxy and the beginnings of heresiology, classically exemplified by Irenaeus's *Against Heresies* that tries to draw up an inventory of all those groups who are in error and who should be excluded from fellowship.[19] This overlap between emergent orthodoxy in both Christianity and Rabbinic Judaism was surely no accident because one of the groups whom the Rabbis were targeting and with whom they were fighting for the hearts and minds of Jews was Jewish Christianity. Conversely, Irenaeus and other Christian heresiologists were targeting *inter alia* Christian groups that still had close associations with Judaism. This emergence of orthodoxy in both camps is one of the major causes of the famous 'parting of the ways' between Judaism and Christianity. This parting did not happen in a fit of absent-mindedness, as Sir John Seeley said of the creation of the British Empire: it was willed by religious elites on both sides, and language was an important instrument in the process.[20]

The Rabbis increasingly identified their opponents as the Christians, with a result that broad terms for heretic, such as *min*, narrowed down (from the third century onwards) to designate specifically Christians. As Christian power grew, a shift in the Rabbinic linguistic strategy can be detected. In the early days the Rabbinic movement seems to have tried to ignore the Christians and in this way subtly to suggest that they were upstarts or to dismiss them sweepingly as 'heretics', people who had strayed from the true faith. But when Christianity became an everyday experience of Jews this no longer worked so well so the Rabbis turned to more direct ridicule and vilification. This can be seen in the emergence of the *Toledot Yeshu* ('History of Jesus') traditions, a scurrilous parody of the Gospels. It is generally recognized that the name used for Jesus—*Yeshu* rather than *Yeshu'a*—was a derogatory deformation of some kind, though just how is disputed. The Jewish anti-Gospel claimed that Jesus was the illegitimate son of Mary and a Roman soldier called Panther or Pander and referred to him as Ben Pandera. Mary shockingly went around with her long hair unbound, the mark of a wanton woman. Jesus's name was avoided: Instead he was referred to as *Talui*, 'the Hanged One' (cf. 'Aher for Elisha ben Abuyah). And so on.[21] It is tempting to see this intensifying anti-Christian rhetoric as charting the loss of power and growing oppression by triumphant Christianity, but I see a problem here. If power is the only factor then we would expect Christian anti-Jewish rhetoric to follow the opposite trajectory, to begin with strident vilification when Christians were the persecuted minority and then subside into more distantly dismissive language as Christians became securely entrenched in power and Judaism the subservient faith. Certainly early Christian writings, starting with the New Testament, use some strong anti-Jewish language ('synagogue of Satan', Revelation 2:9; 'generation of vipers', Matthew 3:7; 'you are of your father the devil', John 8:44; 'children of the devil', 1 John 3:10; 'sons of the evil one', Matthew 13:38; etc.), but far from declining as Christianity became politically more powerful the graph of vilification seems steadily to rise or at least to show little sign of falling. Power then cannot be the whole story. Perhaps bad habits, once learned, were hard to shake off. Certainly the Christian psyche seems always to have needed an ideological 'other' against which to define self-identity. Judaism traditionally has played that role, though today Islam is increasingly taking its place.

THE DESCENDERS TO THE CHARIOT

The second early Jewish group that I want to discuss is the 'Descenders to the Chariot' (*Yoredei Merkabah),* mystics who existed on the fringes of Rabbinic society in Late Antiquity practising, sometimes in conventicles and sometimes alone, trance ascent to heaven to achieve visions of God's celestial throne, the Heavenly Chariot or *Merkabah.*[22] One of the founding movements of the Jewish mystical tradition, the *Yoredei Merkabah* are sociologically a rather shadowy group but a number of things about them are clear. First, they bore an uneasy relationship to the Rabbis who in their day dominated the religious establishment within Palestinian Jewry. The reasons for this uneasiness are not hard to find: Rabbinic authority rested on expertise in interpreting the Written Torah; it was consequently predicated on the cessation of prophecy. By their ascents to heaven, the *Yoredei Merkabah* were effectively engaging in prophetic activity. There was always the danger that they would try to use these experiences to launch a challenge to Rabbinic power. The Rabbinic authorities attempted to impose restrictions on this kind of activity and the speculation it engendered by declaring it esoteric, only to be indulged in by rabbinically trained scholars.[23] The *Yoredei Merkabah,* for their part, did not seem to have been trying to unseat the Rabbis: rather they were attempting to gain recognition from the Rabbinic establishment. They wanted to enter the club, not take it over.

This power relationship is reflected in their language. The Hebrew of the *Yoredei Merkabah* is strange, full of neologisms and Greek loanwords that would have made it difficult for the outsider to understand. It constitutes a very strong religious idiolect, and one of its purposes was probably to reinforce the identity of the group and to keep its teachings from being too readily understood by outsiders. As I suggested, this makes sense if the group in question is not bidding for power but simply wanting to preserve its own distinctiveness. The *Yoredei Merkabah* were not really trying to persuade third parties that they were right and the Rabbis wrong. Despite their strong sense of identity it is hard to find in their literature distinctive self-designations, apart from the title 'Descenders to the Chariot', which simply describes what they do.[24] It is possible that phrases such as 'men of faith' or 'members of the fellowship' or 'sons of proud ones' refer to them collectively, but it is hard to be sure and if they do they do not seem to embody any implicit claim to represent orthodox or normative Judaism.[25] There is also a noted absence of terms for outsiders, at least Jewish outsiders, and again there may be a reason for this for, as I have said, they do not want to set themselves apart from the Community of Israel but to be recognised as 'orthodox' Jews. This is shown by their strategy of appropriation: they try to pass themselves off as good Rabbinic Jews by peppering their texts with references to Rabbis and Rabbinic ideas. The heroes that the group claimed as its founding practitioners—Rabbi Aqiba, Rabbi Ishmael, Rabbi Nehuniah ben Haqanah—were also heroes of the Rabbinic tradition. Any genuine historical link between these great Rabbis and the *Yoredei Merkabah* is highly unlikely. The *Yoredei Merkabah* then represented an interesting case of the use of language by a subaltern group as a way of trying to claim membership of the establishment.

There is, however, another power that plays a central role in the Merkabah texts, namely wicked Rome, the destroyer of the Temple and the oppressor of Israel. In the case of the references and allusions to Rome, the language is unquestionably confrontational and subversive. The *Yoredei Merkabah* saw Israel and Rome in cosmic conflict, a conflict that Israel was bound to win. The fact that the fundamental opposition in their literature was not between the *Yoredei Merkabah* and Rome, nor between the *Yoredei Merkabah* and other Jews, but between *Israel* and Rome, shows how much they wanted to construe themselves inclusively as part of the Community of Israel and as offering a message of comfort and reassurance to all Jews. To do this they drew an implicit but sustained parallelism between God as the heavenly emperor and Caesar as the earthly emperor in such a way as to suggest that Caesar has arrogantly usurped the powers of the heavenly emperor and will be punished by him for it. Israel may be politically oppressed on earth but the *Yoredei Merkabah* had ascended to the heavenly court and can report to her that they have been assured that she is the darling of the heavenly emperor and it is only a matter of time before he asserts his authority and overturns the arrogant earthly kingdom.[26]

The basic idea here is not peculiar to the Merkabah literature but is found also in Rabbinic midrash though without any reference to the ascent to heaven. One midrash wittily puts it in the form of a parable. Once a king was visiting a distant province and he rode into a town in the state coach (*carrucha*) accompanied by the provincial governor. The crowds lining the road wanted to greet him with the cry of *Domine* (the Latin is actually used in the Hebrew text so you are in no doubt who the king is), but they hesitated because they were unsure which of the two figures in the coach was the king. When the king saw their confusion he pushed the governor out of the coach so that no one would be in any doubt as to whom obeisance was due![27] This message is expressed in the Merkabah texts by a clever piece of linguistic appropriation: The angels in heaven are referred to by the collective title 'the celestial family.' The Hebrew uses the Latin *familia* as a loanword.[28] As I have argued at length elsewhere the allusion here is unquestionably to the *familia Caesaris*, the designation used in the Roman administration for the group of imperial slaves and freedmen whom the emperor employed effectively as a civil service to run the empire. The usage here turns sharply on its head the ideology of kingship that emerged increasingly in the Byzantine period and tried to legitimate earthly kingship by seeing the king as God's vicar on earth. The Merkabah texts leave us in no doubt that the earthly emperor has usurped God's power and will be punished for it. Behind the pomp and circumstance of the earthly court they project the menacing vision of the celestial emperor and his *familia* poised to strike the usurper down.[29]

THE DEAD SEA COMMUNITY

A third early Jewish group whose linguistic power-plays will repay analysis is the Qumran community.[30] A few concluding comments will have to suffice to suggest how this analysis could be pursued. In the Qumranites who display a strong sectarian profile, we have a group that is quite definitely out of power: whether voluntarily or under duress, its leaders have gone into exile from Jerusalem and are lurking with their followers in a settlement on the desolate northwest shore of the Dead Sea. But unlike the marginal *Yoredei Merkavah* who aspired to be accepted into the dominant 'club', the Dead Sea sect want to take it over: they saw themselves as a 'government in exile'. They were bidding for power in Israel. They developed their own distinctive religious idiolect that reinforced their separatist identity. One of the key markers of this was the term *Yahad*, 'community', which seems to have been their most specific collective self-designation: They are 'the men of the Yahad'.[31] In origin *yahad* is a noun meaning something like 'unitedness' or 'togetherness', but it seems to have been rarely used if ever in earlier Hebrew in this sense; rather it functioned adverbially in the sense of '*in* union, together' (cf. its augmented form *yahda(y)w*, lit. '(in) its togetherness' equals 'together').[32] The Qumranites however did use it regularly as a noun and because their usage was distinctive it served to denote not just any community but their community. This usage is so distinctive that historians would now have little hesitation if they found the word with this meaning in a Second Temple period text, in seeing a reference to the Qumran group.[33]

An important element of Qumranian discourse is a series of terms for insiders and outsiders. These labels are dominated by a stark dualism that clearly indicates that the insiders (the sect) are good, and the outsiders (everyone else, whether Jews or non-Jews, especially Romans) are bad. The most comprehensive of these binary oppositions is 'Sons of Light' (equals insiders) versus 'Sons of Darkness' (equals outsiders).[34] What is striking about the labels is that they tend to be highly generic: 'sons of righteousness' versus 'sons of falsehood',[35] 'the upright/ perfect in the way' versus 'the wicked/unjust'.[36] Even when phrases such as 'the Poor' or 'the simple folk of Judah who keep the Torah' are employed to denote the members of the Community,[37] they are linguistically made up of transparent common terms and carry within themselves no linguistic clues that they point to a very specific group. As I suggested in the case of the Rabbinic movement, such appropriation of generic language probably implies a claim to normativity: Rabbinical Jews/the Qumran Community are the 'true Israel', everyone else is in error. But there is a problem: As noted above, the more generic the label is the less obvious will be its referent. The Rabbinic movement partially solved this problem by using, asymmetrically, generic labels for insiders and specific labels for outsiders. Qumran opted for greater symmetry, with generic terms on both sides of the binary divide.

How then did Qumran solve the problem of reference? The answer appears to be that they constantly link themselves and their opponents with specific historical individuals. But again there is a linguistic puzzle because these individuals are designated in code: the 'Sons of Light' are implicitly associated with the 'Teacher of Righteousness'[38] and the 'Sons of Darkness' with his opponent the 'Wicked Priest'.[39] There are other references to historical individuals, events and opponents of the Community in the sectarian writings but they are all in code—to the great annoyance of modern historians who would like to know just who they are! Why in code? One explanation is that anonymity was adopted by the Community out of fear of its enemies. But this makes little sense. The opponents of Qumran did not need to read the Dead Sea Scrolls to know that the Qumran Community was implacably opposed to them and I cannot imagine that the Qumran covenanters would have had any compunction in telling their enemies to their faces that they were 'wicked' and doomed to annihilation at the end of days. Rather more meaningful is the suggestion that the coding has a rhetorical function as part of a put-down: you do not dignify your enemy with his proper name. Certainly some of the codenames contain high levels of vilification, for example 'the Spouter of Lies',[40] 'the Rabid Lion Cub',[41] and so forth. But codenames are also used for the good guys as in the 'Teacher of Righteousness'. Perhaps the most satisfactory general explanation is essentially a literary one, namely that the Qumran Covenanters derived such coded language from apocalyptic literature, which we know, played an important role in their worldview. The coding gives an air of mantic solemnity to their discourse and links it to the great prophecies, but I think it makes little sense unless the codenames were pretty transparent to both insiders and outsiders.

Language was important to the Qumran sect: they form a classically logocentric community and more perhaps than any other early Jewish group used ritual incantation (for example in the form of blessing and cursing) as a means of defending themselves and attacking their enemies.[42] The extremes of their language are matched by their fantasies of power and I wonder if one can hypothesise from their case a general rule that the strength of the language is in inverse proportion to the power actually possessed and functions as linguistic compensation for the lack of real power. Put another way: perhaps the grandiose aspirations of the small and powerless Dead Sea Sect were so patently counter-factual and absurd that they could only be sustained by very high levels of hyperbole.[43]

CONCLUSIONS

The Dead Sea Sect and the *Yoredei Merkavah* exemplify two different relationships between the Jewish establishment and a marginal Jewish group and this fact is reflected in their linguistic power-plays. The *Yoredei Merkavah* craved recognition by the establishment (in their case the Rabbinate) and admission into 'the club', the Dead Sea Sect damn the establishment (in their case the Hasmonean party and its successors) and strive to overthrow and replace it. In political terms this is the difference between reform and revolution. An analogy from modern times would be the difference in attitude between the Beta Israel (the Falashas, the Black Jews of Ethiopia) and the Black Hebrews.[44] Although these two groups differ from the *Yoredei Merkavah* and the Dead Sea sect in their beliefs and practices, their relationships to the Jewish religious establishment are somewhat analogous. The Beta Israel long for acceptance and recognition by the Rabbinate, the Black Hebrews damn their fellow Jews and all their works.

The Rabbinic movement's relationship to the Jewish 'establishment' is more complex because, as I have already hinted, owing to the disruption caused by the first and second wars against Rome, there was no obvious establishment for them to confront. Instead there was an open field in which various sectarian movements competed for power. The Rabbinic movement emerged from these skirmishes victorious and became the new orthodoxy. Like the Qumran covenanters they believed they were authentic Israel, but they faced a very different world from the Second Temple period sect. They did not have to displace an entrenched establishment; they did not have to be revolutionary. Rather, they were able to claim power by steadfastly asserting in generally moderate and reasonable language that they represented the middle ground and continuity with the past. It was this unusual historical situation, brought about by external events (the wars against Rome) that shaped their religious rhetoric. In all three cases language, and above all labelling, played a key role in self-definition and the bid for power, but the social and political realities that each group faced determined exactly how they deployed their linguistic resources.

NOTES

1. First formulated in the 1960s and 1970s, Labelling Theory became popular among American sociologists of deviance in the 1980s and 1990s. See H. S. Becker, *Outsiders: Studies in the Sociology of Deviance* (New York: Free Press, 1963); E. M. Schur, *Labeling Deviant Behaviour* (New York: Harper & Row, 1971); P. G. Schervish, "The Labeling Perspective: Its Bias and Potential for the Study of Political Deviance", *The American Sociologist* 8 (1973), pp. 47–57; J. Hagan, "Labelling and Deviance: A Case Study in the 'Sociology of the Interesting'", *Social Problems* 20 (1973), pp. 447–58. An early attempt to apply it to the New Testament is B. J. Malina & J. H. Neyrey, *Calling Jesus Names:The Social Value of Labels in Matthew* (Sonoma, CA: Polebridge Press, 1988); for more recent use by New Testament scholars see T. D. Still, *Conflict at Thessalonica: A Pauline Church and its Neighbours* (Sheffield: Sheffield Academic Press, 1999), esp. pp. 94–98; L. K. Pietersen, *The Polemic of the Pastorals: A Sociological Examination of the Development of Pauline Christianity* (London: T&T Clark, 2004), esp. pp. 29–35.
2. See Hodayot (1QHᵃ) x 32. "I give you thanks, O Lord, for your eye stands guard over my soul (*ᶜeinekhah ᶜamedah ᶜal nafshi*), and you have delivered me from the zeal of lying interpreters (*melitzei kazab*), and from the congregation of the expounders of smooth things (*doreshei halaqot*) you have redeemed the soul of a poor one (*'ebyon*)." The pun, of course, is not certain, nor is the reference to the Pharisees, but the passage seems rich in Qumran idiolect: *'ebyon* in the sense of a member of the community, *melitz* equals "interpreter" (cf. Genesis 42:23), possibly *ᶜeinekhah ᶜamedah ᶜal nafshi* equals "you keep watch over me", as well *doreshei halaqot*; and it is probable that *halakhah* meaning "religious law" was part of the Pharisaic–Rabbinic idiolect.
3. See Babylonian Talmud Shabbat 116a. Sometimes *gilyonim* is used on its own for the Gospels (Tosefta Yadayim 2:13; Tosefta Shabbat 13(14):5). See further note 21.
4. The group thus attacked may respond with a charge of blasphemy against its attackers, if it feels that something that it holds sacred has been treated with serious disrespect. Blasphemy has always been a potent weapon in intersectarian conflict, but the labelling of the act of disrespect as 'blasphemy' can be an effective counter-measure, since societies in general tend to find blasphemy distasteful, no matter against whom it is directed. Another strategy is to accept the negative label and wear it with defiance and even pride. For example, 'Quaker' is an originally pejorative label that the Society of Friends now accepts with pride.
5. For an edition and translation of this remarkable text, see A. P. Hayman, *Sefer Yesira: Edition, Translation and Text-Critical Commentary* (Tübingen: Mohr Siebeck, 2004). Further Y. Liebes, *Ars Poetica in Sefer Yetsira* (Jerusalem/Tel-Aviv: Hotza'at Shoken, 2000).
6. See War Scroll III–V and VI 2–3.

7. For some remarks of the early Jewish philosophy of language and of names, see P. S. Alexander, "The Etymology of Proper Names as an Exegetical Device in Rabbinic Literature", in D. T. Runia & G. F. Sterling (eds.), *The Studia Philonica Annual* 16 (2004), pp. 169–87.

8. C. Hezser, *The Social Structure of the Rabbinic Movement in Roman Palestine* (Tübingen: Mohr Siebeck, 1997), offers the fullest account of the Rabbinic movement from a sociological perspective.

9. See e.g., Mishnah Yadayim 4:4–6. For negative uses of the verb *parash* and of the noun *perushim*, see Mishnah Pirqei 'Abot 2:4; Tosefta Sanhedrin 13:5; Babylonian Talmud Rosh ha-Shanah 14a; Jerusalem Talmud Berakhot 9:7 (14b). These and similar references should not be used to challenge the standard view that the Rabbis are the spiritual heirs specifically of the Second Temple Period Pharisees.

10. Possibly by accident, since there are few texts from the pre-70 period that can be identified for certain as Pharisaic. Paul in Acts 23:6 claims that he is a "Pharisee, a son of Pharisees", but the setting is the Sanhedrin, and he is deliberately trying to play off the Pharisees against the Sadducees. To Agrippa he says, "I belonged to the strictest sect of our religion and lived as a Pharisee" (Acts 26:4)—a statement that seems to indicate a certain pride in the title. Similar pride seems to be in evidence at Philippians 3:5, "A member of the people of Israel, of the tribe of Benjamin, a Hebrew born of Hebrews; as to the law, a Pharisee."

11. See further P. S. Alexander, "'The Parting of the Ways' from the Perspective of Rabbinic Judaism", in J. D. G. Dunn (ed.), *Jews and Christians: The Parting of the Ways A.D. 70 to 135* (Tübingen: Mohr Siebeck, 1992), pp.1–25; P. S. Alexander, "Jewish Christians in Early Rabbinic Literature", in O. Skarsaune & R. Hvalvik (eds.), *Jewish Believers in Jesus—The Early Centuries* (Peabody, MA: Hendrickson, 2007), pp. 659–709.

12. See e.g., Mishnah Berakhot 9:5; Rosh Ha-Shanah 2:1–2; Sanhedrin 4:5; Tosefta Shabbat 13(14):5; Tosefta Megilla 4(3):36–37. I see no reason to deny that *min*, "heretic" is derived semantically from *min*, "kind".

13. See W. Horbury, "The Benediction of the Minim", in W. Horbury, *Jews and Christians in Contact and Controversy* (Edinburgh, Scotland: T&T Clark, 1998), pp. 67–110.

14. For Elisha ben Abuyah referred to as *'Aher*, see Babylonian Talmud Hagigah 14a, 15a; 3 Enoch 16:2–4 (Schäfer, *Synopse* §20). Some early mediaeval sources call him *'Ahor*, "renegade", but this is secondary.

15. Tosefta Sanhedrin 13:4–5; Hullin 1:1.

16. Mishnah Sanhedrin 10:1 famously denies an *Epiqoros* a share in the world to come: see the exposition of this in Talmud Yerushalmi Sanhedrin x1 (27d–28a). Further, see H.-J. Becker, "'Epikureer' im Talmud Yerushalmi", in P. Schäfer (ed.), *The Talmud Yerushalmi and Graeco-Roman Culture*, vol. 1 (Tübingen: Mohr Siebeck, 1998), pp. 397–421.

17. For *Tzeduqi*, see Mishnah Niddah 4:2; Tosefta Hagigah 3:35.

18. But see M. D. Goodman, "Sadducees and Essenes after 70 CE", in S. E. Porter, P. Joyce, & D. E. Orton (eds.), *Crossing the Boundaries: Essays in Biblical Interpretation in Honour of Michael D. Goulder* (Leiden: Brill, 1994), pp. 347–56. This is not to deny that the priestly class retained some sort of social cohesion and organization after the destruction of the Temple in 70 CE. See P. S. Alexander, "What happened to the Jewish Priesthood after 70?", in Z. Rodgers (ed.), *Festschrift for Sean Freyne* (forthcoming).

19. For a critical text of Irenaeus's *Adversus omnes Haereses*, see A. Rousseau, L. Doutreleau, and others, in the Sources Chrétiennes series 100, 152–153, 210–211, 293–294 (Paris: Éditions du Cerf, 1962–1985). A useful English

translation can be found in the *Ante-Nicene Fathers* (Edinburgh, Scotland: repr. T&T Clark; Grand Rapids, MI: Eerdmans, 1993), 1, pp. 309–567.

20. "We [the English] seem, as it were, to have conquered and peopled half the world in a fit of absence of mind". Sir John Seeley, *The Expansion of England* (1883), Lecture 1.

21. Though the *Toledot Yeshu* was not composed till the early Middle Ages, many of the traditions it contains are found in much earlier Jewish texts. Peter Schäfer recently argued that the Rabbinic traditions about Jesus show much deeper knowledge of the Gospels, specifically Matthew and John, than has often been supposed. See P. Schäfer, *Jesus in the Talmud* (Princeton, NJ: Princeton University Press, 2007); see further P. S Alexander., "Yeshu/Yeshua ben Yosef of Nazareth: Discerning the Jewish Face of Jesus", in G. J. Brooke (ed.), *The Birth of Jesus: Biblical and Theological Reflections* (Edinburgh, Scotland: T&T Clark, 2000), pp. 9–22; J. Maier, *Jesus von Nazareth in der talmudischen Überlieferung* (Darmstadt: Wissenschaftliche Buchgesellschaft, 1982). William Horbury's unpublished dissertation, *A Critical Examination of the Toledoth Yeshu* (Doctoral dissertation, University of Cambridge, 1970), remains important. See further W. Horbury & S. Krauss, *The Jewish-Christian Controversy From the Earliest Times to 1789* (Tübingen: Mohr Siebeck, 1996). *Pantheros* is probably not a deliberate deformation of Greek *parthenos* ("virgin"); see Schäfer (2007), p. 98.

22. P. S. Alexander, "3 Enoch", in J. H. Charlesworth (ed.), *The Old Testament Pseudepigrapha*, vol. 1 (New York: Doubleday, 1983), pp. 223–315, provides a readily available translation of one of the main texts, with notes and introduction. The standard edition is P. Schäfer, *Synopse zur Hekhalot Literatur* (Tübingen: Mohr Siebeck, 1981); the only complete translation is in German: P. Schäfer & K. Herrmann, *Übersetzung der Hekhalot-Literatur*, 4 vols (Tübingen: Mohr Siebeck, 1991–1995). The classic introductions to this are G. G. Scholem, *Major Trends in Jewish Mysticism*, 3rd ed (New York: Schocken, 1954); G. G. Scholem, *Jewish Gnosticism, Merkabah Mysticism and Talmudic Tradition*, 2nd ed (New York: Jewish Theological Seminary of America, 1965). But much has been written since, see P. S. Alexander, "Mysticism", in M. D. Goodman (ed.), *The Oxford Handbook of Jewish Studies* (Oxford: Oxford University Press, 2002), pp. 706–708. Most of the more recent studies have continued to concentrate on the *ideas* in the texts. Less has been done on the sociology of the movement behind them, and its relationship to Rabbinism, and even less on its highly distinctive language and style. Its place within the thought-world of late antiquity has been dominated by the debate over whether or not it is Gnostic, but Vita Daphna Arbel's recent study *Beholders of Divine Secrets: Mysticism and Myth in the Heikhalot Literature* (Albany: State University of New York Press, 2003) argued for strong links with ancient Near Eastern myth. This raises again the similarities with the *Chaldean Oracles* and with Neoplatonism, which utilised this ancient Near Eastern tradition—a comparison drawn many years ago. See P. S. Alexander, "The Historical Setting of the Hebrew Book of Enoch", *Journal of Jewish Studies* 28 (1977), pp. 170–171. One does not have to subscribe to Simo Parpola's highly speculative views ("The Assyrian Tree of Life: Tracing the Origins of Jewish Monotheism and Greek Philosophy", *Journal of Near Eastern Studies* 52, 1993, pp. 161–208) to recognise the persistence of the ancient Near Eastern myths into late antiquity, and their "philosophical" transformation in Neoplatonism and Hermeticism, nor to see the urgent need to re-assess radically our naive post-Enlightenment assumptions about the primitive nature of their thinking.

23. See Mishnah Megillah 2:1, and the parallels in the Tosefta and the two Talmuds. The texts are analysed in D. J. Halperin, *The Merkabah in Rabbinic Literature* (New Haven, CT: American Oriental Society, 1980).

24. Schäfer, *Synopse* §199.

25. In a chain of transmission that echoes Mishnah Pirqei 'Abot 1, 3 Enoch 48D:10 (Schäfer, §80) relates how Metatron revealed the secret of the Merkabah "to Moses, Moses to Joshua, Joshua to the Elders, the Elders to the Prophets, the Prophets to the Men of the Great Synagogue, the Men of the Great Synagogue to Ezra the Scribe, Ezra the Scribe to Hillel the Elder, Hillel the Elder to Rabbi Abbahu, Rabbi Abbahu to Rabbi Zira, Rabbi Zira to the Men of Faith, and the Men of Faith to the Faithful". It seems likely that "men of faith" (*'anshei 'amanah*) and "faithful" (*ba‘alei 'emunot*) — the repetition is typical of Heikhalot style — are self-designations of the *Yoredei Merkabah*. It is also possible that when Rabbi Ishmael is addressed as "Son of Proud Ones" (*ben ge'im*) the title denotes a master of Merkabah lore (Schäfer, *Synopse* §§200, 225, 239, 403, 579, 583, 601, 778). The meaning of the term is obscure, but since *ge'im* is sometimes used in Heikhalot texts to denote the angels (Schäfer, *Synopse* §§1, 799) it is possible *ben ge'im* denotes someone who consorts with the angels. The very neutral term "members of the fellowship" (*haberim*) is used in the importance séance passage in Heikhalot Rabbati 15.1–22.2 (Schäfer, *Synopse* §203; cf. 584), but it is unclear whether it is a self-designation of the group, or, in context, alludes to the students of the Yeshivah.

26. P. S. Alexander, "The Family of Caesar and the Family of God: The Image of the Emperor in the Heikhalot Literature", in L. Alexander (ed.), *Images of Empire* (Sheffield, England: Sheffield Academic Press, 1991), pp. 277–97.

27. Genesis Rabba VIII 10.

28. 3 Enoch 12.3–5, Schäfer, *Synopse* §15; 16.1, Schäfer, *Synopse* §20.

29. Alexander (1991), pp. 287–297.

30. For a recent, reliable introductions to the Dead Sea Scrolls and the Qumran community see J. G. Campbell, *Deciphering the Dead Sea Scrolls*, 2nd edition (Oxford: Blackwell, 2002); P. R. Davies, G. J. Brooke, & P. R. Callaway, *The Complete World of the Dead Sea Scrolls* (London: Thames and Hudson, 2004). The standard English translation is G. Vermes, *The Complete Dead Sea Scrolls in English* (London: Penguin Books, 2004).

31. Community Rule IX 5–6.

32. F. Brown, S. R. Driver, & C. A. Briggs, *A Hebrew and English Lexicon of the Old Testament* (Oxford: Clarendon Press, 1966), p. 403; L. Koehler & W. Baumgartner, *The Hebrew and Aramaic Lexicon of the Old Testament*, trans. & ed. M. E. J. Richardson (Leiden, The Netherlands: Brill, 2001), vol. 1, pp. 405–406.

33. See C. A. Newsom, "'Sectually Explicit' Literature From Qumran", in W. H. Propp, B. Halpern, & D. N. Freedman (eds.), *The Hebrew Bible and its Interpreters* (Winona Lake, IN: Eisenbrauns, 1990), pp. 167–87. One might compare the Arabic noun *al-qa‘ida*, which etymologically means, "the foundation" or "the base" (H. Wehr, *A Dictionary of Modern Written Arabic*, ed. J. M. Cowan, 3rd printing (Wiesbaden, Germany: Harrassowitz, 1961), p. 780), but which has come, of course, to designate a specific Islamist terror network led by Osama bin Ladin (al-Qaida/al-Qaeda). How this came about is unclear. The "base" originally referred to may have been the guerrilla training camps in Afghanistan, but the linguistic development is probably similar to *Yahad*: a generic term is used idiolectically by a particular group as a self-designation that then becomes accepted in this specific sense by the wider world.

34. See especially the War Scroll I 1, 8, 10, 11, etc.
35. Community Rule III 21–22.
36. Community Rule IV 22–25.
37. Pesher Habakkuk XII 2–6.
38. Damascus Document I, 8–11; Pesher Psalms³ III 15–17; Pesher Habakkuk VIII 1–3.
39. Pesher Habakkuk VIII 8; IX 9; XI 4.
40. e.g. Pesher Habakkuk X 9.
41. Pesher Nahum 3–4, i 6–7.
42. See P. S. Alexander, "'Wrestling Against Wickedness in High Places': Magic in the Worldview of the Qumran Community", in S. E. Porter & C. A. Evans (eds.), *The Scrolls and the Scriptures: Qumran Fifty Years After* (Sheffield, England: Sheffield Academic Press, 1997), pp. 318–37.
43. On this phenomenon see P. S. Alexander, "The Evil Empire: The Qumran Eschatological War Cycle and the Origins of Jewish Opposition to Rome", in S. M. Paul, R. A. Kraft, L. H. Schiffman, & W. W. Fields (eds.), *Emanuel: Studies in Hebrew Bible, Septuagint and Dead Sea Scrolls in Honour of Emanuel Tov* (Leiden: Brill, 2003), pp. 17–31.
44. By the Black Hebrews I mean here the followers of Ben Carter, some of whom emigrated to Israel in 1969 and settled in the Dimona area; see F. Markowitz, "Israel as Africa, Africa as Israel: 'Divine Geography' in the Personal Narratives and Community Identity of the Black Hebrew Israelites", *Anthropological Quarterly* 69 (1996); J. H. Boykin, *Black Jews: A Study in Minority Experience* (Miami, FL: Boykin, 1996), pp. 193–205; T. Parfitt, *The Lost Tribes of Israel: The History of a Myth* (London: Phoenix, 2003), pp.111–112. More generally, see T. Parfitt & E. Trevisan Semi, *Judaising Movements: Studies in the Margins of Judaism in Modern Times* (Richmond, Surrey: Curzon Press, 1999). The Beta Israel or Ethiopian Jews, large numbers of whom emigrated to Israel in the 1980s and 1990s, have been much studied: see e.g., S. Kaplan, T. Parfitt, & E. Trevisan Semi (eds.), *"Between Africa and Zion": Proceedings of the First International Conference on Ethiopian Jewry, Venice 1993* (Jerusalem, Israel: Ben-Zvi Institute, 1995).

5 Who Are the Others?

Three Moments in Sanskrit-Based Practice

Jacqueline Suthren Hirst

In this essay on Sanskrit, one of the classical languages of India, I examine the changing ways in which 'opponent others' are characterised at three different points in the development of Sanskrit-based traditions. I focus initially on the work of the great Advaita Vedantin thinker Shankaracharya (c. 700 CE) to show how various fluid and shifting boundaries operate between different groups in his works.[1] I differentiate between, on the one hand, *mlecchas* (foreigners), others whom he simply ignores, and, on the other hand, 'opponent others', those who have to be understood and negotiated with, rivals within a Sanskritic universe of discourse. I argue that Shankara was trying to locate a variety of groups (not just Buddhists and Jains) as 'outside the Veda', while identifying Advaita as a proper Vedic exegetical tradition. Simultaneously, I suggest, he was seeking to incorporate aspects of current devotional practice to Vishnu, in a bid to secure the position of his own school in a competitive market involving ritualist brahmins, rising devotional traditions, and Jain and Buddhist movements amongst others. This enables us to challenge for their lack of fit both the 'world religions' model of religion and the 'six orthodox schools of Indian philosophy' model, which are each embedded in their own intertwining networks of religion, language, and power.

This is thrown into relief by two briefer case studies: firstly a consideration of nineteenth-century Christian missionary discourse in Sanskrit or Sanskrit-based Bengali and the replies of the great reformist thinker, Rammohun Roy (1772?–1833), and a later brahmin thinker, Nilakantha Goreh (1825–1885); and secondly the way the Vishwa Hindu Parishad (World Council of Hindus) has positioned itself in relation to the world religions model current in British Religious Education in the late twentieth century. Power relations in these colonial and postcolonial situations clearly affect the shifting ways in which the 'wholly other' and the 'opponent other' are characterised, intimately bound up as these characterisations are with constructions and deconstructions of what counts as (a) 'religion'. I argue that this alerts us to the likely operation of power relations in Shankara's context where the historical data are less certain. Conversely the fluid and different boundaries that Shankara marks point up 'religion' as a construction that shifts, and is shifted by, the way language is used to label (opponent) others.

The idea of the six major world religions is a commonplace one in popular discourse.[2] Along with it goes a set of assumptions including the view that religion is a primary, exclusive identity.[3] In other words, a person is either Hindu or Christian or Muslim, so 'others' are those who belong to different religions.[4] Scholars have frequently drawn attention to the complex history of such constructions and to the violence they have engendered in South Asian contexts amongst others. Nonetheless, essentialised religion is seen as the key in much contemporary political analysis of South Asia, even as scholars of religion work to deconstruct such notions.[5] In this chapter, I argue that paying close attention to the way others are characterised and categorised at different points in history enables us both to challenge the idea of religions as permanent, essentialised, discrete systems and to see how such views come to be constructed. In examining different constructions of 'others', I suggest, we are able to detect varying (perhaps otherwise submerged) issues of power, as well as the changing role and function of Sanskrit in relation to such constructions.

To demonstrate this fully would be a massive task. Here I confine myself to the three examples mentioned above, one precolonial, one colonial, and one diasporic postcolonial. Through them I shall indicate how issues of religion, language, and power emerge variously in such contexts. Paying attention to this requires us to reject the world religions' model of essentialised 'isms'[6] demarcated with fixed clear boundaries throughout history. Through these three examples, I also interrogate another model still prevalent in scholarly discourse, that of the so-called six systems of Indian philosophy. I show that the relation of the 'six schools of Indian philosophy' to 'Hinduism' is intimately linked with modern constructions of the latter, but that a very different picture of how these schools are envisaged in relation to each other and contemporary norms obtained in the time at which Shankara was writing. I shall, however, argue that he too was involved in negotiating issues of boundary formation and power.

In exploring the ways 'others' have been characterised, I take as a starting-point the distinction Jonathan Z. Smith makes between 'strategies that portray the out-group as *different* but comprehensible and strategies that emphasize the *otherness* or unintelligible alienness of the barbarian.' Key to Smith's contrast is the idea that 'otherness' blocks language and conceptualization; 'difference' invites negotiation and intellection.'[7] We shall see that this contrast apparently fits Shankara's differentiated treatment of groups who inhabited his South Indian world very neatly. I, however, draw further on both Sheldon Pollock's work on Sanskrit as a cosmopolitan language and the notion of identity formation as the 'marking of symbolic boundaries' that 'requires what is left outside . . . to consolidate the process', drawn on, among others, by the sociologist, Stuart Hall.[8] I thereby seek to make more complex our understanding of the extent to which characterisations of others have been necessary to the way the 'self' group has viewed itself at these different points. Let us turn now to the first of these.

SHANKARA AND HIS OTHERS

Background

Shankaracharya was one of the greatest teachers in the brahminical philosophical school of Advaita Vedanta.[9] Providing precise historical background for figures like him is difficult. While there are masses of literary, philosophical, and other texts in Sanskrit, Sanskritists otherwise have what historians call 'bad data' in many cases, including his.[10] We can, however, say that Shankara probably lived in South India around 700 C.E. If this is the case, this was at a time and in a region when devotion to the Supreme Lord as Shiva or as Vishnu was on the increase. Simultaneously, as rice production started to grow, the brahmins who would later run massive temple complexes in the south became stronger in competition with Jains and Buddhists who tended to operate at the maritime margins.[11] These devotional *bhakti* brahmins were also in competition with ritualist brahmins who presented themselves as the true guardians of the Veda and of a socioritual order that could challenge that espoused by various Buddhist dynasties from the Mauryas (4th to 2nd centuries B.C.E.) onwards. Shankara himself was primarily a commentator on the Sanskrit texts of the Veda, in particular, on the texts known as the Upanishads or Vedanta (c. 900 BCE to the turn of the Common Era). While the Upanishads themselves contain many different explorations, Shankara's nondualist school holds that *brahman*, the ultimate reality that grounds the cosmos, is nothing other than *atman*, the self or principle of consciousness that grounds all sentient beings. Realisation of this liberates a person from the otherwise endless cycle of rebirth. Within the world of rebirth, however, socioritual distinctions must be preserved to maintain proper order.

Who then were Shankara and his others? In the following, I shall differentiate between *mleccha*s (foreigners), others who are simply ignored by Shankara, and his 'opponent others', those who have to be understood and negotiated with, as rivals within a Sanskritic universe of discourse, in terms of whom Advaita's own identity is carefully positioned.[12] I argue that Shankara was trying to locate a variety of groups as 'outside the Veda', while identifying his own Advaita Vedanta school as a proper Vedic exegetical tradition. Simultaneously, I suggest, he was seeking to incorporate aspects of current devotional practice to Vishnu, in a bid to secure the position of his own school in a competitive market involving ritualist brahmins, rising devotional traditions and Jain and Buddhist movements amongst others. As well as allowing us insight into the way his 'religious others' were organised, this will enable us to start challenging both the 'world religions' model of religion and the 'six orthodox schools of Indian philosophy' model, models that are each embedded in their own networks intertwining issues of religion, language, and power.

Sanskrit and the Marking of Otherness

If first we return to the notion of six world religions, we might label Shankara as 'Hindu' and look for representatives of the other religions in his writings. However, since to call Shankara 'Hindu' would be anachronistic, I have preferred to use the label 'brahminical'.[13] Shankara was a brahmin, a member of those minority élite groups that alone were allowed to transmit the authoritative Vedic texts. Shankara also had a clear preference for his pupils to be brahmins, renouncers if possible, although technically anyone 'twice-born', that is member of warrior or merchant groups, was allowed to hear the Vedas. He taught in a world of brahmin teachers and their pupils, a world in which many Buddhist teachers were also themselves brahmins by background. He was, however, well aware of other social groups; his numerous illustrations draw on the daily lives of people from kings to artisans. In such a plural context, Shankara operated with a series of concentric boundaries to do with qualification to study the Veda. These boundaries demarcate the twice-born from the majority servant group, brahmins within the twice-born, and within the brahmins those who seek liberation through an Advaitin interpretation of Vedanta. What, though, of 'other religions'?

In his commentaries, Shankara mentions Buddhists and Jains. We also know that in the South India of his day there were established communities of Christians and of Jews.[14] Of these he makes no mention. They are, in Smith's terms, truly others, in relation to whom there is no conceptualisation. We may question, then, whether they could, in Stuart Hall's terms, be 'a constitutive outside', to consolidate any process of identity formation, since they simply do not feature.[15]

Strictly speaking, however, they are 'other' not because they belong to other religions, but because they do not participate in the same linguistic world of discourse. They do not communicate in Sanskrit. In this sense, they are beyond a very strong boundary, a boundary that is fundamental to Shankara's identity as a cultured Sanskrit-Veda-transmitting brahmin. As Pollock pointed out in discussing how Sanskrit becomes a cosmopolitan literary language in South, and indeed Southeast, Asia in the first millennium of the Common Era, before this time Sanskrit was limited to being a liturgical language of brahmins.[16] It was only after the turn of the era that political inscriptions started to occur in Sanskrit and literature was created in that language. A language then demarcated an area of cultural activity and, in Shankara's day, Sanskrit demarcated not only the field of literature and political clout, but was the appropriate language in which to discuss matters of soteriology. Its hegemony in such matters is clear. Whereas early

Buddhist and Jain texts were composed in Prakrit vernacular languages of different kinds, by the second century CE not only were Mahayana Buddhist scriptures composed (or 'discovered') in Sanskrit, but discussions between Mahayana Buddhist, Jain and brahminical schools were entirely conducted in Sanskrit. Sanskrit alone was the language for such negotiation and conceptualisation.

It may be for similar reasons that members of different ethnic groups are largely absent from Shankara's writings too. Again, we can be fairly sure that Arab traders were known along the (south-) western coast of India by his day. Places such as Mathura in North India, which Shankara does mention, had earlier been under Indo-Greek rule and influence, yet neither Arabs nor Greeks nor other 'outsiders' are worth even a passing reference. They do not feature in the texts on which he comments nor in the examples from contemporary life with which his exegesis abounds. They are simply *mleccha*s, the foreigners, those who cannot speak Sanskrit, as the unmellifluous *ml* in their name suggests.[17] They are strictly others, in Smith's terms, those in relation to whom language and conceptualisation are blocked.[18]

In this respect Shankara is more extreme than some of his sources and commentators. We know, for example, that Shankara was familiar with the *Manusmriti* (c. 200 CE) from which he quoted on numerous occasions, though not on the subject of *mleccha*s.[19] This text on the duties of the different ideal social groups and stages of life contains many apparent contradictions. It lays down very strict guidelines and then, sometimes in the very next verse, opens the way to exceptions to the rule. We can see this at work in the way it handles *mleccha*s. On the one hand *mleccha*s are defined as those who are beyond the geographical reach and jurisdiction of socioritual order (*dharma*) encoded in Sanskrit. On the other hand, the *Manusmriti* compilers are pragmatic enough to realise that foreigners have actually ruled parts of the country the text considers to fall within the purviews of *dharma*. The text therefore explains that foreign kings, including Greeks and Scythians, were really one-time *kshatriya*s, members of the second ideal social group of rulers and warriors. These *kshatriya*s had, however, fallen because they failed to perform due rituals or consult brahmins (*cf. Manu* 10.41–44). Those of their posterity who did actually demonstrate their protection of the socioritual order, consulting brahmins and allowing *dharma* to flourish, could be incorporated back into the picture, since they acted as true *kshatriya*s. In Hall's terms[20] the *Manusmriti* thus includes a series of boundaries producing frontier effects beyond which are the *mleccha*s. Yet these boundaries are permeable in the world of *Realpolitik*, for they allow the foreign king whose action places him within the sphere of *dharma* to be located within the conceptual system.

Shankara was well aware of the purview of correct socioritual order. At one level, he wished to locate his school within its sphere by contrast with, especially, Buddhist practice that rejected this social construction, at least in theory. In this, Shankara showed himself part of the contemporary milieu. However, it would be incorrect to see this as a straightforward division between two religions, Hinduism and Buddhism. As Ballard argued of popular religion in the Punjab, there are other ways of articulating different dimensions of that which we might label as 'religion' and package in single 'systems'.[21] For Shankara and his contemporaries, the relation between one's search for liberation within a *sampradaya* or teaching tradition and everyday life in the socioritual world was itself a matter of intense debate and varying articulation. It is to that world of competing teaching traditions we now turn.

Opponent Others in a Sanskritic Universe of Discourse

Shankara is to be positioned in a world of teaching traditions, many of which have (or come to have) a soteriological intent. Each teaching tradition both promulgates a particular view in Sanskrit (*darshana*) and represents a form of organisation that transmits this view. Each tradition looks back to its key teacher and his teaching and tries to help its pupils to engage critically with and understand this teaching. In so doing, it examines the views of other schools in order to provide refutations of their positions and to establish the truth of its own. In Smith's terms, these are not 'others' beyond conceptualisation, but very much those with whom one negotiates and engages intellectually.[22] I call them 'opponent others'.

Shankara's opponent others in this context include, but are not exhausted by, Materialists (Lokayatikas), Buddhists of various types, and Jains, along with members of those six paired schools which have come to be identified as 'orthodox'.[23] The former three are often referred to as *nastika* ('heterodox') by contrast with the latter six which are identified as the *astika* schools ('orthodox').

While nineteenth-century Europeans such as Monier-Williams wanted to map 'atheism' onto 'heterodoxy' and 'theism' onto 'orthodoxy' because of their own Christian presuppositions about correct belief, it is normally accepted that the *nastika* schools were those that rejected the Veda and its socioritual practices, while the *astika* schools were those which accepted its authority.[24] However, this was a construction that was only in the process of being established in Shankara's day. When we look at his actual usage, we see a rather different picture, a picture in which Shankara is indeed negotiating the Vedic orthodoxy of his own school, but rejecting that of other schools that came to be identified as *astika*. We can trace this in the way he labels his opponent others and the way he discusses their teachers.

Firstly, then, Shankara may refer to his opponent others by the name of their school or group of schools (Naiyayika, Bauddha, etc.). He may also describe them as members of a transmitting organisation ('the red-robed ones', i.e., Buddhists; 'the naked ones', i.e., Digambara Jains). But these are not constant terms and much more often he will label opponents according to the position they hold (e.g., 'those who hold that the effect is not latent in the cause', i.e., members of various schools who rejected the notion of causality that Shankara adapted from the Sankhyan school).This enabled Shankara to group his opponent others in various ways as he negotiates the position of his own school, though he did not make use of the terms '*astika*' and '*nastika*' in so doing. Rather, for example, Shankara linked the Buddhist view on momentariness with that of knowers of Nyaya, Sankhya, and Mimamsa philosophy who teach that the individual does not exist as the permanent self (*Brihadaranyaka Upanishad* commentary 2.1.20).[25] He thus showed that none of them holds a Vedic view. More damning still, Shankara castigated those who 'think of themselves as exponents of the Upanishads', because they joined forces with the purveyors of logic and, in their fear of Sankhya, follow the Vaisheshika understanding of consciousness (2.3.6). In so doing, he distanced those who might be his most direct rivals in interpreting the Upanishads from the true Advaitin interpretation and pressed his point home by a series of fairly uncharacteristic pejorative comments.[26] These tactics provide rhetorically effective ways of removing views which form obstacles to the development of the Advaitin pupil's correct understanding. But they are also ways of aligning different viewpoints and schools, so that they are distanced from the authority of the Veda.

Secondly, Shankara discussed the teachers of other schools. He made it clear that Kapila, the purported founder of Sankhya, ostensibly an orthodox school, is on a par with the Buddha. This is criticism indeed, since the founder of one of the key 'heterodox' schools is held by Shankara to be the author of—possibly malignantly—confused teachings. The criticism of Kapila is important, since some of the cultured, that is those of high social prestige and Vedic learning, were following Sankhya (*Brahma Sutra* commentary 2.2).[27] They needed to be shown that their erroneous views on mind-matter and selves were 'outside the Veda'. Here we see Shankara jockeying to establish his school within the Vedic ambit and trying to exclude others from it, in competition for social power, prestige, and pupils.

However, whereas Shankara appeared to be ousting Sankhya and Yoga from the Vedically-authorised sphere, he simultaneously seemed to be including another group whose Vedic credentials are very dubious. The Bhagavatas were worshippers of Vishnu. In Shankara's treatment, they are associated with the Pancharatrikas, a sect of Vishnu-worshippers who had their own originally non-Vedic corpus of Sanskrit texts. Nonetheless, he sanctioned their temple worship, provided it focused attention on *brahman* as the sole reality and thus was conducive to an Advaitin understanding. He did though reject the theology of the Pancharatra texts. By contrast, Shankara rejected outright another devotional group, the Maheshvara worshippers of Shiva, along with Nyaya, Vaisheshika, and Sankhya, whose teachers were often Shaivas themselves, as also having teachings that are 'outside the Veda'.

Nineteenth-century European presentations of the schools of Indian philosophy tended to ignore the devotional schools because they were operating with an Enlightenment assumption about the difference between 'religion' and 'philosophy' that prioritised the rationality of the latter. But to use this lens misrepresents the social context of Shankara's day and his own attitudes and boundaries. The devotional traditions of his day were engaging in the Sanskritic world of discourse by developing their own sectarian Sanskrit texts. They were gaining power at a social level, attracting brahmin teachers and pupils to their forms of worship and requiring attention from exegetes like Shankara, who may well have drawn his own pupils from a Vishnu-worshipping milieu.

In this complex context, Shankara put forward the Vedantically-given Advaitin teaching that would lead to liberation. But this is no forest-dwelling sage of modern oleographs, cut off from the world. For Shankara, the contending centres of power were those of the Buddhists and Jains who had enjoyed patronage from local rulers but in the South India of his day were finding their maritime base undermined by the rice-producing hinterland. In the struggle between the ritualist Purva-mimamsaka brahmins and those associated with rising devotional traditions, Shankara both aligned Advaita Vedanta as a Mimamsa (that is, proper Vedic exegetical) tradition and allowed that devotion to Vishnu may be a step toward Advaitin truth. He thus negotiated actual situations of competition and power, while teaching in the end the need to transcend all such worldly preoccupations.

There are several symbolic boundaries being marked and breached here in their absence as much as in their presence. Firstly, though Shankara certainly recognised the six schools that were to be seen as the six classical schools of orthodox Indian philosophy and sometimes dealt with them in their associated pairs, he marked no hard and fast boundary between them and, on the one hand, the heterodox Veda-rejecting schools (Buddhist, Jain), or, on the other hand, the originally non-Vedic Sanskrit sectarian schools (Maheshvara, Bhagavata), whose texts would provide the foundation for the practice of some of the most influential devotional schools of what would become known as Hinduism.[28] Rather, he judged each of them in accordance with his Advaitin interpretation of the Vedic Upanishadic texts and his desire to draw them in as pupils. He has then two 'hard' boundaries where language and power interact. The outer marks the Sanskrit universe of discourse within which proper intellection and negotiation between opponent others takes place. The inner marks the correct Vedic interpretation given in his Advaitin understanding. Neither is identical either with boundaries between 'religions' or between the six orthodox schools and others. Between the two is space for variously intersecting teaching traditions, interpretations of social order, and forms of worship, some of which are to be rejected out of hand, others of which are to be allowed in so far as they lead towards Advaitin understanding.

Between Shankara and the nineteenth century, to which we turn next, there was a plethora of ways of negotiating these different intersections, not only in Sanskrit but in cosmopolitan vernaculars and local languages in South Asia. As European missionaries and indologists sought to gain knowledge of the 'religions of India', a category that they developed as their knowledge increased, it is unsurprising that they relied, amongst others, on brahmin pandits (and hence on Sanskritic traditions) whom they saw as the appropriate specialists.

TWO NINETEENTH-CENTURY ENGAGEMENTS

It is often held that 'Hinduism' is a nineteenth-century construct, a view that is strongly rejected by those who since that period have learned to view it as *sanatana-dharma*, 'the eternal teaching'. Through painstaking research into the work of English, Dutch, German, and French missionaries in the seventeenth and eighteenth centuries, Will Sweetman showed a much more complex picture of knowledge emerging through their interactions.[29] David Lorenzen also argued that the 'Hinduism' of the famous indologist and comparative religionist, F. Max Müller (1823–1900), is a fair representation of Puranic understandings that date back over one thousand years.[30]

Nevertheless, it is certainly the case that particular constructions of Hinduism as a religion comparable with Christianity did develop in nineteenth-century colonial contexts of power. In this section I argue that the notion of the (six) orthodox schools of Indian philosophy played a role in such constructions. The history of European awareness of these schools, of their grouping as six orthodox schools and of their relation to the 'religion' of Hinduism is complex. Suffice it to say that the 'six main schools among the brahmins' from 'antiquity' were identified by 1740 and described by Sir William Jones (1794) and then in increasing detail by H. T. Colebrooke, whose 1823–27 lectures, published serially, were widely read in Pauthier's French translation of 1833 (published in revised book form in English in 1858).[31] Alongside this developing understanding of 'antiquity' was another picture based on contemporary regional specialisations of Bengali pandits in Nyaya and North Indian pandits in Vedanta. These were the only two 'schools' included in 1821 on the Sanskrit curriculum of the newly set up Poona Hindu College, along with *dharmashastra,* grammar, astronomy, aesthetics, and Veda.[32] However, by the early 1870s, the head of the school in Poona, Mahadeo Moreshwar Kunte, had started a publication in Marathi, *Saddarsanadarpana* (*Reflection on the Six Schools*), 'to introduce the philosophical systems in Sanskrit to Marathi readers.'[33] Clearly insider categories, and their reorganisation by outsiders and reintroduction to insiders, are involved here. The following examples will tease this out further and show how developing notions of 'others' are linked with self-presentations.

My argument is focused around two debates. The first was conducted in Bengali and English from 1821 for two years between the Baptist Serampore missionaries and the famous reformer Rammohun Roy (1772?–1833), writing under the pseudonym of the pandit Shivuprusad Surma.[34] The second took place nearly two decades later, provoked by the publication in 1839 of John Muir's *Matapariksha* in Sanskrit ('An Examination of Religions').[35] In each case, I show that disputes around the different schools both reflected missionary emphases on correct belief as central to true religion and contributed to the rhetoric of Hinduism as a religion within which difference was included and harmonised, by contrast with Christianity which excluded and rejected it. Here then missionaries participated in a modern form of debate with opponent others in which negotiation and intellection were central and in which Hall's process of symbolic boundaries producing 'frontier effects' is clearly visible.[36] The way the 'opponent other' is constituted is indeed part of the way of defining self.

The Serampore Missionaries and Rammohun Roy

On 14th July 1821, a Bengali weekly newspaper, *Samachar Darpan*, carried a letter 'shewing the unreasonableness of all the Hindoo Sastras'[37] and inviting a response. *Samachar Darpan* was a production of the Mission Press at Serampore, set up in 1818 to convey secular knowledge and create an informed public in Bengali that would then be ready to listen to the (Christian) truth.[38] Its turn to a direct attack on authoritative Hindu texts seems to be what provoked Rammohun to reply, aware as he was of the potential for widespread circulation of a newspaper, compared with earlier face-to-face discussions and publications dedicated to such views.[39] Since his initial reply in Bengali was rejected by *Samachar Darpan*, he published it in both English and Bengali, along with an English version of the original critique, in the first two numbers of his own publication, *The Brahmunical Magazine*, created for this purpose. A reply, in English only, was published in *The Friend of India* (no. 38), another production of the Serampore missionaries.

Rammohun was disappointed that the discussion had been diverted from Bengali, with its primarily Hindu readership, to English and so primarily a European and Christian readership, and that a bilingual response had not been offered to *The Brahmunical Magazine* itself. In his view, the initial intention of the missionaries, writing in Bengali to persuade educated Hindus away from the incoherence of their own writings, represented an abuse of colonial power. It was important for him to engage in this disputation about authoritative Sanskrit texts in Bengali to show by counterargument and comparison the incoherence and hence falsity of 'their own religion', Christianity. Yet when the missionaries refused to pursue this in Bengali, presumably because they realised it could be counter-productive, Rammohun continued the debate in English, aware of his other audience.

The original letter took each of the ('orthodox') *shastra*s in turn: Vedanta, Nyaya, Mimamsa, Yoga, and Sankhya (omitting only Vaisheshika, often subsumed under Nyaya). It sketched out its key teachings on God and the soul, and then raised questions indicating the problematic and often contradictory nature of each of these in the writer's opinion. The likely author of this letter was the Serampore Baptist missionary, William Ward, who in 1811 in his *Account of the Writings, Religion and Manners of the Hindoos* had already discussed the Hindoos' 'six durshunus' as 'six Systems of Philosophy'.[40] He elaborated on these in the second edition of 1822, including translations of primary sources for each school.[41] By taking each *shastra* in turn, his intention seems to have been to show the comprehensive incoherence of the various Hindoo texts and doctrines.

Rammohun contributed further to the construction of 'the Hindoo religion' as being primarily based on these *shastra*s as 'immediate explanations of the Vedas, our original Sacred Books' by treating the *shastra*s together in his first number.[42] He leaves it to the second issue of his magazine to show how the Puranic and Tantric texts, also criticised in the letter, are only authoritative insofar as they are in accordance with the Veda, so that what is inconsistent in them can easily be by-passed. This, he argued, is in contrast with Christianity. Its incoherent view of the Man–God or God–Man and of God as both Son and Father is rooted in its most authoritative source, the Bible, so is of far greater consequence and cannot be ignored. He stressed against this the coherence of the Vedically-based *shastra*s in their teaching on God as one and immaterial, even if they disagree on less important subjects.[43]

In the first section of this chapter, we saw Shankara negotiating a position of authority based on correct Vedic interpretation from which he marginalised not just Buddhists and Jains, who had what we would regard as other scriptures, but also schools such as Sankhya, whose founder's teachings are placed on a par with those of the Buddha. These, along with the rising devotional schools conducting ritual and theology in Sanskrit, are his rivals amongst whom he must establish the power of Advaita, power both to liberate but before that to attract pupils in the competitive market place of his day. In early nineteenth-century Bengal, the opponent others between whom intellection and negotiation is required in the context of an unequal distribution of power are advocates of two separate religions ('*dharma*' is the term they use here in Bengali). Both conversant, at least to some degree, with the teachings on the originary Sanskrit texts collectively held to form the foundation of the 'Hindoo' religion, they start the discussion in Bengali. This opens the discussion in the newly designated language of the educated élite at the core of British jurisdiction in India, which is being formed through the printing press.

The different Sanskrit opponent others have been reconvened. Gone are the Buddhist and Jain participants; only those deemed 'Hindoo' remain.[44] And far from needing marginalising as opponent others from the single correct Vedic interpretation, they need presenting as a group: either a group whose views on God and soul are all contradictory, and who therefore provide the foil to the claimed coherence of Christianity, as true religion, or as a group whose views all agree on the single correct Vedically-based interpretation of the one immaterial God, though they may differ on less important matters. Adherents of each are being constructed as Christians and Hindus who oppose one another in terms of doctrine and primary identity, identities that are connected for Rammohun, writing forcefully in the preface to the first edition, with the unequal power of the conquering colonial and the simple vegetarian native respectively.

Two years later in the preface to the second edition, it is rather as others with different attitudes that Rammohun constructs his opponents. His tone has changed to one of sorrow that the missionaries will no longer carry out the conversation in Bengali. He defends himself against any suspicion of opposing Christianity on the grounds that

> it is well-known to the whole world, that no people on earth are more tolerant than the Hindoos, who believe all men to be equally within the reach of Divine beneficence, which embraces the good of every religious sect and denomination.

Rather, he continues,

> I was influenced by the conviction that persons who travel to a distant country for the purpose of overturning the opinions of its inhabitants and introducing their own, ought to be prepared to demonstrate that the latter are more reasonable than the former.[45]

The (Christian) opponent other is shown to be less rational than those he accuses of lacking rationality, even as boundaries are being drawn around a scripturally-based and coherent religion of the same kind as that opponent other's. However, by contrast with Christianity, Rammohun affirmed that the Hindu religion can find room within itself for diversity on all but the most important matters and outside itself can recognise the Divine beneficence that the missionaries wish to confine.

In the background, beyond discussion in Rammohun's current context, stand the Muslims ('Mussalmans'), who 'upon their conquest of India, proved highly inimical to the religious exercises of Hindoos'.[46] A potential contrast with Hindu tolerance as they will later become, the 'Mussulmans' are used here rhetorically by Rammohun, along with the Greeks and Romans who mocked their Jewish subjects, to appeal to the English to live up to their own claims, forebear to interfere with the religious practices of others (as the missionaries were doing) and administer justice with equity and impartiality.[47]

The Matapariksha and Its Brahmin Opponents

Whereas Rammohun was a Hindu reformer, conversant in English, influenced by Unitarianism and happy to be buried in Bristol, the three pandits who responded to the challenge of another missionary, John Muir (1810–1882), were initially of a far more conservative tendency.[48] Yet like Rammohun's conversation with the Serampore missionaries, their debates both drew on the idea of the (six) Hindu philosophical schools forming a whole and contributed to the modern notion of Hindu 'tolerance'. Like Rammohun too, they were multilingual, conducting different aspects of the debate in Sanskrit, Hindi, and other modern Indian vernaculars, as well as being familiar with English.

I focus here on the third of those who responded to Muir: Nilakantha Goreh (1825–1885), a Chitpavan brahmin from a Maharashtrian family settled in Banares. In the fifth chapter of Muir's Sanskrit *Matapariksha* (5.163–64), Muir as the teacher moots that Mimamsa, Nyaya, and Sankhya were mutually contradictory and were refuted by the three means of proof that Muir used throughout 'to test religions, accept the true one (*saddharma*) and reject the false (*anrita*) ones'.[49] Further, Yoga is rejected as blasphemous, since as renunciation of the world it denies the principle of community so important in Muir's Christian understanding. In his 1845 response in Sanskrit, *A Verdict on the Truth of the Shastras*, Nilakantha argued at some length that while there is indeed only one correct way of understanding the Lord's nature—that is, according to Vedanta—this does not mean that there are no other ways of achieving salvation (*mukti*). The classical *shastras*, like Sankhya and Nyaya philosophy, are provided by a compassionate God. The *darshana*s based on them are for those who cannot comprehend the truth of Vedanta immediately. So too are the various *marga*s or devotional paths of the worshippers of Vishnu or Shiva, which can lead indirectly to the truth of Vedanta. Further, the *darshana*s other than Vedanta are not there to refute it but to help in understanding it.

Here, then, Nilakantha marks out a boundary that contrasts the teaching of the Vedas and *shastra*s with that of Christianity. It also promotes the idea that the different schools are not contradictory but can each contribute towards the true understanding found in Vedanta. Here Nilakantha articulates the kind of inclusivism by hierarchy that Hacker identified as characteristic of Hinduism: one view is seen as the truth, but others are included and subordinated to it, contributing to its realisation.[50] It is important to note, however, that far from extending this inclusivist approach to include all religions as (eventually) paths to the same goal, Nilakantha views Christianity as a Dharma of delusion that will lead its adherents to hell worlds; as *mleccha*s (foreigners), Christians are debarred from even the possibility of advancement open to once-born Hindus.[51] In this, his approach and outcome are rather different from Rammohun's. For Rammohun sought a common truth in all (Hindu) schools, which united them over their differences, and indeed saw belief in the One True God as shared across religions, including the Unitarian version of Christianity to which he was attracted.

Nilakantha's inclusivism seems to be in accordance with Vedantin doxographies, which incorporated both the so-called schools of philosophy and devotional traditions. However, Nilakantha makes no mention of Buddhist, Jain, and materialist positions that are not germane in the new quest to define Hindu boundaries. Nonetheless, for Nilakantha as for Rammohun, engaging with the missionary critique does entail defining the boundaries in terms of correct beliefs and reliable scriptures.[52] Here his understanding of the place and role of the schools (albeit alongside other traditions) has an important place. Indeed later, after his own conversion to Christianity, one of Nilakantha's refutations, now of Hindu views, was entitled *Shad-darshana-darpana*, 'Mirror of the Six Schools'.[53] It was quickly translated into English by Fitz-Edward Hall as *A Rational Refutation of Hindu Philosophical Systems*.[54] The various editions of this and others of his works show the continuing importance of this way of marking the boundaries between Christians and Hindus in Indian Christian circles. The opponent others of Shankara and the classical schools are shifted and regrouped to provide boundaries of a different kind.

For Rammohun and Nilakantha, then, the context is one of both colonial and missionary power. The language of their debates is bound up with this context. The Serampore missionaries used Bengali as the language they are fostering via the printing press to generate a Bengali-reading educated élite whose views they hope to sway. Muir chose Sanskrit, the proper language of debate about the schools, to engage conservative pandits (who are nevertheless well-informed in English as well as in traditional Sanskrit education, and who also pursued aspects of the debate in Hindi and other modern Indian vernaculars). Rammohun responded in Bengali, but, rebuffed as his arguments may be too persuasive if conveyed to that public, publishes in both Bengali and English, appealing to the much-vaunted impartiality of the colonial power against the current missionary attempt to undermine 'the Hindoo religion'. Like Nilakantha later, he used the debate about the schools to demarcate a boundary between the rationality of the 'Hindoo' religion that can incorporate difference but agree on the ultimate truth (or for Nilakantha that builds via difference towards the ultimate truth) and the irrationality of Christianity (which, in addition, for Nilakantha spurns the Veda and socioritual order and so disqualifies its adherents from anything other than hell worlds). In Hall's terms,[55] the development of identity via the production of symbolic boundaries is indeed linked with frontier effects, here developing contentions about rationality, equity, and tolerance. In the modification of Smith's terms[56] that we have used throughout, intellection with opponent others is central to this process.

RECONFIGURING OPPONENTS BY THE HINDU RIGHT

Our final snapshot of the way 'others' are conceptualised in Sanskrit-based traditions comes from a diaspora textbook produced in 1996 for 'teachers engaged in teaching Hinduism as part of religious studies' in English schools. As its second edition of 1998 makes clear, it is a production of the Vishwa Hindu Parishad (UK), a member of the 'World Council of Hindus' that is part of the Sangh Parivar's loose confederation of organisations of the Hindu right.[57] Its six chapters cover topics selected to address syllabus content as then required by public examining boards and Local Agreed Syllabuses for Religious Education.[58] It is both constrained by a world religions framework (which has become fundamental to English and Welsh Religious Education, via the 1994 *Faith Working Groups Report*, the 1994 Model Syllabuses and the more recent National Framework for Religious Education) and seeks to shift the understanding of Hinduism as a religion separate from Buddhism, Sikhism (and Jainism) presupposed by that framework.

Hindutva (Hinduness) in Hindu nationalist discourse is not simply a question of religion, but of identification with India as fatherland (*pitribhumi*) and holy land (*punyabhumi*). All those considered indigenous, and indeed all those who will subscribe to the foregoing, are in these terms 'Hindus'. Explaining this in terms of religion, the textbook points out that 'Hindu religious leaders prefer to use the name "Sanatana Dharma" or Hindu Dharma instead of Hinduism'.[59] But whereas in the nineteenth-century usage we considered above, '*sanatanadharma*' designated 'the Hindoo religion' based on the (six) orthodox systems of philosophy (and including Hindu devotional traditions but excluding Buddhist and Jain schools),[60] now the term is much more expansive: 'Buddhism, Sikhism and Jainism all come within the fold of this Sanatana (eternal) Dharma (laws of nature)'. The Buddhist canon and Jain Kalpa Sutra, while acknowledged as rejecting the Vedas and hence as being 'Nastika', 'remain firmly within the fold of Hinduism.'[61] Those who were amongst Shankara's fiercest opponent others, though within the Sanskrit universe of discourse, and who were edited out of the conversation by missionary preconceptions about orthodoxy and the so-called Vedic-based schools, are now no longer opponent others at all, but subsumed within the wide embrace of Hinduism, as reformist schools showing its capacity to tolerate critique. That such a position is widely rejected by many Sikhs and Jains is nowhere mentioned.

A different form of silence treats Indian Islam. The references in passing are to Mughal invaders, oppression, and political upheaval (sometimes placed alongside that caused by the British) without mention of the patronage of temples, elevation of Hindu court officials, and so on that were also features of Mughal rule.[62] This does indeed constitute Muslims as others in a variation of Smith's terms,[63] blocking conceptualisation beyond the stereotype of the conquering aggressor (a motif that we already noted above was part of British colonialist discourse and was picked up to challenge English fair play by Rammohun Roy).

The book's actual treatment of 'the Six Schools of Hindu Philosophy: The Darshan Shastras' comes in the chapter on Scriptures.[64] It is not a major part of the presentation, but nonetheless the comments in this section are telling for our discussion about the way different constructions of the six schools relate to different self-presentations. The Sanskrit tradition is invoked with the opening comment that "the Sanskrit word for philosophy is "Darshan"'. 'The six systems of Hindu thought' are then presented by key teacher and doctrine. The Charvaka or Lokayata (Materialist) school is next mentioned as an atheist school 'which lost ground in a free and fair fight with other philosophies'. This again bolsters the view of Hinduism as tolerant (unlike the, literally other, unmentioned religions of Christianity and Islam) since, despite this materialist school's atheism, 'it was neither banned nor suppressed.' It is further pointed out that atheists in the Hindu community, who 'may not believe in God-the-Creator', still remain Hindus.[65]

The book explains the apparent contradictions between the six systems in terms of a progression from 'truth to higher truth to the highest truth', using another form of the inclusion by hierarchy we noted in Nilakantha's response to Muir. Both take it that the highest truth is that of Vedanta that 'takes the best elements from all these systems and harmoniously combines them'. In the Vishva Hindu Parishad explanation, 'Nyaya and Vaiseshika prepare the mind for philosophical thought, Sankhya explains the nature of the world and Yoga shows the way of concentration and self-control'.[66] It was indeed the case that Advaita Vedantins, including Shankara, incorporated Nyaya forms of reasoning, adapted Sankhyan understandings of causality and allowed Yogic renunciation as preparatory to Advaitin teaching. So in this respect, the relation of the schools envisaged here has very long roots. Very different, however, was Shankara's castigation of the errors of all these opponent others in matters of truth. But using a similar strategy to Rammohun, the VHP book tries to stress the common beliefs of all the (six) systems: the immortal self, the misery of the world, ignorance as the cause of bondage to rebirth, liberation as the goal. The differences are merely superficial. By reglossing the common truths to hold that 'one can be happy only by realizing God and obtaining true knowledge about one's real nature', the Vishva Hindu Parishad book then draws on the neo-Hindu view popularised by thinkers such as Swami Vivekananda and Sarvepalli Radhakrishnan that 'different religions of the world are different pathways leading to the same goal, i.e. God or reality'.[67] This is supported by a reference to Gandhi. And yet there is a certain dissonance with the treatment of the truly others of this book.

For these truly others, in Smith's terms, are the aggressive and intolerant Muslims and Christians who wait in the subtext, notwithstanding the claim that all religions lead to God. Indeed, this claim is part of the self-presentation of inclusive Hinduism, contrasted silently, as for Rammohun (and Radhakrishnan), with the exclusivist truth claims associated with Christianity and Islam. The contexts of power here are not only the politics of modern South Asia (the Sangh Parivar-linked BJP party was jostling for power in India at the time the book was published) but of the British diaspora where the politics of representation and the demands of the education system have entrenched religion as a primary identity. And increasingly 'tolerance' has become an essential ingredient of Hindu self-definition even as polarisation from 'intolerant' Muslims and Christians has produced diaspora-funded violence in the subcontinent. Yet the stereotype of the Muslim aggressor has its roots in colonial justifications of power as Rammohun's appeal to a shared rhetoric of the other hints, while the discourse of tolerance originates in nineteenth-century responses to Christianity. This leads me to my concluding remarks.

RELIGION, LANGUAGE, AND POWER: SOME CONCLUSIONS

It has been my aim in examining three different moments in Sanskrit-based discourse to demonstrate how the conceptualisation of 'religious others' is constantly being reconstructed in different contexts of power. If we take each example in turn, we can see how different forms of intellectual, economic and political power are linked with various understandings of what a 'religious other' might be and how such others are to be portrayed. In particular, we can see highlighted the shifting ways in which the 'wholly other' and the 'opponent other' are characterised in discourse that remains Sanskrit-based, and thus how these are intimately bound up with different constructions and deconstructions of what counts as (a) 'religion'.

I start this concluding review with my second and third examples where the power relations, while more complex than this essay can discuss, are clear. My second example was drawn from a colonial context of contested political and intellectual power, between British missionaries and rising Indian Hindu élites with (changing) colonial rule providing the backdrop. These factors influenced the emerging construction of two homogenised religions, Hinduism and Christianity, as comparable systems to be judged by the same criteria, notably, adherence to consistent, coherent, and unified beliefs based on primary scriptural texts. Linked with this, we saw a specific discourse of Hindu tolerance and inclusivism starting to take shape. This was contrasted with the behaviour of imperial rulers, Christians or 'Mussulmans', whose intolerance was either specified or adumbrated, condemned or reproached as being against their own best principles. The 'opponent other' in this context is clearly the speaker for the comparable but opposing (and incoherent) religion. The 'wholly other' is either the intolerant ruling power and its allies (which Rammohun appeals to the missionaries as British themselves not to be) or those religious traditions, Buddhist and Jain, which have no (political or intellectual) significance in the Hindu–Christian polemics being developed.[68]

My third example, from the late twentieth century, involved the way the Vishva Hindu Parishad negotiated the 'world religions' model prevalent in British school Religious Education, given their own reconceptualisation of Hinduism in terms of the *hindutva* ('Hinduness' = 'Indianness') of the Hindu right. Operating within a specific British diasporic context of the politics of representation, the Vishva Hindu Parishad approach has also to be located in a wider postcolonial South Asian context.[69] Certain 'world religions', that is Jainism, Buddhism, and Sikhism, are now located as within the boundaries of an all-embracing Hinduism, which is both tolerant and inclusive. Both these terms are employed continuously with, though in very different ways from, the colonial usages we summarised above. The Jain, Buddhist, and materialist 'opponent others' of Shankara, ignored by Rammohun and Goreh, have become absorbed into the larger Hindu 'self'. By contrast, outside the boundaries of a reconceptualised Hinduism lie Islam and Christianity, a silent foil. More than a century—including the traumas of the Partition of India and Pakistan, recent communal violence in South Asia and Islamophobia in the West—has strengthened the portrayal of Muslim rulers as intolerant, and heightened the *hindutva* condemnation of continued Christian conversions. In such diasporic and global contexts, where religious identity has become primary through processes such as those we observed in our second example, the perceived need to differentiate Hindus as tolerant helps to position these 'wholly others' as the silent foil.

The negotiation of differential power relations—economic, political, and intellectual—in these colonial and postcolonial examples is clear and, I have argued, alerts us to their likely operation in Shankara's context, where the historical data are less clear. In the eighth-century South Indian picture of my first example, then, we know that the attempt to control the correct interpretation of Vedic texts was hotly contested, as was the need to manage rising devotional traditions. However, I suggested that this may not just have been a matter of intellectual rivalries, but of competition for patronage and the allegiance of the 'cultured' as rice production shifted economic power away from Jains and Buddhists at the maritime margins. Shankara's context was, though, one where teaching traditions, socioritual order and political identities were not yet articulated in terms of the single systems of homogenised (world) 'religions' each with their own scriptures that we saw emerging in our colonial examples. Shankara's 'opponent others' were those belonging to rival traditions based on the views of different teachers. Fierce criticism of them (not a rhetoric of tolerance) was used to establish the truth of a single position, that of Advaita Vedanta. Those who followed teachers opposed to this truth, whether brahminical or Buddhist, were equally castigated as being outside the Veda.

Shankara's 'wholly others' were the *mlecchas*, those outside the Sanskrit realm of discourse. They are completely unmentioned in his works. If they do function as a silent foil, it is in marking that linguistic boundary within which alone liberation from rebirth was held to be possible. Shankara thus has two 'hard' boundaries, which Smith and Pollock helped us to identify: Advaitin truth equated with correct Vedic interpretation and the world of Sanskritic discourse.[70] Yet between the two, there lies a range of other more negotiable boundaries, where different people can be aligned and re-aligned according to the issue in hand. They are not rigidly presumed to belong to one group whose primary identity is their 'religion'. And, while the Veda is central, this boundary does not work straightforwardly to divide 'Hindus' from 'Buddhists' and 'Jains', nor six orthodox schools from the heterodox, but to support Shankara's Advaitin interpretation, to incorporate some devotional groups and not others, and to contest the allegiance of the 'cultured'. While issues of religion, language and power can thus be seen to be intertwined in all three of these moments of Sanskrit-based practice, the varying ways in which 'others' are characterised and positioned demonstrate clearly the constructed nature of our modern picture of six or more 'world religions'. We have seen snapshots of how such a picture developed, linked with a view that makes religion a primary and exclusive identity. We have also seen how pictures of one's own tradition as a rational, tolerant system can be painted, contrasted in various ways with the conflicting, incoherent, or intolerant systems of one's opponent, or wholly, others.[71] Being alert to such types of discourse, whether Sanskrit-based or not, is surely vital in a world where the media projection of violence between 'religions' so powerfully shapes global 'common sense'.

NOTES

1. See for example, *Brahma-Sūtra-Bhāṣya of Śaṅkarācārya,* trans. Swami Gambhirananda, 3rd ed. (Calcutta: Advaita Ashrama, 1977); The Bṛhadāraṇyaka Upaniṣad with the commentary of Śaṅkarācārya, trans. Swami Madhavananda, 5th ed. (Calcutta: Advaita Ashrama, 1975).
2. The six are held to be Judaism, Christianity, Islam, Hinduism, Buddhism, and Sikhism (which exclude, in the South Asian case for example, Jain, Parsee, and tribal traditions, apart from homogenising those named).
3. On the development of this notion in relation to the term 'Hindu', see M. Searle-Chatterjee's chapter in this volume.
4. Though, as J. Zavos shows in this volume, there is also a discourse that speaks of 'people of faith' contrasted with those who do not believe or who use violence and so cannot be real people of faith.
5. See J. Suthren Hirst & J. Zavos, 'Riding a Tiger? South Asia and the Problem of "Religion"', *Contemporary South Asia* 14:1 (2005), pp. 3–20 (special issue *Teaching Across South Asian Religious Traditions*).
6. e.g. Hinduism, Judaism.
7. J. W. Laine, 'The *Dharma* of Islam and the *Dīn* of Hinduism: Hindus and Muslims in the Age of Śivaji', *International Journal of Hindu Studies* 3 (1999), pp. 299–318 p. 300, quoting Jonathan Z. Smith, 'Differential Equations: On Constructing the "Other"', Thirteenth Annual University Lecture in Religion, Arizona State University, 1992, p. 10, italics in original.
8. S. Pollock, 'The Sanskrit Cosmopolis, 300–1300: Transculturation, Vernacularisation and the Question of Ideology', in J. E. M. Houben (ed.), *The Ideology and Status of Sanskrit* (Leiden, The Netherlands: Brill, 1996), pp. 197–247; S. Pollock, 'The Cosmopolitan Vernacular', *Journal of Asian Studies* 57 (1998); S. Hall, 'Introduction: Who Needs Identity?', in S. Hall & P. du Gay (eds.), *Questions of Cultural Identity* (London: Sage, 1996), p. 3.
9. Sanskrit names and terms have been anglicised in the main body of the text to help nonspecialist readers unfamiliar with the standard system of diacriticalised transliteration. Inconsistencies in the representation of particular sounds in Sanskrit are linked with the need to minimise distortion of pronunciation due

to English stress patterns, the need to represent more than one Sanskrit sound by a single letter in roman, variant spellings in Sanskrit and different historical precedents in anglicising particular terms. 'Th' is an aspirated sound, similar to English 'hot*h*ouse', not as in English 'then' or 'thin'.

10. Pollock (1996), p. 201.
11. See e.g., R. Champakalakshmi, 'Religion and Social Change in Tamil Nadu (c. AD 600–1300)', in N. N. Bhattacharyya (ed.), *Medieval Bhakti Movements in India* (Delhi, India: Munshiram Manoharlal, 1989), pp. 162–173.
12. cf. P. Alexander's chapter in this volume.
13. For varying uses of the term 'Hindu', see M. Searle-Chatterjee in this volume.
14. There were also Arab traders settled from about the eighth century. See R. Thapar, *Early India: From the Origins to AD 1300* (Berkeley: University of California Press, 2002), p. 332.
15. Hall (1996), p. 3.
16. Pollock (1998), p. 10.
17. Romila Thapar noted that '*mleccha* represents a cultural event rather than a linguistic fact.' She did however accept that '*mleccha* may have been an onomatopoeic sound imitating the harshness of an alien tongue'(p. 236). See R. Thapar, 'The Image of the Barbarian in Early India', in R. Thapar (ed.), *Cultural Pasts: Essays in Early Indian History* (Delhi, India: Oxford University Press, 2000).
18. Smith (1992).
19. For an English translation of *Manusmṛti*, see W. Doniger, with B. K. Smith, *The Laws of Manu* (Harmondsworth, England: Penguin, 1991).
20. Hall (1996).
21. R. Ballard, 'Panth, Kismet, Dharm te Qaum: Four Dimensions of Punjabi Religion', in P. Singh (ed.), *Punjabi Identity in a Global* Context (Delhi, India: Oxford University Press, 1996), pp. 7–38.
22. Smith (1992).
23. i.e., Nyāya ('logicians') and Vaiśeṣika ('categorisers'); Sāṃkhya ('enumerators') and Yoga (practitioners of mental self-control); Pūrvamīmāṃsā (ritualist exegetes of the earlier Vedic texts) and members of other Vedānta schools (exegetes of the later Vedic texts, the Upaniṣads, holding different views on the nature of *brahman* and *ātman*).
24. cf. M. Monier-Williams, *Hinduism* (London: Society for Promoting Christian Knowledge, 1906), p. 49.
25. For an English translation, see *The Bṛhadāraṇyaka Upaniṣad With the Commentary of Śaṅkarācārya*, trans. Swami Madhavananda, 5th ed. (Calcutta, India: Advaita Ashrama, 1975).
26. J. G. Suthren Hirst, 'Who Were the Tārkikas? The Place of Polemic in Śaṃkara's Bṛhadāraṇyakopaniṣadbhāṣya', in J. Ganeri (ed.), *New Developments in Indian Philosophy and Logic: Papers from the 13th World Sanskrit Conference* (Delhi, India: Motilal Banarsidass, forthcoming).
27. For an English translation, see e.g., *Brahma-sūtra-bhāṣya of Śaṅkarācārya*, trans. Swami Gambhirananda, 3rd ed. (Calcutta, India: Advaita Ashrama, 1977).
28. So, for example, the richest temple in India, the Veṅkateśvara Temple in Tirupati, Andhra Pradesh, belongs to the Śrīvaiṣnava tradition that worships Viṣṇu and his consort using Vaikhānasa rituals but Pañcarātra theology.
29. W. Sweetman, *Mapping Hinduism: 'Hinduism' and the Study of Indian Religions 1600–1776* (Halle, Germany: Verlag der Franckeschen Stiftungen zu Halle, 2003).
30. D. Lorenzen, "Who Invented Hinduism?", *Comparative Studies in Society and History* 41 (1999), pp. 630–659.
31. 'Il y a eu dans l'Antiquité parmi les Brahmanes, six principales Ecoles' . . . 'Nyāyam, Vedāntam, Sankiam, Mimamsa, Pātanjalam, bhassyam, sont

ce qu'ils appellent simplement les six Sciences, qui ne sont que six Sectes ou écoles', letter sent in 1740 from Jesuit, Jean François Pons, as cited in Sweetman (2003), p. 142, note 84. See also H. T. Colebrooke, *Essays in the Religion and Philosophy of the Hindus*, new edition (London: Williams & Norgate, 1858) and J. G. Suthren Hirst, 'Tracing the Six Schools: Some European Constructions', *Religions of South Asia* (forthcoming).

32. M. M. Deshpande, 'Pandit and Professor: Transformations in the 19th Century Maharashtra', in A. Michaels (ed.), *The Pandit: Traditional Scholarship in India* (Delhi, India: Manohar, 2001), pp. 119–153. *Dharmaśāstra* involved the study of the extremely extensive texts on *dharma* (duty), such as the *Laws of Manu* mentioned above.

33. *Ṣaḍdarśanadarpaṇa*, mentioned in M. M. Deshpande, 'Aryan Origins: Arguments from the Nineteenth Century Maharashtra', in E. F. Bryant & L. L. Patton (eds.), *The Indo-Aryan Controversy: Evidence and Inference in Indian History* (London: Routledge, 2005), pp. 407–433.

34. cf. D. Killingley, *Rammohun Roy in Hindu and Christian Tradition* (Newcastle upon Tyne, England: Grevatt & Grevatt, 1993), p. 120f. The 'Serampore Three' were William Ward, Joshua Marshman, and William Carey.

35. The translation is Richard Fox Young's. See R. F. Young, *Resistant Hinduism: Sanskrit Sources on Anti-Christian Apologetics in Early Nineteenth Century India* (Vienna, Austria: Publications of the de Nobili Research Library, 1981). *Mata* ('thought') is a common synonym for 'system of thought' or 'viewpoint'.

36. Hall (1996).

37. Rammohun Roy's characterisation. See the preface to the first edition of *The Brahmunical Magazine* in K. Nag & D. Burmani (eds.), *The English Works of Raja Rammohun Roy*, part II (Calcutta, India: Sadharan Brahmo Samaj, 1946), p. 138.

38. D. H. Killingley, 'The Hindu Response to Christian Missions in Nineteenth-Century Bengal', in K. Ballhatchet & D. Taylor (eds.), *Changing South Asia: Religion and Society* (London: School of Oriental and African Studies, University of London, 1984), pp. 113–124, p. 114.

39. See Rammohun's first reply in *The Brahmunical Magazine*, 1821, as cited in Nag & Burmani (1946), p. 143.

40. W. Ward, *Account of the Writings, Religion and Manners of the Hindoos*, 4 vols. (Serampur, India: Missionary Press, 1811), vol. 1, p. 329f.

41. W. Ward, *A View of the History, Literature and Mythology of the Hindus: Including a Minute Description of Their Manners and Customs and Translations From Their Principal Works* (London: Kingsbury, Parbury & Allen, 1822). His translations were much criticised by, for example, H. T. Colebrooke.

42. *The Brahmunical Magazine*, Preface to the Second Edition, as cited in Nag & Burmani (1946), p. 139.

43. 'The commentators, in their interpretation of the Veda, though they differ from each other on subordinate subjects, yet all agree in ascribing to him neither *form* nor *flesh*, neither *birth* nor *death*', conclusion of issue number 1, italics in original, in Nag & Burmani (1946), p. 150. On Rammohun's Unitarian-influenced view of 'the One True God', see Killingley (1993).

44. Buddhists were long gone from India in terms of significant political influence. A Materialist position is mentioned by Ward (1822), but brought under the umbrella of the 'others', perhaps free thinkers.

45. Nag & Burmani (1946), p. 140.

46. Preface to the First Edition, in Nag & Burmani (1946), p. 138.

47. The difference of the English from their Muslim predecessors was a key part of colonial rhetoric.

48. Though Haracandra Tarkapañcānana from Calcutta was acquainted with Unitarian and free-thinking ideas and Nīlakaṇṭha Goreh went on to convert to Christianity. See Young (1981).

49. Summary of *Mataparīkṣā* 1.3–13 in Young (1981), p. 73. The proofs are: that the founder of the scripture concerned had the power to work miracles; that the scripture is seen to be holy; and that it is universal, not confined to one race (*vaṃśa*).

50. P. Hacker "Inklusivismus", in G. Oberhammer (ed.), *Inklusivismus: eine indische Denkform* [Inclusivism: an Indian form of thought] (Vienna, Austria: Publications of the de Nobili Research Institute, 1983).

51. Young (1981), p. 163.

52. Boundary-making was not confined to issues of belief. Christian rejection of the Vedas and the duties of the ideal social groups and stages of life was as problematic for Nīlakaṇṭha, whose explanation of Christianity as a '*Dharma of delusion*' tried to account for this. See Young (1981), pp. 153–161.

53. *Ṣaḍdarśanadarpaṇa: Mirror of the Six Schools: Hindu Philosophy As Examined by a Benares Pandit* (Allahabad: North India Christian Tract and Book Society, 1st ed., 1860; Calcutta, India: Calcutta Christian Tract and Book Society, 6th ed., 1950).

54. F. Hall (trans.), *A Rational Refutation of Hindu Philosophical Systems*, 2nd ed. (Madras: Christian Literature Society for India, 1897 [1861]).

55. Hall (1996).

56. Smith (1992).

57. N. K. Prinja (ed.), *Explaining Hindu Dharma: A Guide for Teachers*, 2nd ed. (n.p.: Vishwa Hindu Parishad U.K., 1998).

58. Prinja (1998), p. 3.

59. Prinja (1998), p. 9.

60. In the later nineteenth century it would develop with the Arya Samaj as its 'other'.

61. Prinja (1998), p. 126, cf. pp. 47–49 & p. 7.

62. See e.g., Prinja (1998), pp. 48, 49, 72, 105, 107.

63. Smith (1992).

64. Prinja (1998), pp. 158–160.

65. Prinja (1998), p. 159. Compare Monier-Williams' attitude, mentioned above.

66. Prinja (1998), p. 160.

67. Prinja (1998), p. 160.

68. Buddhist traditions had died out in India long before. Jain ones were not part of the challenge from either Ward or Muir, perhaps as little known (Ward does not treat them in his expositions of the 'six durshunus'), as ruled out from the construction of Hinduism as based on the six orthodox systems (Muir/Goreh) or as not yet impinging as a current economically and politically significant separate 'religion' (Jain influence being concentrated in western India). Christian missionaries had only relatively recently (i.e., since 1813) been allowed by the British power in Bengal to proselytise.

69. On the politics of representation, see G. Baumann, "Body Politic or Bodies of Culture? How Nation–State Practices Turn Citizens into Religious Minorities", *Cultural Dynamics* 10 (1998), pp. 263–280.

70. Smith (1992); Pollock (1996, 1998).

71. cf. the essays by Gregory and Zavos in this volume.

6 The Continuum of 'Sacred Language' From High to Low Speech in the Middle Iranian (Pahlavi) Zoroastrian Tradition

Alan Williams

INTRODUCTION

In this chapter I consider religious language on two axes for the purpose of analysis: the vertical axis of register, from 'sacred' and 'high' down to 'low' speech, that is execration, insult, calumny, and the disparaging names religious groups call one another; the horizontal axis of mode of use and reception ranging from the 'emic' mode of religious usage by religious traditions themselves to the 'etic' mode of academic terms.[1]

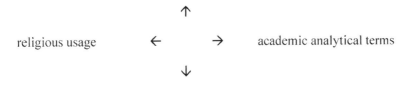

sacred language/divine speech

↑

religious usage   ←   →   academic analytical terms

↓

curses, insults, low speech

There is confusion in the academy about how scholars may use religious language: they generally reject derogatory interreligious name calling, yet they assent to such 'sublime' notions as 'sacred language' and 'divine speech', so as not to offend believers. In a discussion of Zoroastrian language, I consider the ideological power which extends along the spectrum from sacred high use to low execration.

The controversial secularist writer Ibn Warraq opened his *What the Koran Really Says*, an edited collection of essays by an assortment of Qur'an scholars, with the following (it would seem deliberately provocative) words:

> My wish . . . is to dispel the sacred aura surrounding the Arabic language, the Arabic script, and the Holy Arabic Scripture—to *desacralise*,

if I may coin a term—and put them back into their historical, linguistic, and Middle Eastern sectarian milieu; to show that each—language, script and text—is inexorably related to the Semitic, Aramaic/Nabatean, and Monotheist background respectively, and that each can and must be explained by the normal mechanisms of human history.[2]

Although the juxtaposition of Ibn Warraq's italicised *desacralise* with 'Holy Arabic Scripture' may seem shocking to some, to me and to historians of religion in general 'desacralisation' (that is, translating religious transrational language into rational language) is a necessary and accepted procedure for locating the object of our study in the public, academic domain, as opposed to the theologically defined domain of a particular faith community. But sacred language—Qur'anic language included—does not just emerge solely in the high range of a glorificatory, transcendent lexicon: sacred language also resorts to execration, insult, and indeed a 'low' lexicon of negative, critical, and insulting terms of abuse for all that of which it disapproves and from which it wishes to distance itself. We may more easily regard religious 'low language' of interreligious insults as being the result of accidents of human social, linguistic, and cultural intercourse: there would then be no need to desacralise execration, for example. However, as Ibn Warraq forcefully implies there is a tendency among scholars of religion, as if in imitation of believers' own deference in this regard, to draw back from the deconstruction of 'sacred language' as being beyond the pale of criticism.

In the conditions of present-day conflict between the West and Islamism, the case of the Arabic of the Qur'an is the most visible example of this assertion and protection of the (Qur'anic) sublime over and above academic criticism. However, in this essay I shall not deal with Arabic but rather the Iranian group of 'sacred' languages, not just because my research specialism lies more in that latter area, but also because the dualistic system of Zoroastrian thought is, I consider, a vivid example of a general principle in religious language which is not so visible, yet is just as present in the monotheisms of the 'Abrahamic' traditions. I take the example of the Zoroastrian textual language known as Pahlavi (c. 4th–10th century CE), also called Middle Persian.[3] This is a conservative, retrospective, esoteric, hieratic language in which the majority of Zoroastrian theological and exegetical texts is preserved. Pahlavi is notoriously problematic. In terms of its linguistic form it is grammatically anarchic and it is highly cryptic in its orthography: as the Pahlavi language developed, scribes adopted a system of combining ideogrammatic spellings borrowed from imperial Aramaic alongside Iranian words spelled phonetically in a modified Aramaic alphabet. The language is also religiously problematic, as it communicates a much more ancient stratum of Iranian religion from the Avestan Gathic texts attributed to the prophet Zarathushtra from the end of the second millennium BCE: thus it renders a prehistoric religious tradition in terms of the theological debates and contingencies of late antiquity. First, however, I shall address the problem of academics taking 'sacred language' as being sublime.

'SACRED LANGUAGE'

It is a proposition of this essay that 'sacred language' is a problematic category for the academic study of religion. However, *pace* Ibn Warraq, much as the academic scholar would wish to desacralise sacred languages in order to analyse them soberly in linguistic, cultural, and historical context, it is necessary to recognise the primary functions of the sacred status afforded to scriptural languages. One function is that strict control of the language (whether it be Hebrew, Sanskrit, Avestan, Arabic, etc.) by religious authorities safeguards the 'magical', or perhaps better 'transformative', power of that language. For the modern academic community, on the other hand, the term 'sacred language' is used in a different way, not as a descriptor of an essential reality as it is for the religious community that associates itself with it but as a meta-term, that is, an analytical ('etic') term. From this academic perspective there are no self-evidently, intrinsically, or universally *sacred* languages, just as there are no self-evidently, intrinsically, or universally *sacred* rituals, prophets, or temples. To assume that there are such would be to *participate* in religion, rather than to study it. Just as scriptures exist only in relation to a faith community, so languages are sacred only in relation to a particular faith community also. This is by definition an analytic perspective: it is not one shared by most religious communities (with the exception—though the interpretation is different—of some universalist belief systems, such as Theosophy, Baha'ism perhaps and some more 'mystical' theologies). It is more usually the case that groups only attribute sacredness to their own scriptures; Hindus, for example, do not believe that the Arabic Qur'an or Buddhist Pali canon stand above all other books, and most Christians, Jews, and Muslims do not believe that Avestan, Sanskrit, and Tibetan are in any real sense 'sacred languages'. They may, however, like academics, recognise that scriptures are sacred to others. Zoroastrians, Hindus, and Tibetan Buddhists, for example, do not believe that the name of God is the unpronounceable tetragrammaton YHWH. As William Paden succinctly put it, who among the Irish thinks that the River Ganges is holy?[4]

In the past, in Religious Studies and Theology and in the specialised areas of Buddhist, Christian, Hindu, Islamic, Jewish, Zoroastrian, and other studies, academics have often implicitly accepted the notion of 'sacred language' in a somewhat essentialist manner. This has resulted in one or other of two types of scholarly religious prejudice:

1. *against* another religion, because the scholar privileged his or her own faith community—as for example in some of the notoriously

bigoted tracts against other religions from the eighteenth, nineteenth, and twentieth centuries;[5]

2. *for* a particular religion, where the academic acts virtually as *defensor fidei* and as part of the religious tradition rather than according to scientific principles of the academic study of religion.[6]

Since biblical studies has managed to unfetter itself from the control of ecclesiastical authorities in most Western universities, academics are now generally able to apply the modern methods of historical, literary, linguistic analyses, and criticism to which other, nonsacred texts and documents are subjected. Indeed, in many respects biblical studies has led the way in developing critical methods and theories. The 'sacred language', however, is an evanescent entity, whose presence is sensed by the scholar who has been exposed to the aura of the devotion and enthusiasm of the faith community which imbues it with 'numinous' power—even sometimes through his or her own 'devotion' to the language as a result of the long, dedicated apprenticeship required for expertise. Yet, as others are saying throughout this volume, both in religious practice and in society, religious language in general and a 'sacred' languages in particular have a political role: among other things a sacred language serves metonymically to establish the superiority of the particular group which sacralises it over other, 'lesser' languages. Academic students of religion can retain 'sacred language' as a meta-term, in the sense that they recognise it as a way of thinking among some of the people and texts they study. They then avail themselves of a range of theories to explain the *raison d'être* of such 'sacred languages' (as social facts). Thus they can happily accept the *religious* reality of such a category, and the potency it wields over and above such a term as 'scriptural language'. However, I suggest that they should not allow the values of the faith community to leach into the academic world. They have so leached into academia in the past; two types of prejudice are apparent in the history of the academic study of religion, namely either to 'remain at home' with their enthusiasm for an essentialist understanding of their *own* religion aggressively (type 1 above), or alternatively to celebrate defensively the religion they study (type 2 above). Both prejudices have for a long time diminished the credibility of the study of religion as a serious discipline.

PROFANITY

Both prejudicial tendencies in the academic study of religion are due to the failure to look at 'sacred' languages historically and sociologically. In order to look further into this difficulty, I propose briefly to turn our attention to the opposite end of the language spectrum, which could perhaps be given its old-fashioned name, profanity, where speech is eminently human: the insulting names one religious group uses of other groups, not to mention the self-congratulatory names it gives itself. The names religious people call their opponents and themselves serve to protect and foster the authenticity and authority of their belief system: they are part of the self-perpetuating rhetoric of religious language. In the mind of the believer their own superiority, not to mention the inferiority of the rival faith community, is inevitably closely linked with their assurance of the superiority of the word of their revelation, their prophet, and the sacred language of that word. Thus 'sacred language' operates in an aggressive and defensive way to preserve the exclusivity and superiority of one 'faith' group/tradition over another. Though it is almost certain that, given the probable intellectual profile of the potential reader of this volume, I am so to speak 'preaching to the converted', I still find it necessary to urge that academics must at all costs avoid their complicity in the religious activity of faith communities, even if by religious affiliation they are insiders to that particular faith community outside academic life.

Some years ago, in the course of writing a chapter about translation theory (or rather the lack of it!) in the study of religions and theology, I found the term 'linguistic imperialism' useful with regard to 'sacred languages'.[7] It is of course a very widely used term, nearly always with reference to the case of the English/American-English language and its role as a weapon in the arsenal of Western cultural imperialism. Linguistic imperialism is the means by which a 'centre' country dominates 'periphery' countries by making them use its language. I would argue that linguistic imperialism also features as a real factor in the history of religions, ancient and modern: I would contend, though I admit that I do not demonstrate it adequately in this chapter, that it is a political factor that we, as scholars of religion who are 'experts' in just those 'sacred languages', may for many possible reasons choose to ignore: I suggest that generally it is because the liberal arts academy tends to accept that 'sacred language' is after all really something rather special. Discomfort with a notion such as 'sacred linguistic imperialism' may be as simple as a basic resistance, even in academic work, to what Ibn Warraq boldly termed 'desacralisation'.

On the other hand, for some others in academia the suggestion that the sacredness of such 'sacred languages' as Arabic, Aramaic, Avestan, Hebrew, New Testament, Greek, Pali, Sanskrit, and Tibetan is a social, political and cultural construct of linguistic imperialism serving as a tool for domination and ideological coercion by one group over another may be too obvious to need arguing. It is not for them I am writing, nor for those members of a faith community who would find the idea to be a deeply offensive and disrespectful assault on faith traditions, striking at the very 'heart' of religion. Between these two opposed camps, however, there are cohorts of troops not sure which side, if they must, they must defend. What is highlighted in any case is the great power conserved in the notion of a sacred language. By way of illustration of this power, I shall revert briefly to the Islamic example, because of the doctrine of *i'jaz* or 'inimitability': Qur'anic Arabic is asserted to be both fundamentally untranslatable and morphologically and rhetorically superior to all other languages for the purpose of containing divine speech. This assertion is made not only by classical Arab thinkers of the eleventh century CE down to authorities of the present day, but also strongly implied and occasionally asserted by some Muslim academics in the West.[8] The result is that Qur'anic Arabic is more or less unquestioningly accepted as being so superior by millions of other Muslims whose first languages are other than Arabic.

Scholars of religion may observe, but need not accept as true, religious assertions about the nature of the world. One such fundamental assertion is that the Qur'an is a miracle that proves the veracity of Islam. It is one thing for a writer to explain, as Hassan Mustapha does, that 'Linguistically and stylistically, the Qur'an is the masterpiece of the Arabic language.'[9] It is a different matter, however, for an academic to affirm the quintessentially *divine* nature of the Qur'an and to assent to any proscription upon and declaration of the impossibility and invalidity of translation of the Qur'an. There is in fact a long-standing, ancient tradition of dissent from this hard-line proscription on translation of the Qur'an. However, the insistence that the Qur'an is untranslatable leads to much more than a problem for translators—it is among many other things an assertion of the Qur'an's inviolability to rational discussion.[10] However, for several reasons, I have chosen to discuss another religious tradition in order to consider the constructed nature of the concept 'sacred language' and the problems it causes scholars and translators. I move to the far less controversial area (for Westerners, though not of course for Parsi and Iranian Zoroastrians) of the old pre-Islamic religion of Iran that survives into the present era as 'Zoroastrianism', also known as Parsiism, Mazdaism and, to the faithful themselves, simply as the 'Good Religion'.[11]

ZOROASTRIANISM: A DUALISTIC SYSTEM OF RELIGION REFLECTED IN RELIGIOUS LANGUAGE

One apparently straightforward task of lexicographical work, as of translation in general, is the finding of target language translation equivalents to terms in the source language. However, in the translation of religious texts there is often a difficult problem finding equivalents for words from other cultures: it is not that there are no equivalents in the target language, but that that the nearest equivalents are already put to another use there. Lynn Long, author of one of the few books that directly addresses the problems of translating sensitive religious texts, has put it succinctly: 'the holy resists translation, since the space it needs in the target language is often already occupied; available vocabulary is already culturally loaded with indigenous referents.' It is, she continues, 'a cultural interface that requires translation, but at the same time defies it.'[12] The process of translation is nowadays seen differently from the way it was viewed in the past as a result of developments in linguistic, literary, and philosophical theories of translation. It is no longer expected that it will always be possible to find exact conceptual equivalents to terms in the source language. Generally this would not necessarily be regarded as a weakness in translation technique, but rather as an acknowledgement of the complex nature of language in its context, which expresses concepts particular to a religion and situation, and may be charged with strongly affective, subjective meanings. Translators are prepared to have to use a number of strategies of translation other than that of fixing straightforward *term for term* translations. To take some examples from the study of Zoroastrian religious texts (which could be replicated, *mutatis mutandis*, in practically any other religious tradition): neither the common noun 'god' nor the proper name 'God' is adequate as a translation of the Pahlavi (Middle Persian) proper noun *Ohrmazd* (Avestan *Ahura Mazda*) 'Wise Lord'; the reason is that the theological character of Ohrmazd/Ahura Mazda does not correspond to that of the God described in Jewish or Christian biblical scriptures, nor indeed to that of the Qur'anic Allah. But these are proper nouns and it may be objected for that reason alone they are problematic. But no—for very similar reasons the Pahlavi common noun *yazad* is not adequately translated as 'god' or 'God', nor angel, sprite, daemon, peri, or any other exotic concoction of the thesaurus. Like its Avestan antecedent *yazata*, it refers to a 'being worthy of worship' (from the root *yaz-* 'worship'), which is not uncreated and omniscient like the creator Ohrmazd/Ahura Mazda, yet which is a spiritual being with a great degree of autonomy from its creator. Many examples could be given to show how particular religious terms are problematic for the academic translator and how they cannot be translated directly into terms of another religion.[13] Each of such translations is approximate; they trail too many theological roots of Western monotheism to be adequate without explanatory footnotes. A larger context must be given as explanation before such translations of basic terms can become usable in order to avoid the English reader having to manage a whole new lexicon of Iranian terms. Basic terms such as 'God', 'orthodoxy', 'theology', 'religion', and so forth must be thought about carefully before they are used in the discussion of relations between religious traditions. Scholars, translators, and teachers are well-versed in this problem of explaining the technical terms of one faith-community to readers and students who belong to others or to none. The method is relatively scientific and objective, treating the terms with the appropriate critical tools of historical and linguistic research. Nevertheless, sometimes a field is so little known in the larger world of scholarship and general readership that the difficulty of explaining concepts from the source culture is much more difficult and almost requires a re-education. Just such a case is Zoroastrianism.

One factor that makes an understanding of Zoroastrian texts so difficult is that Zoroastrian theology is not at all familiar territory to generalists in the study of religion and specialists in fields other than Iranian studies. In spite of its proven influence on the history of Jewish, Christian, and Islamic theology, Zoroastrians were more or less oppressed under Islamic rule.[14] They were only grudgingly accepted as a *dhimmi* (*ahl al-dhimma*, 'people of the covenant or obligation') community allowed to pay the *jizya* tax to in order to have a right to exist as a community, because they were not acknowledged in Islamic law to have a legitimate prophet or scripture and to be 'people of the book', as were Jews and Christians.[15] The Zoroastrian community of Iran suffered the cessation of its theological, exegetical activity in the Islamic period after the writing down of the surviving written and oral religious traditions in the Pahlavi books of the ninth/tenth century CE. Theological activity seems virtually to have ceased after the tenth century. The Pahlavi books, written in a form of Aramaic script, had been difficult for Muslim scholars to read; the New Persian language, in Arabic script, could be easily understood by Muslim authorities. Early in the Islamic period (eighth century CE) a group of Iranian Zoroastrians had abandoned Iran to find refuge in Gujarat, India, and later became known as the Parsis ('Persians'). Whilst the Parsis managed to thrive in India, and eventually rose to become India's leading industrial and entrepreneurial community from the eighteenth to twentieth centuries, their theological traditions remained more or less in stasis until they were challenged and startled into activity by European missionary polemics and scholarly investigations in the nineteenth century.[16] In the modern period, whilst Western philological scholarship on the Avestan and Pahlavi texts has helped to bridge the gap of centuries, it remains questionable how far Western scholars have been able to overcome their own Christian, Jewish, Muslim and other ideological backgrounds in deciding what and how they write about Zoroastrianism. An emerging principle of postmodern academic study is to attempt to understand terms in their own indigenous contexts, and only then to reflect on their historical and philosophical significance, rather than to view 'other religions' in the mode of the religious polemicist's discourse. Zoroastrian texts in Pahlavi have to be considered in the light of their dualistic theological background from the ancient Avesta and the binary coding of its terminology which resulted from the cosmic and ethical dualism of its Avestan theological conception. Christian, Jewish, and above all Muslim polemicists from antiquity to premodern times sought to berate, ignore, or belittle the theological dualism of Zoroastrianism largely because they did not know, or care to know, the system in its own terms.[17]

More so than other religious traditions, the Zoroastrianism of the ninth-century books is conceived within a comprehensively dualistic framework. This is not only a *theological* dualism, but also one that pervades ritual, moral, and social structures. Binary coding of good and evil, light and dark, is not unique to Zoroastrianism, as it is found in other religious ideologies. But it is the type, intensity, and pervasiveness of the dualism that is exceptional and, most importantly, it is the degree to which Zoroastrian dualism has been (sometimes deliberately) misunderstood that compounds the problem of understanding it now. Yuri Stoyanov began his study of the history of dualism by explaining why it was from the outset a stumbling block in the Western tradition.

> The term "dualism" itself was introduced in 1700 by Thomas Hyde to describe religious systems such as Manichaeism that conceive of God and the devil as two coeternal principles.[18] Following Hyde's terminological innovation, however, Christian Wolff introduced the term into philosophical discourse to define philosophical systems like Deckart's which posit that matter and mind are two distinct substances.[19] Subsequently the term came into use for philosophical descriptions and discussions of Cartesianism, the mind-body problem and doctrines of transcendence. In more general terms, the term dualism came to be applied also to philosophical systems which contained important pairs of oppositions, like that of Plato, with its dualities between the mortal body and the immortal soul, or the world perceived by the senses and the world of eternal ideas, comprehended by the mind; or the Kantian distinction between the phenomenal and the noumenal world.[20]

Before looking at its use of 'low' language, I shall sketch some of the key characteristics of Zoroastrianism, particularly its specific form of dualism. To do this we have to take note of an old conflation of two different uses of the term, the original coinage of Hyde's as a term of religio-historical significance, and the later philosophical use.

The Italian historian and comparative religionist Ugo Bianchi has attempted in many works to understand different types of religious dualism, not solely in the so-called 'high' religions of antiquity with their written scriptures, but also in those religious traditions that had come to light through ethnographic study, from Californian Native American societies to the Maui of Polynesia. Bianchi expounds a brief taxonomy of dualism,[21] as it is found across the world. He explains,

> dualism means the doctrine of the two principles: more precisely, the doctrines of all those religions, systems and conceptions of life which admit the dichotomy of the principles which, whether or not they are co-eternal, cause the existence of that which exists or seems to exist in the world.[22]

Bianchi applies a categorization that depends on answers to three questions according to which, he says, all dualistic positions, whether systematic, mythological, or otherwise, are bound to give an answer to each of these three alternatives:[23]

Question 1: Is it (a) radical dualism or (b) softened dualism?

Definitions: (a) radical dualism admits two principles from the very metaphysical beginnings; and (b) softened dualism exhibits only one principle in the beginning, while a second principle––somehow deriving from the first––acts in the coming into existence of the world or of constituent parts of the world, for example, matter, or body, or the inferior soul deriving from an inferior demiurge.

Bianchi gives a number of examples of religions of radical and softened dualism, thus:

(a) Radical dualism	(b) Softened dualism
Catharism	Bogomilism
Empedocles	Plato's *Timaeus*
Heraclitus	Some Cathar trends
Manichaeism	
Orphism	
Platonism	
Some Indian Dualism	
Zoroastrianism	

Question 2: Is it (c) dialectical dualism or (d) eschatological dualism?

Definitions: (c) Dialectical dualism admits two principles whose relation is productive and eternally irreducible, although one of them is often conceived as 'good' and the other as 'evil' in the ethical or metaphysical sense of the word; and (d) Eschatological dualism admits that the evil is to be evacuated at the end of history.

Bianchi gives examples:

(c) Dialectical dualism	(d) Eschatological dualism
Empedocles	Bogomilism
Heraclitus	Catharism
Indian Atman-Maya	Gnosticism
Orphism	Manichaeism
Platonism	Zoroastrianism
Theosophy	

Question 3: Is it (e) pro-cosmic dualism or (f) anti-cosmic dualism?

Definitions: (e) Pro-cosmic dualism contends that the creation is good, and evil comes from outside into it; and (f) Anti-cosmic dualism contends that the evil comes from inside the world, from a substance essentially negative or illusory intrinsic to this, such as matter, or body, or the inferior soul.

Examples:

(e) Pro-cosmic
    Zoroastrianism

(f) Anti-cosmic
    Manichaeism
    Catharism
    Orphism
    Bogomilism
    Gnosticism
    Hindu Trends

Zoroastrianism emerges in Bianchi's taxonomy as a unique form of dualism: It is the only religious tradition to be characterised by radical, eschatological, pro-cosmic dualism (a, d, e). He remarks that the first two alternatives, radical or soft, are the least important; that from the metaphysical point of view the second pair of alternatives is most relevant, that is, whether the dualism is dialectical or eschatological. But he notes that 'in relation to the conception and the practice of life . . . it is the third, that between pro-cosmic and anti-cosmic dualism, that is the most salient.'[24] As Bianchi concludes, the position of Zoroastrianism between all the possible forms of dualism is the most specific one. I can only concur with his very succinct and telling characterisation of the theological perspective of this religious tradition. Theologians and historians of religions have not only confused Zoroastrian dualism with the anti-cosmic forms, they have also understood it as a form of ditheism, bitheism, or duotheism, which the ancient and medieval texts are very clear in denying. Ohrmazd (Ahura Mazda) is opposed not by a rival divine *being* but rather by a *nonbeing* Ahreman,[25] whose status is the antithesis of existence, yet who is present as a parasite of the material universe that he invaded out of lust for the existence of Ohrmazd's creation on which he now feeds: 'Ahreman never existed and does not exist'.[26]

The key principle of Zoroastrian ethics and eschatology is that humankind is urged and instructed to destroy Ahreman and his legions by denying him a place in their (minds, words, and) bodies. As the sixth book of the *Denkard* put it:

> It is possible to put Ahreman out of the world in this manner, namely, every person, for his own part, chases him out of his body, for the dwelling of Ahreman in the world is in the body of humans. When he will have no dwelling in the body of humans he will be annihilated from the whole world; for as long as there is in this world a dwelling for a small demon even in a single person, Ahreman is in the world.[27]

This radical, eschatological, pro-cosmic dualism is expressed consistently in a long line of tradition from antiquity to early, pre-colonial modernity.[28] The language of the most important religious texts is very precisely worded to specify the theological principles and imperatives of Zoroastrian dualism. In the most philosophically sophisticated exegetical text of the tradition, the third book of the *Denkard*,[29] we find that all propositions, and their constituent terms, are posited along with their conceptual opposites; every proposition is examined in terms of a counter-proposition, which is objectified as just as black is opposed to white. A proposition is formed as the rational, correct formulation of the truth: the contradictory term is regarded as nothing more than a lie. The dualistic structuring of Zoroastrian thought is, however, expressed in other more amplified ways than just semantic and lexical parallelism and opposition of terms and propositions. Traditionally, through strict adherence to a purity code that embraced all areas of Zoroastrian life there is seldom, if ever, a neutral area between what is coded as 'good/true' and 'evil/false': for there doubt and hesitancy would be entertained.[30] Most pertinent to us for the purposes of this volume with its focus on the naming and labelling of 'others' is that the priestly authors struggled above all to find resolutions to the dilemmas posed by the contingencies of the physical social world, which the hostile spirit, Ahreman, was thought to have invaded.[31] Muslims in particular are seen as wicked and evil,[32] and even as devilish,[33] opponents of the 'Good Religion'; yet because they were in positions of power they could never be named, only mentioned anonymously in these terms. Both terms are epithets of the archdemon, Ahreman, perpetrator of evil in the universe. All the ninth century CE Pahlavi books and even the late Persian Zoroastrian books that followed them (e.g., *Sad Dar Nasr*, *Sad Dar Bondahesh*, and the *Revayats*, down to the late sixteenth century Persian poem *Qesse-ye Sanjan*) are written in the same confrontational, polarised style as is manifest in the dualism of its theology.

I have outlined the theological background because it turns out to govern the lexicon both of self-referential nomenclature and of the sobriquets and terms of abuse directed at opponents and members of other religions. For example, the style and vocabulary of Pahlavi texts have a spatial, dynamic metaphorical scheme that is strongly characteristic of the Zoroastrian thought they express.[34] Many types of nominalization of abstract notions into moral, spiritual, and other religious reifications are based upon a spatial, polar opposition between here:there; up:down; high:low; inner:outer, and so forth. This is of course not at all unique to Zoroastrian thought, but it is the type and intensity of the polarisation that is so characteristic.[35] The religious system posits the 'mental' (invisible, spiritual)[36] existence of good spiritual agencies that are characterised as being spatially, as well as conceptually, opposed to their counterpart reifications. In general, this is a profoundly different way of writing from that of mainstream writers in Jewish, Christian, and Islamic religious discourse. In both the Bible and Qur'an, the omnipotent divine being seems always to be theologically central: the constant focus of the discourse is the will and speech of God demanding human moral and actual response.

This interaction and complex relationship between God and 'Man', may even be said to dominate the discourse of the Abrahamic religions. This is expressed by setting greatest emphasis on the *verbal*, that is dynamic and interactive, components of language as distinct from emphasis in Zoroastrian texts on the substantive, nominalised forms which are so typical of their discourse. Sometimes in the Abrahamic traditions there is an emphasis on reification of abstractions (an obvious example is the Muslim names of God and named angelic presences), but both their existence and independence as entities are limited by the strictly monotheistic cast of the respective theologies. Zoroastrian theology has few such constraints if any, namely the whole pantheon of autonomous divine *amahraspands* ('blessed immortals') and *yazads* ('worshipful ones') who collaborate with their creator Ohrmazd and who are opposed by an equivalent pandemonium of evil spirits.

The Pahlavi language and Zoroastrian religious tradition reflect one another's character. The writing was constrained to be stylistically, aesthetically, and philosophically in keeping with the austere, priestly regime of the religion. It is known from the Pahlavi books and from studies of ritual practice in modern times that just as the sacred liturgy and its precincts must be kept in a state of high purity, so the words used in the religious texts had to remain pure of all that was deemed to be foreign. There was a special demonic (*daevic*) vocabulary comprising nouns and even verbs, which was only ever used of demons and their wicked cohorts of the sinful. There was even an inverted orthography used for the name of the arch-demon Ahreman, which was literally a graphic striving to keep the language of religious utterance as pure as possible from the pollution of evil. In this system of thought, change, and evolution are the inevitable characteristics of this world's cosmology, in the movement away from original perfection, down through the mixture of this world, in the two states and the three times; this takes place until the eschatological attainment of perfection. The particular definition of this cosmological metamorphosis is a central organizational theme of the religion: The guardians of the religion were obliged, by whatever means they had, to keep clearly in mind the processes of the three times of creation, mixture, and separation.[37] Other, intrusive philosophies and religions, whether they be Christian, Jewish, Muslim, Buddhist, Manichaean, or other 'false doctrines', all have in common the fact that they confuse and contradict these revealed truths about the spiritual world and the soteriology that ensues: they distort Zoroastrian epistemology. The form of language in the Pahlavi books is an exercise in careful, orthodox speech: moderation, observance of the rule, which may be summed up as righteousness. The apparent neutrality of the words is the act of resistance to any eccentricity from the norms of tradition, which can be as much linguistic as actual. This means that the language is carefully controlled and positioned by the writers of *Denkard* III. As H. H. Schaeder said, the practitioner of bad *zand* ('interpretation, exegesis') is with good reason called a *zandik* or 'heretic'.[38]

It is on the basis of their particular understanding of dualism that the writers of the *Denkard* established their defence of Zoroastrian theology and vigorously attacked Jewish, Christian, and particularly Islamic theologies as wholly misconceived and destructive of the truth. The third book of the *Denkard* is the most theologically sophisticated of all the Pahlavi books extant, as it examines the dogmatic and moral principles of the Zoroastrian religion from the perspective of a rational systematic exposition. It is an energetic inquiry *apologia* of the true faith, which is at the same time self-defensive and aggressive towards other systems of belief. The underlying argument is arranged around two central foci:

1. an elaboration of the rational arguments of Zoroastrian dualism and correction of errors made by Judaism, Christianity, and Islam;
2. an explanation of the cosmogony and anthropology of Zoroastrian lore, which is intended to integrate the current understanding of physical nature into the dualistic metaphysics of the religious tradition.

In spite of the writer's insistence on the traditional nature of this exposition from the ancient sages,[39] passages in *Denkard* III appear to be a vigorous rearguard action and response to attacks on specific Zoroastrian doctrines by Muslim clerics and theologians. Muslims were not mentioned by name for fear of reprisal and punishment under Islamic law. They and those of other faiths are referred to as *keshdaran* 'religious teachers'; but this is not nearly so polite as it sounds: the *keshdaran* are those who hold or profess *kesh*, derived from a much older Avestan word,[40] which occurs as early as *Yasna* 49 in the *Gathas* to mean the *false* profession of faith, as in 49.3: 'however it has been fated for this world that the truth is to be saved for its good preference, that deceit is to be destroyed for its false profession'.[41] The *keshdaran* are members of other religions (*jud denan*). Again, 'other religions' does not quite translate *jud denan* because *jud* means other in the sense of 'anti-', so *jud-ristag* (*ristag* = 'sect') does not mean just 'another sect', but rather 'heretical, schismatic'. The foundation upon which everything is said to rest throughout *Denkard* III is the principle of the 'Good Religion' revealed to Zarathushtra and transmitted through the ages by the Ancient Sages. Central to the philosophy of the *Denkard* is the unity of three notions prized as quintessentially Zoroastrian: 'the Good Religion', 'right measure' (i.e. the mean between excess and deficiency) and 'innate wisdom'.[42]

Paradoxically, in view of the closed nature of the Pahlavi language to outsiders, the discussions of the *Denkard* seem to be addressed to the circumspectly named *keshdaran* (false) religious teachers of other faiths. They are 'interlocutors' of the text. Islamic doctrines are the most energetically disputed of all subjects, without any direct reference to the name of either Islam or of Muslims, for certain of these were felt to be not just offensive to Zoroastrian sensibilities, but illogical, impossible (because self-contradictory) and devilish (in their power to corrupt). The writer does not constrain himself to attacking these thinly disguised doctrines of the Islamic faith. There is a deeper cause, which implicates not just the Christian faith, but also, and fundamentally, Judaism as culpable. The writer, Adurbad, is no respecter of the Jewish prophets. He is extremely rude about them, including Abraham and Moses, pillars of the tradition, because they are said to have inherited the teachings of a demon, Dahag. The author also attacks the doctrine that Muhammad is the last of the prophets. The *Denkard* objects that in the very terms of the Muslim doctrine of prophecy, the last of the prophets would announce and inaugurate an age of immortality and justice. But such is not the case, since Islam has inaugurated a regime of conquests and violence. The main targets for the *Denkard*'s attack are the Islamic doctrines of divine omniscience and omnipotence in connection with human sin and their chastisement of the fires of hell. On this subject the argument of the *Denkard* (which like much religious polemic tends to simplify and vulgarise the logic of the theology under attack) is along the following lines: if man must suffer eternal hell for the sake of his conduct that is within the foreknowledge of God, then God is effectively the cause of what has led man to his downfall, if God is, as Zoroastrians understood Muslim belief, the author of the evil desire (*varan*) as much as of its contrary, wisdom. The alleged illogicality of the Muslim belief is that the ruin of men seems to have been brought about by the divine will itself. As Adurbad sees it, in Islam God seems to allow evil to exist and thereby participates in it: this is incompatible with the Zoroastrian understanding of the supreme creator-divinity. Islam is referred to as 'evil religion'[43] as distinct from 'the Good Religion' of Zoroastrianism. Perhaps most disparaging of all for Persians/Iranians, Muslims are 'non-Iranian', that is Arab and 'enemy'.[44] In all this terminology there is embedded the double theological foundation of the dualism described above: (a) it expects and urges the future victory of wisdom in Zoroastrian eschatological scheme, and (b) it distances falsity from truth spatially, in low speech set far apart from the sublimity of the high speech of the discourse of truth. In fact, what we call 'Zoroastrian religion' today is traditionally characterised as 'the wisdom-worshipping teaching, against the demons'. A late, sixteenth-century Zoroastrian poetic text in Persian, the *Qesse-ye Sanjan* ('Ballad of Sanjan') tells of the downfall of the Good Religion brought about by the invading Muslims, again without mentioning them by name, but instead calling them 'infidels'[45] and later 'wicked devils'.[46] This language may be mapped as belonging within the spectrum of the sacred language on ancient principles of the tradition. It is the rejection of the outsider as intrinsic to the fight for survival; equally it is the affirmation of belief in the ultimate eschatological victory of those inside the truth. At the fulcrum point of the text it is announced:

95   When the millennium year of Zartusht came,
        the limit of the Noble Faith came too.
     And when the kingship left King Yazdegar,
        when infidels arrived and took his throne,
     From that time forth Iran was smashed to pieces.
        Alas! That land of faith now gone to ruin! . . .

110 . . . So it is better we should go away
        to Hend and leave behind the wicked devils.
     So let us all escape henceforth to Hend,
        in fear of our existence, for our faith.[47]

CONCLUSION

This essay has touched upon several issues other authors have addressed in this book. I conclude by offering four interlocking points which, I hope, summarise the argument of the essay.

1. I suggested that proper academic use of the term 'sacred language' is as an object of study, that is, *as an analytical tool* to discover the conditions and characteristics that seem to permeate religion with such trans-rational power to persuade and control.
2. Religious adherents' use of sacred language is *as part of their participation* in the religious tradition to appropriate the trans-rational power that, it is believed, permeates the sacred language.

I have argued in this essay that points 1 and 2 have been, and to some extent still continue to be, blurred and confused in some academic work on religion.[48] I further conclude that:

3. For religious adherents control of language is paramount, so that purity and profanity are not mixed together, and so that the apparently separate languages of benediction and malediction are not perceived to be derived *from the same source*. The polarities of for example light and dark, good and evil, blessed and wicked, are posited as being discrete categories that must be kept absolutely distinct: they thus become self-perpetuating, enduring, mythic realities[49] that are perceived to be objective, as opposed to subjectively or socially contingent.

This last point may appear to derive from my over-immersion in the workings of the dualistic Zoroastrian system that I outlined in the course of the chapter; but I would argue that such boundary/category maintenance is, as Mary Douglas demonstrated in her work following in Durkheim's and Mauss's footsteps, fundamental to the operation and perpetuation of 'religion' in general.

The above tendency to divide up language in order to render up mythic categories is, I suggest, an inbuilt and powerful feature of religious language precisely because it affords protection to the religious believer from rational analysis of the religious process itself, outlined in 4 below, the very rational analysis which is the *sine qua non* of the academic study of 'religion':

4. The strong *invocatory* category of language of benediction, glorification, and sanctification ('high language' normally deemed to be the essence of 'sacred language') is mirrored in the equally strong *apotropaic* category of language execration, denunciation and insult.

Just as we may diagnose the latter category as performing social, political, and psychological functions, so, I would argue, the former must also be investigated analytically in order to discover the functional operations of this 'high language'. However, if academic scholars do *not* investigate sacred language analytically, from top to bottom, but resort to a type of *virtual participation* in the religious tradition they study, then the conclusions drawn out in points 1, 2, 3 and 4 are unavailable, and even unwanted.

NOTES

1. Referring to the pair of terms first coined by Kenneth L. Pike in 1954, and discussed in his essay, 'Etic and Emic Standpoints for the description of Behavior', most recently reprinted in R. T. McCutcheon (ed.), *The Insider / Outsider Problem in the Study of Religion,* Herndon, VA: Cassell Academic, 28–36.
2. I. Warraq (ed. & trans.), *What the Koran Really Says: Language, Text and Commentary* (Amherst, NY: Prometheus Books, 2002), p. 13.
3. See A. V. Williams, "Pahlavi" in R. E. Asher & J. M. Y. Simpson (eds.), *The Encyclopaedia of Language and Linguistics,* vol. 6 (London: Pergamon, 1994), pp. 2898–2899.
4. W. Paden, *Religious Worlds: The Comparative Study of Religion,* 2nd ed. (Boston: Beacon, 1992), p. x.
5. In Iranian Studies the most notorious example is that of J. Wilson, *The Pársí Religion: As Contained in the Zand-Avastá, and Propounded and Defended by the Zoroastrians of India and Persia, Unfolded, Refuted and Contrasted with Christianity* (Bombay, India: American Mission Press, 1843).
6. In this category there is an *embarras du choix* of examples, continuing down to the present day, but to my mind nothing can rival the purple prose of Geoffrey Parrinder's closing paragraph of G. Parrinder, *Avatar and Incarnation: A Comparison of Indian and Christian Beliefs* (Oxford: Oxford University Press, 1983).
7. A. V. Williams, "New Approaches to the Problem of Translation in the Study of Religion", in P. Antes, A. W. Geertz, & R. R. Warne (eds.), *New Approaches to the Study of Religion* (Berlin: de Gruyter, 2004), vol. 2, *Textual Comparative and Cognitive Approaches,* pp. 13–44.
8. See for example H. Abdul-Raof, *Qur'an Translation Discourse Texture and Exegesis* (Abingdon, England: Routledge, 2001). It is as if, as has often been said by Muslim writers, the Qur'an is untranslatable on the premise that the

book has 'senses' that are exclusive to Qur'anic Arabic, so that even attempting to render such senses in non-Qur'anic Arabic is doomed to failure (H. Mustapha in *ibid*, p. 201, citing Imam Shatby c. 1133–1193). This is to peer into a very technical field, but let me just make the point that in 1936 Sheikh Mustafa al-Marāghi, Rector of Al-Azhar in Cairo, formally announced in a letter to the prime minister of the time that rendering the meanings of the Qur'an into any language cannot be termed Qur'an. This resulted in a formal legal opinion, a *fatwa*, to the effect that translating the Qur'an was allowed from a *Shari'a* point of view, but with the stipulation that any such translation must be called 'a translation of an interpretation of the Qur'an or an interpretation of the Qur'an in language X, and not a translation of the Qur'an'. The problems and questions that this raises for not just translators and scholars of the Qur'an, but generally for religionists, go way beyond this essay. In summary not only should not the Qur'an be translated, it is maintained that it cannot be translated, as its having been sent down from the divine world in Arabic is believed to be intrinsic to its being. Strictly speaking, any translation that is made is regarded not as a translation in the common sense of the word, but as a form of exegesis; hence if such is done, it is maintained it should be done only by Muslims. These strictures have not prevented the making of many translations into Western languages since the Latin translation by Robert of Chester, sponsored by Peter the Venerable, Abbot of Cluny, in 1143. It remains, however, perhaps the most problematic of all texts to translate, not only because of the linguistic challenges it poses (which are considerable), but because of its status as inimitable, untranslatable, divine revelation. However, Western scholars have been far from daunted by the protective, reverential Muslim attitude towards their most holy scripture, and in some cases they have appeared to take extreme liberties with the text, such as for example Richard Bell, whose 1937 translation rearranged the suras of the Qur'an in what he argued, was the original chronological order. As with other, non-Muslim scriptures (e.g., the Bible), one way of indicating that the translation is intended to be subordinate to the scriptural text is to place it in parallel to the original text on facing pages. Several translators have used this strategy, including N. J. Dawood, *The Koran*, parallel edition (London: Penguin, 1990). A. J. Arberry's *The Koran Interpreted* avoided the prohibition of translation by announcing in its title its exegetical intention. Ironically, however, Arberry chose to experiment with stanza form in his translation, both in prosodic and visual styles, in order to emulate the quality of the original—which to the traditionalist viewpoint must have transgressed the spirit of the tradition, if not the letter.

9. H. Mustapha, "Qur'an Translation", in M. Baker (ed.), *Routledge Encyclopedia of Translation Studies* (London: Routledge, 1998), p. 200.

10. For a forceful attack on the tendency for academic idealisation of the Qur'an, see M. B. Schlub's review of Abdul Raof (2002) in *Middle East Quarterly*, Fall 2003 on the Middle East Forum website at http://www.meforum.org/article/573.

11. Pahlavi *weh den*, Avestan *vohu daena*, New Persian *beh din*.

12. L. Long, (ed.), *Translation and Religion: Holy Untranslatable?* (Clevedon, England: Multi Lingual Matters, 2005), p. 1.

13. A few examples may suffice to demonstrate this: *yazišn* is not really 'sacrifice'; *asrō, dastwar* are not properly 'priest'; *dādgāh* is not exactly 'temple'; *yašt* is not 'worship'; *niyāyišn* is not 'prayer'; *sōšāns* is not 'saviour'; *paygāmbar* is not 'prophet'.

14. There has been a sea change in scholarly attitudes to Iranian influence on these three religions in recent years particularly since the ground-breaking

work of the late Professor Mary Boyce, doyenne of Zoroastrian studies for three decades until her death in 2006. See M. Boyce with F. Grenet, *A History of Zoroastrianism*, vol. 3, *Zoroastrianism Under Macedonian and Roman Rule* (Leiden: Brill, 1989), chapter. 9, "Zoroastrian Contributions to Eastern Mediterranean Religion and Thought in Greco-Roman Times", pp. 361–490.

15. Arabic *ahl al-kitāb.*
16. See further J. R. Hinnells & A. V. Williams (eds.), *Parsis and Their Diaspora in India and Abroad* (London: Routledge, 2007).
17. This persists, in more subtle terms, in modern times. See e.g., the Swiss Catholic theologian Hans Küng on Zoroastrian dualism in H. Küng, *On Being a Christian*, trans. E. Quinn (London: Collins, 1977).
18. T. Hyde, *Historia religionis veterum Persarum* (Oxford: 1700), cap. 9, p. 164.
19. C. Wolff, *Psychologia rationalis* (Frankfurt: 1743), § 37.
20. Y. Stroyanov, *The Other God: Dualist Religions from Antiquity to the Cathar Heresy* (New Haven: Yale University Press, 2000).
21. U. Bianchi, 'The Category of Dualism in the Historical Phenomenology of Religion' *Temenos* 16 (1980), pp. 10–25.
22. Bianchi, 15.
23. Bianchi, 16.
24. Bianchi, 16f.
25. See further A. V. Williams, "Dēw", in E. Yarshater (ed.), *Encyclopaedia Iranica*, vol. 7, fasc. 3 (New York: Routledge and Kegan Paul, 1994); A. V. Williams, "Demons in Zoroastrianism"; "Zarathushtra"; "Zoroastrian Philosophy in the Denkard"; "Zoroastrianism" and "Zurvanism", in O. Leaman (ed.), *Encyclopedia of Asian Philosophy* (London: Routledge, 2001).
26. Pahlavi *ahreman hamē nē būd ud nē bawēd*, in *Dēnkard* VI. 278 in S. Shaked (ed. & trans.), *The Wisdom of the Sasanian Sages: Dēnkard VI by Āturpāt-i Ēmētān* (Boulder, CO: Westview, 1979), p. 108. The ninth century CE *Dēnkard* 'Acts of The Religion'.
27. *Dēnkard* VI. 264 in Shaked (1979), p. 103; my translation.
28. Mary Boyce wrote many books in which she argued for the continuity of the tradition of Zarathuštra's procosmic, ethical dualism that is so clearly distinguished from, and misunderstood by, the monotheisms of the so-called Abrahamic traditions of Judaism, Christianity, and Islam. See for example M. Boyce, *Zoroastrianism: Its Antiquity and Constant Vigour* (Costa Mesa, CA: Mazda, 1992).
29. There is a French translation of this work by J. de Menasce, *Le troisième livre du Dēnkart* ['The third book of the *Dēnkart*'] (Paris: Librairie C. Klincksieck, 1973).
30. See A. V. Williams, "The Body and the Boundaries of Zoroastrian Spirituality", *Religion* 19 (1989), 227–239; A. V. Williams, "Zoroastrianism and the Body", in S. Coakley (ed.), *Religion and the Body* (Cambridge, England: Cambridge University Press, 1997), 155–166; A. V. Williams, "Zoroastrian and Jewish Purity Laws: Reflections on the Viability of Sociological Interpretation", in S. Shaked & A. Netzer (eds.), *Irano-Judaica III* (Jerusalem: Ben-Zvi Institute, 1994), 72–89.
31. For further discussion of this, see A. V. Williams (ed. & trans.), *The Pahlavi Rivāyat Accompanying the Dādestān ī Dēnīg*, 2 vols (Copenhagen: Royal Danish Academy of Sciences and Letters, 1990), vol. 1, Introduction, pp. 10–18.
32. Pahlavi *druwand.*
33. Pahlavi *dēv.*

34. For a more detailed discussion of this and what follows, see A. V, Williams, "Lexicography and Zoroastrian Meanings in the Pahlavi Books", in C. G. Cereti & M. Maggi (eds.), *Middle Iranian Lexicography* (Roma: Istituto Italiano Per l'Africa e L'Oriente, 2005), pp. 387–398.
35. See for example the work of George Lakoff on metaphor, particularly G. Lakoff & M. Johnson, *Metaphors We Live By* (Chicago: University of Chicago Press, 1980).
36. Pahlavi *mēnōg*.
37. Pahlavi *bundahišn, gumēzišn, wizārišn,* definitively studied in M. Boyce, *A History of Zoroastrianism*, vol. 1, *The Early Period* (Leiden: Brill, 1975), chapter 9, "The Two States and the Three Times".
38. *Iranische Beiträge I, Schriften der Königsberger Gelehrten Gesellschaft,* 6 Jahr, Heft 5, Halle 1930, 274f.
39. Pahlavi *pōryōtkēšān.*
40. Avestan *tkaēša.*
41. Avestan *atcā ahmāi varənāi . . . nidātəm/ ašəm sūidyāi tkaēšāi rašayenhē druxši.*
42. Pahlavi *weh dēn, paymān, asn xrad.*
43. Pahlavi *agdēn* as distinct from *wehdēn.*
44. Pahlavi *an-erān* and *dušmen.*
45. Persian *joddinān.*
46. Persian *divān-e dorvand.*
47. These passages are extracted from my new translation and critical edition (in preparation), which features in A.V. Williams, "'Strung Beautifully the Pearls of Past Events': On the Structure and Poetic Unity of the *Qesse-ye Sanjan*", in Hinnells & Williams (2007). See also A.V. Williams, "The Zoroastrian *Qesse-ye Sanjān* and Judah Halevi's *'aliya* to Eretz Israel: Reflections on Two Contrasting Journeys in Faith", in S. Shaked & A. Netzer (eds.), *Irano-Judaica V: Studies relating to Jewish Contacts With Persian Culture Throughout the Ages* (Jerusalem: Ben Zvi Institute for the Study of Jewish Communities in the East, 2003).
48. See for example the debates and controversies about the re-theologisation of religious studies that have raged in the pages of the journal *Method and Theory in the Study of Religion.*
49. In the Barthesian sense.

7 Articulating Anglicanism
The Church of England and the Language of the 'Other' in the Eighteenth Century

Jeremy Gregory

Given that the orientation of most of the other essays in this volume is to de-stabilize (what are often thought to be) English language cultural assumptions about the ways in which we use the term 'religion' (and the power relations and linguistic connotations associated with the concept) from the vantage-point of other languages and cultures, my contribution to a book entitled *Religion, Language and Power* is to interrogate English usage in a historical context. My focus is on the Church of England in the late seventeenth and eighteenth centuries, and I will explore the ways in which that Church represented itself and its rival Christian denominations (and to some extent other religious traditions), both as part of its efforts to maintain its dominant position in English society and in its attempts to gain power in New England and elsewhere. In particular, I will examine how the Church portrayed and labelled its Christian competitors by the use of stereotypes and stock descriptions in the public sphere, primarily through the medium of print culture such as sermons, tracts, and pamphlets—although it would be interesting to see how far this spilled over into visual languages and imagery too.

In a collection of this kind my topic may be of some significance since 'Christianity' has often been viewed as a monolithic entity—especially from within a comparative religion perspective. But at least since the Reformation, and indeed right from the very start of its history, as the rich literature on heresy and deviance in the early and medieval Church indicates, it patently was not.[1] And while it may no longer be fashionable to use the conceptual models of 'the other'/'the them and us', as developed by Emmanuel Lévinas, Edward Said, Peter Sahlins, and others, as an entry into the ways in which 'the' Christian religion viewed 'other' religions; it may have some purchase in examining the ways in which the Church of England and its Protestant and Catholic rivals depicted each other.[2] The 'other' could be found as much within England and within alternative forms of Christianity as in any imagined Africa, America, or Asia.[3] In this light it may also be instructive to examine how far the negative attributes appended to a competing version of Christianity could be transferred to (and from) those placed on non-Christian religions, so that for example in the Protestant mindset Roman Catholicism was often seen as sharing the attributes of 'pagan' religions, and vice versa. Of course some of the criticisms made of Said—that not all Christians in all places and all times viewed contending religions as 'other', that in certain periods and places there is evidence of considerable interchange between 'rival' religious faiths, and that there may have been an 'occidentalisation' as well as an 'orientalisation' of religion—may be applied to the ways different Christian denominations viewed their opponents.[4] For instance, Protestants of a variety of persuasions within Britain could bond against the Papist 'other';[5] Protestants and Catholics themselves could unite under the umbrella of 'Christendom' against the threat from the Islamic 'other';[6] and, at the end of the eighteenth century, Protestants and Catholics could join together against the 'other' represented by the atheism and destruction associated with the French Revolution.[7] Moreover, with regard to its Christian rivals, the Church of England alternated between deciding whether Catholicism or Protestant nonconformity was the greater threat. Thus the object of the language of the 'other' depended on the power politics shaped by the immediate political and social context and was indeed a shifting target. Nevertheless, as I hope to show, even as the target shifted, the linguistic armoury deployed in the language of 'the other' remained remarkably constant and persistent.

My reason for concentrating on the Church of England is that it presents us with an obvious opportunity to look at the relationship between a religious denomination and the issue of power. Within England (and in Wales and Ireland), the Church of England was the established Church and thus had (indeed has) a uniquely political role; its bishops sat (sit) in the House of Lords and technically between 1673 and 1828 it was illegal to hold a public office without being an Anglican. Further, the ways in which England and Wales were divided into parishes arguably made the Church structurally the most powerful organisation in the country. Although the Toleration Act of 1689 gave certain freedoms to other (Trinitarian) Protestant groups, historians have debated its significance in power terms.[8] J. C. D. Clark argued that until 1828–32 England was to all intents and purposes a confessional state with a formidable Anglican political and social hegemony but as we will see below Clark probably underestimates the degree to which the Toleration Act altered the ways in which the Church tried to maintain its privileged position.[9] However, this is not the only 'power' context in which the Church of England operated in the eighteenth century. In Scotland members of the Episcopal Church were an often harried minority under the Presbyterian powers that be,[10] and as I will briefly explore in a short coda to this chapter, in New England the Church was a small nonconformist group where within Connecticut and Massachusetts at least Congregationalists were the establishment.[11] In what ways did the different 'power' contexts in which the Church found itself affect the language it used to describe itself and its rival 'others' and how far was usage within Old England transferred across the Atlantic?

In asking questions such as these, this chapter will also aim to interrogate the relationship between the three co-ordinates of the book's title: Is this a co-equal trio of 'Religion', 'Language', and 'Power', or is one more important than the others? Are these discrete entities or are they so inextricably bound up with one another that it becomes impossible to separate them out? It may be that 'religion' can only be expressed through language (broadly defined to recognise that rituals, ceremonies, and performances are in themselves languages) but perhaps particularly in the post-Reformation Protestant world where the concentration on 'the Word' gave a prominence to spoken and written words that was not necessarily true of other religions or periods.[12] In this context, words, whether preached from the pulpit, read on the printed page, or shouted in the street, could become instruments of hegemony, weapons of confrontation, and tools of subversion. We might also ask whether it was access to channels of power that determined how language was used, or conversely whether it was language that determined access to power. Language could be an implement to be drawn on but it could also be a controlling vision—a way of seeing—which could shape people's attitudes, assumptions, and behaviour. The choice of words used implied issues of power, and this was especially so when describing and labelling others given that in the period under discussion depictions of other religious groups were seldom—if ever—done even with the intention of providing an objective account. Descriptions of self and 'other' religions were generally polemics.

The manner in which the Church of England labelled and described itself and its rivals (both in Old and New England) during the long eighteenth century was shaped by three events: the Reformation of the sixteenth century; the Civil War of the mid-seventeenth century; and the 1689 Toleration Act. It was, after all, the Reformation that shattered the notion of a universal Western Christendom, making it no longer possible even for Church leaders to imagine Christianity as a uniform and monochrome religion that spoke with a single voice—and one way for rival Christian groups at the Reformation and after to deal with other Christian denominations was to deny that they were a real religion at all, at its most extreme seeing them as a 'false' Church or Anti-Christ.[13] What is also noticeable at least from the perspective of the Church of England is that discussions of 'religion' in the centuries after the Reformation were almost always conducted (either explicitly or implicitly) with reference to another Christian denomination or rival religion since a prime method of articulating what a particular denomination or religion stood for was to show what it was not. This meant that a vital aspect of self-definition necessitated defining the 'other' and this ensured that, at least from the Reformation onwards, the language of religious labelling and representation operated through a binary polarity in which religious discourse was structured around a comparison of opposites.

Binary thinking was a crucial way in which the nexus of religion, language, and power operated in the post-Reformation Protestant world, and it may be worth asking how far this is true of other periods and other cultures too. It is also worth asking why there was such an emphasis on binary polarities, on opposites, on inversion and on a black-and-white way of thinking. Writing about the immediate post-Reformation period, and with particular reference to Puritanism, Patrick Collinson proposed that there were several reasons for what he has termed 'the piebald mentality': biblical precedent ('he who is not for me is against me') and the early modern habit of mind of discussing all subjects antithetically, this being, he suggested more speculatively, a characteristic of the early modern personality (which of course begs all sort of questions about whether there was something that could be so termed).[14] What is interesting for our purposes is how far the broader Protestant world shared in what Collinson has seen as Puritan sensibilities and how far 'Puritan' habits of thought were absorbed within post-Restoration Anglicanism.

The advisedly Protestant use of the language of binary polarity developed in its self-identification against Popery, which ensured that after the Reformation whatever aspect of religion was concerned—whether it be Church organisation and structure; the roles of clergy and laity; issues of Church and state; questions of belief, doctrine, and worship; or debates about what made a good Christian—was almost always debated (either explicitly or implicitly) with reference to a 'Popish' antitype or inversion.[15] It might be argued that discussing religion in terms of binary opposites was not a new development (as both biblical injunctions and the representation of 'heretics' in the medieval period demonstrate) but it can certainly be maintained that the Reformation sharpened the use of polarities—and this had consequences for topics that might seem to have stood outside the confines of religion since, arguably after the Reformation, the dominant thought structures in Western Europe became fixated with the issue of polarities in ways in which they had not been before.[16] Moreover, the Church of England (along with all other Protestant denominations) could find Popery everywhere (nonconformists groups, of course, found it still lurking within the established Church); it became a short-hand for anything not approved of or deemed perverse by the Protestant orthodox. For example, Popery was often linked to notions of absolutism, tyranny, and violence, but in ways that might at first sight appear contradictory, it could also represent all kinds of 'disorder', ranging from moral and sexual laxity to corruption, inefficiency, and political insurrection.

Second, to most people living in late seventeenth- and eighteenth-century Britain (or at least to members of the Church of England's hierarchy), the Civil War and Interregnum was remembered as a time when the world was turned upside down, creating political and social dissolution and anarchy that was intrinsically linked to religious sectarianism and fanaticism.[17] This 'sectarian' vocabulary of 'the other' could be used against anyone who did not conform to the Church, and in the century and a half after 1660 it became a useful weapon to use against any new religious movement and to warn of the inherent propensities of religious groupings that did not adhere to the established Church. In striking ways, too, the Reformation and Civil War came together as the Church saw itself as the victor of both the Reformation (over Catholicism) and the Interregnum (over Protestant dissenters). This reinforced the use of binary polarity and enabled Anglican religious discourse to maintain that 'Popery' and the disorders associated with the Civil War were intimately related (including perpetuating the idea that Jesuit machinations were behind the anarchy of the Interregnum).[18]

Against my insistence on the importance of binaries, it might be suggested that although many of the ways in which the Church articulated its position did depend on the use of binary polarities it also employed triads, often presenting itself as a middle ground between the authoritarianism of Rome and the licence of Protestant dissent. But although this was certainly a favoured conceit, what is noticeable is that the main thrust of such presentations was to show that in fact both the extremes of Popery and Nonconformity had very similar consequences. Finding over-arching agreements and similarities between the Church's varied opponents reinforced the language of the 'other' and strengthened the Church's view of 'them and us'.

Some further consequences emerged for the ways in which the Church dealt with its rivals in the context of the Reformation and the Civil War. Religious representations depended on associating contemporary religious groups with the perceived attributes of their forbears. All Catholics were seen as being potentially the same as those against whom the Reformation had been initiated; all Nonconformists could be envisaged as being on the verge of wanting to start a second Civil War. Moreover, any new religious group could be inserted into a past paradigm that made them more understandable and manageable by fixing on them a whole baggage of negative attributes. Additionally, these negatives could also be transferred backwards to religious groups in the past. For example, Edward Gibbon's highly influential late eighteenth-century critique of the rise of Christianity within the Roman Empire (where he accused early Christian monks of indolence, passivity, and sometimes sexual misdeeds) in effect transferred Protestant criticisms of Popery to Christianity per se.[19]

A third event that shaped the ways in which the eighteenth-century Church of England dealt with its rivals was the Toleration Act of 1689, which meant that that the Anglican Church had to fall back on the powers of persuasion rather than on the mechanisms of persecution to maintain its hegemony.[20] Deprived of the advantages of working in a fully confessional state (*pace* J. C. D. Clark), the Church could no longer rely on active and exclusive state support to maintain its position in society and had to find other ways in which to build up and sustain its place against its rival 'others'. Clergy could not trust in the combined efforts of the spiritual and secular courts to impose Anglicanism in the parishes, and it was through the medium of print, and in the public sphere, that the Church increasingly attempted to retain its social and political position.[21] Through an endless stream of printed sermons, tracts and pamphlets the Church articulated its language of 'the other' against its religious competitors in what was essentially a contested space for power. Arguably, what was distinctive about the period after 1660, and especially after 1689, was the move to competition between religious groups, since one of the effects of the 1689 Act was to encourage members of the laity to shop around, ensuring that the Church had to enter the market place. This made the Church develop strategies both to win people over from its competitors and to retain its own members. Recent scholarship has shown how a commercialization of culture and leisure developed in this period: in tandem with this was a commercialisation of religion.[22] And in 'selling' the Church against its rivals of Catholics, Dissenters and the diversions of a secular society, the Church utilised a range of opportunities—social, educational and cultural—to bolster up its position within society.[23] In dealing with its rivals, and intrinsic to the ways in which it carried on its competition, the Church counted on a series of stereotypical and stock descriptions designed to present both Catholics and Protestant Nonconformists in an unflattering light, and which were deployed through a whole range of media, from tracts and pamphlets to sermons and satirical prints.[24]

Reasons of space do not permit me to give a full analysis of the stereotypes used by Anglicans to describe their opponents. Rather, what I want to highlight are three (inter-related) dominant vocabulary clusters—or what Roger Fowler has termed lexical collocations—which the Church of England deployed to articulate its position *vis à vis* its competitors and to articulate 'the other'.[25] In these vocabulary clusters, stereotypes, stock images, and language associations became weapons with which to attack religious rivals. In the rest of this essay I will examine how language was used in these word clusters and tease out some of the implications for understanding the Church's power politics and how it defined 'the other'.

The first lexical collocation I will discuss, and one into which the others could fit, centred on the vocabulary of 'enthusiasm'. For seventeenth- and eighteenth-century Anglican writers, 'enthusiasm' was always a term of abuse, meaning a deluded and false religion that would lead to disastrous social and political consequences (and for English writers after 1660 this was invariably short-hand for the upheavals of the English Civil War). From the mid-seventeenth century, the cause of enthusiasm was perceived to have shifted from the devil to madness, pride, or misguided religious notions, which tended to increase the blame placed on the individuals concerned rather than seeing them as instruments or victims of a superior power. Against 'enthusiasm', religious writers in the century and a half after 1660 pitted the reasonableness inherent in their own religion, which, they maintained, led to moderation and to the improvement of society. Enthusiasm implied a self-centred religion; reason and moderation, on the other hand, led the individual to work with and for society.

The starting point for exploring eighteenth-century understandings of 'enthusiasm' is Ronald Knox's classic study of 1950.[26] Knox's work was essentially an exploration of key figures who have been labelled 'enthusiasts', particularly of the seventeenth and eighteenth centuries, although his starting point were the Corinthians written to by St Paul. As a taxonomy, it remains a useful resource, albeit telling us more about Knox's own preoccupations as an early twentieth-century Catholic convert than being a nuanced study of the enthusiasts themselves. Indeed the book itself was initially conceived as a polemic, "to be a kind of rogues' gallery, an awful warning against illuminism", although as Knox himself recognises, the finished product is a more sympathetic and benign treatment of many of the 'enthusiasts' since he found their writings more appealing than those of the writers against enthusiasm, dismissing these authors as "dull dogs".[27] Knox may well be right that the writings of enthusiasts such as Wesley et al. are more religiously musical than those of his opponents who wrote against him (although that is not a judgement I want to make here). What intrigues me more is the way in which the language of enthusiasm operated and how it worked as a discourse of power. To a certain extent, of course, the labelling of individuals and groups as enthusiasts can be viewed as part of a perennial Weberian tension between established institutions and charisma,[28] and some have suggested that it also mirrors a divide between elite and popular religiosity.[29] However, it seems to me that those who created the language of enthusiasm could also usefully be seen as operating within a Saidian framework, where the 'enthusiast' could be identified as 'the other'. Although Knox was more concerned with the religious beliefs of those who were labelled enthusiasts, I am more interested in the construction of enthusiasm as a concept by its critics. Just as Said saw Orientalism as an indicator of Western supremacy over the East (and thus worth studying), so the articulation of the language of enthusiasm can be viewed as one of the ways—and perhaps the most powerful way—by which the Church of England during the long eighteenth century tried to contain those who represented a threat to its position.

Knox suggested that the vogue for discovering and denouncing enthusiasm started with George Hickes' *The Spirit of Enthusiasm Exorcised,* which was preached before the University of Oxford in 1680, appropriately on Act Sunday.[30] In fact, there had been a number of full-dress investigations into the topic before then, including Meric Casaubon's *A Treatise Concerning Enthusiasme* (1654), which in the midst of the emergence of a range of religious options during the Interregnum, wanted to show that enthusiasts were neither divinely nor devilishly inspired, and that the visions and trances supposedly experienced by the enthusiasts could be explained by natural causes.[31] Moreover, as a short-hand for a de-based religion, the word 'enthusiasm' was in common currency before then and featured for example in *Gangraena*, the denunciation of the new religious groups of the 1640s by the Presbyterian Thomas Edwards.[32] There were also several other titles before Hickes' that concentrated their attack on the Quakers as the most obvious and the most extreme kind of enthusiasts.[33] As a term of opprobrium, 'enthusiasm' was remarkably transferable and this allowed writers to reassign a whole series of negatives which had been placed on one religious group onto other religious groups. In this way, any non-Anglican group could be attacked with the 'enthusiast' label. In 1688, for example, Henry Wharton published his *The Enthusiasm of the Church of Rome Demonstrated in Some Observations Upon Ignatius Loyola*,[34] and in trying to come to terms with the new Methodist movement of the 1740s George Lavington, the bishop of Exeter, wrote an influential pamphlet entitled *The Enthusiasm of Methodists and Papists Compared* (1749–51) that lumped onto the Methodists the language of two centuries of Protestant anti-popery.[35] Lavington's hostile criticism of Methodism was based on the simple methodological premise that "the spirit of enthusiasm was always the same, operating in much the same manner, on all sects and Professors of Religion",[36] and this point echoed one of the earliest printed critiques of the movement, *Enthusiasm No Novelty: Or, the Spirit of the Methodists in 1641 and 1642* (1739) that deliberately tarred the new movement by association with the Civil War sectaries (on the title page the author quoted Ecclesiastes: 'there is no new thing under the sun') and anachronistically called the Civil War sects 'Methodists' at least eighty years before the term was coined by the Wesleys.[37] Methodists were, according to these analyses, not only 'religious' enthusiasts, they were also socially and politically unstable. Lavington's critique of Methodist enthusiasm was but the most wide-ranging of a host of similar titles which took a similar tack, such as A. T.'s *Enthusiasm Delineated, or the Absurd Conduct of the Methodists Displayed* (1764), Samuel Roe's *Enthusiasm Detected, Defeated* (1768), and Joseph Eyre's *A Dispassionate Inquiry into the Probable Causes and Consequences of Enthusiasm* (1798) that declared that "generally speaking, it produces evil".[38] And so pervasive was the horror of enthusiasm, and so crucial was the need to disassociate oneself from it, that even those who were labelled 'enthusiasts' would rarely if ever have considered themselves as 'enthusiasts' at all (although some late seventeenth-century Quakers claimed that 'Enthusiasm was above atheism' and identified positively with the label).[39] John Wesley, for instance, the arch-proponent of 'enthusiasm' for many Anglican writers after 1740, himself attacked enthusiasm on several occasions, stressing the importance of reason in religious matters and tending to associate himself with religious *zeal* rather than with religious enthusiasm.[40]

As a device for linking religion, language and power, the construction of the term 'enthusiasm' was a brilliant invention. All kinds of horrors and prejudices could be encapsulated in a single word, and merely calling an opponent 'enthusiast' placed him or her within a framework that could be readily understood and gave their actions consequences that were already known. By accusing individuals or groups of being enthusiasts they were made both more containable (by fitting them into a straight-jacket of past precedent) and, conversely, perhaps more frightening than they were (by suggesting that what their predecessors as enthusiasts had done, they would also do). The treatises and attacks against enthusiasm that I have noted above, it seems to me, operate in ways very similar to the Orientalist discourses analysed by Said. Like Orientalism, enthusiasm was a highly schematic concept that depended on a "set of representative figures, or tropes", and accounts of enthusiasm, to quote Said's analysis of Orientalist texts, were "all declarative and self-evident; the tense they employ is the timeless eternal; they convey an impression of repetition and strength; they are always symmetrical to, and yet diametrically inferior to, a [Church of England] equivalent, which is sometimes specified, some-times not." [41]

Just as Said argued that philosophically Orientalism is a form of "radi-cal realism", in that descriptions and labels become reality, that it is rhe-torically "anatomical and enumerative" and that psychologically it is a "form of paranoia", so can similar things be said about the way in which the language of enthusiasm operated.[42] And if Orientalism is a distorting lens, so enthusiasm was too. Said viewed Orientalism as a "closed system", which is ultimately anti-empirical, given that according to him, no amount of evidence can dislodge the Orientalist position, and this seems to have been true of those who found enthusiasts in their midst.[43] Indeed, those on the look-out for signs of enthusiasm may have been so hyper-vigilant that not only did they exaggerate and misinterpret the behaviour of those they called 'enthusiasts', they may actually have invented some of the enthusi-astic groups they lambasted. For example, historians of the 1640s and 50s have debated how large a group the Ranters (precisely the kind of radi-cal religious group that emerged in the Interregnum and spurred Edwards and Casaubon to publish against outpourings of enthusiasm) were. One interpretation has argued that they were purely the creation of the fevered Anglican imagination, (given that all the evidence we have for their exis-tence comes from hostile sources).[44]

A second language-cluster, and one that was often vital to the con-struction of the discourse of enthusiasm, was the use of gendered imagery and vocabulary. From the earliest days of the Reformation, the Church of Rome was associated with the whore of Babylon, and the resulting mas-culinisation of Protestantism versus the feminisation of Popery was part of that process of binary opposition I have noted above. To Protestant eyes, the feminisation of Rome was viewed in wholly negative terms. The beguiling 'femininity' of the Roman Church (surely akin to Said's 'exotic sensuousness'[45] of the Orient) allowed her to be depicted as a blowsy siren, a scarlet woman or a painted harlot: The surface glitter of popish ceremonies and images supposedly appealing to what was most fallen and corrupt in carnal humanity. Against this, the Church of England harnessed to itself the language of masculinity (we often think of 'Christian manliness' as being a mid-nineteenth-century concept, but the connection between the two was an eighteenth century commonplace).[46] And just as eighteenth century understandings of masculinity stressed magnanimity and benevolence, so the Anglican Church prided itself on being magnanimous and benevolent too. Conversely, just as both Catholics and Nonconformist sects after 1660 were tarred with the same brush of being king-killers, they were both viewed as being 'feminine', 'unmanly' and 'effeminate' (and the link between these is itself testament to the flexibility and fluidity of this gender polarity since effeminacy and unmanliness could also be associated with passivity). As numerous Anglican commentators found, an easy way of stirring up opposition to Nonconformity was to highlight its relationship with the female, as a sign of its weakness and irrationality, and indeed Bishop Lavington noted in his critique of Wesley and his followers that "the greater Part of the Dramatis Personae in the Tragi-Comedy of Methodism appears to have been Actresses."[47] It is striking too how far vices attached to representations of Nonconformists (they were described as 'peevish', 'shrewish', 'volatile', 'giddy') were also negative attributions placed on women (by male writers).[48]

A third series of vocabulary associations was concerned with the linguistic pairing of moderation versus violence. In obvious ways this was related to the previous two vocabulary clusters, since just as enthusiasts were deemed to lack sense and moderation in their religious views, so too they were deemed to be immoderate in the ways in which they propagated their religion. And if the Church could be linked with the ideals associated with eighteenth-century concepts of masculinity in its efforts to work for the good of society, then its competitors could be associated with violent and destructive, even bestial and savage behaviour that worked towards the breakdown of civility, sociability, and humanity. Reading the sermons that were delivered at the annual meeting of the Society of the Propagation of the Gospel in Foreign Parts (SPG), I have been struck by the ways that Anglican preachers consistently drew on an antithesis between violent Catholic models of mission work and enlightened Protestant models of conversion. These sermons were of course fund-raising devices; they have to be seen as part of the propaganda of the Society in its quest for monies for missionaries, schools, catechists, and books. As such, they shed light on how one confession dealt with its competitors, and do not necessarily have any bearing on the reality of Catholic mission activity. There were various prongs to this attack such as criticism of the ways in which Jesuit missionaries accommodated Christianity to native American rituals—thereby de-basing it—and the use of bribes and 'trinkets'—rather than understanding—as a basis for conversion.[49] But the centre of the attack was usually a concentration on the ways in which the Catholics had 'converted' the native Americans by torture—one preacher talked of the 'bombs' and 'machines' that Catholic powers had used to terrorise them.[50] Part of the issue here is that whereas Catholic missions had been active in the New World from fairly early on in the sixteenth century, Anglicans and other Protestants were relatively late to the field, and to displace criticism for their tardiness Anglican preachers dwelt on the unsavoury methods of their rivals. The SPG preachers could claim that Native American Catholic converts—however numerous—were only nominal Christians. And, they maintained, the violence inflicted on them had made the Indians despise all kinds of Christianity. By contrast, it was argued, the SPG missionaries would bring Christianity to the Native Americans through instruction, education, and by the example of their own charitable and moderate behaviour. These, it was suggested, were more like the conversion tactics used in the primitive and apostolic church. An example of the Anglican view of Catholic violence is found in this excerpt from the sermon delivered by White Kennett, the dean of Peterborough, to the Society in 1712. This sermon was a review of the various impediments to "planting and propagating the Gospel of Christ", and included a long discussion of the "the exercising of Force and Cruelty to compel" the Indians to convert, "instead of the persuading and convincing of them".[51] The printed sermon contained a graphic instance of how Anglican discourse highlighted the violence associated with its rivals:

The horrible ways of converting the Poor Indians by the Bigots of the Church of Rome, would draw Tears, and make hearts to bleed ... Men hunted down like Beasts, and devoured by the Dogs; Women and Children maimed, and hang'd, and burnt in one and the same way of execution. This Relation is given by a *Spanish* Bishop settled in those parts. When the *Spaniards* first landed in the Isles, there were above Five Hundred Souls; they cut the throats of a great part of these, and carried away the rest by Force; to make them work in the mines of Hispaniola—As for the Continent, 'tis certain, and what I myself know to be true, that the *Spaniards* have ruined Ten kingdoms there bigger than all *Spain*, by the commission of all sorts of Barbarity and unheard of Cruelties. They have driven away or killed all the Inhabitants, so that all these Kingdoms are desolate to this Day—We dare assert, without Fear of incurring the Reproach of exaggerating, That in the Space of the Fourty Years, in which the *Spaniards* exercised their intolerable Tyranny in this New World, they unjustly put to Death above Twelve Millions of People, counting Men, Women, and Children. And it may be affirm'd without Injury to Truth, upon a just Calculation, That during this Space of Time above Fifty Millions have died in these Countries—They valued them Worse than Beasts—They ripp'd up Women with Child, that Root and Branch may be destroy'd together. They laid Wagers one with another who should cleave a Man down with his Sword most dexterously at one Blow. Or who should run a Man through after the most artificial manner. They tore away Children out of their Mother's Arms, and dash'd out their Brains against the Rocks. Others they threw into the Rivers, diverting themselves with this brutish sport &c. They set up Gibbets, and hang'd up Thirteen of those poor Creatures in Honour to Jesus Christ and his Twelve Apostles, as they blasphemously express'd themselves; kindling a great Fire under those Gibbets, to burn those they had hang'd upon them &c.[52]

Just as there was an Anglican/Protestant pornography (with stories of young girls being seduced in the Confessional by lecherous Catholic priests), so there was a genre of Anglican/Protestant blood-and-guts that dwelt on the physical atrocities employed by the Catholic 'other'. The mindless and gratuitous violence and cruelty displayed in this extract was seen as a testimony to the unnatural and perverse nature of Popery, and, in tellingly similar fashion, Said remarked that "Islam came to symbolize terror, devastation, the demonic".[53] In contradistinction to the detail given to popish methods of conversion, White Kennett summed up Anglican methods much more succinctly: "I would only observe to you, that the Soft and Salutary Methods of Conversion, taken by this Society, are of a more Christian Nature; are far from breathing out any Threatenings, or any Slaughter, any Conquest of Slavery of the People of the Land."[54]

There are a number of questions that emerge from this discussion that have relevance to the wider concerns of this book. How far was the use of the lexical collocations associated with 'enthusiasm', gendered imagery, and the polarity of moderation/violence (all of which could overlap, since women were deemed more susceptible to 'enthusiasm' than men, and 'enthusiasm' could also result in violence and bloodshed) a feature of a particular moment within the history of a particular branch of the history of Christianity, or how far was it a more widespread phenomenon in discussing religious 'others'? Further, did the use of vocabulary clusters change with changing power relations? My evidence would suggest that it could do, but not in any straightforward way. Some of the descriptors do seem to have been 'reversible', so that those in power in New England used similar word associations to those in power in Old England. In New England, Congregationalists accused members of the Church of England of being separatists ('Episcopal separatists') and as being a threat to community and order.[55] In similar fashion, Congregationalists could portray Anglicans in New England as being disruptive of social norms (breaking up families, etc.); they also argued that for Anglicans religion was just a sham, a political interest rather than a real religion (thereby casting the Church of England in popish guise).[56] Against this, Anglicans appealed to the language of toleration to allow them some minority status and to attack the privileges of the Congregationalist establishment, just as late seventeenth- and eighteenth-century Nonconformists in England challenged Anglican privileges.[57] These are clear instances of how changes in power could change the use of linguistic descriptions between religious groups.

But sometimes the language proved remarkably resilient. Eighteenth-century Anglicans in North America charged American Congregationalists with being no better than seventeenth-century English sectaries. Of particular interest here was the Anglican reaction to the 'Great Awakening', that explosion of religious enthusiasm in North America during the late 1730s and 1740s. This allowed Anglicans to claim that not only were Congregationalists in mid-eighteenth-century America the same as those in mid-seventeenth-century England, this was contemporary proof of their 'enthusiasm' (one report from Rhode Island in 1760 claimed that Anglicans were surrounded by "Quakers, Baptists, Fanaticks, Ranters, and some infidels", and the list was extended in 1763 to include "Deists, Diggers, Levellers, Sabbatarians, and Brownists" in language identical to that used in the English Civil War).[58] It also allowed moderate Congregationalists ('Old Lights') to accuse their 'New Light' rivals of continuing the enthusiast tradition. Charles Chauncy, a leading New England Old Light minister, preached and published a sermon in 1742, *Enthusiasm Described and Caution'd Against*, which read remarkably like Anglican critiques of Methodism.[59] Likewise, Congregationalists in New England accused Anglicans of being power-crazed Laudians (relying heavily on the memories of the early seventeenth century), despite the fact that the Anglicans only made up about four percent of the population of New England; they could be also charged with being 'effeminate and effete'.[60]

I want to end up by asking: What was the effect of these religious labels and stereotypes? And how far did the language used determine what people saw and felt, and how did it affect their behaviour? I think there is no doubt that one way in which Anglican hegemony was maintained within England was through the power of these representations of both the Church and its rivals, even when they contradicted other kinds of evidence. The negative connotations associated with Popery lived on well into the nineteenth and twentieth centuries, despite the fact that eighteenth-century English Catholics were almost as suspicious of Rome as their Protestant contemporaries.[61] It is also clear that early Methodists were very reluctant to see themselves as separatists. They did not want to be associated with the Civil War sects, and many went out of their way to define themselves as loyal members of the Church, operating in what might be termed a 'both/and' relationship rather than a Saidian 'them and us'.[62] Nevertheless, for much of the century the overwhelmingly dominant—but not the only—Anglican response to the emergence of Methodism was to categorise it in terms of the linguistic clusters I have explored above.[63] To complicate matters further, for the long eighteenth century at least, social historians of religion are increasingly aware that in practice many men and women attended a variety of religious denominations (a not untypical mid-century pattern was to attend the Church of England in the morning, a Nonconformist meeting in the afternoon and a Methodist meeting in the evening).[64] Are we seeing here a division between religious leaders and professionals who had a vested interest in maintaining sharp and clear boundaries between religious groups, and the behaviour of at least some members of the laity, who, in the context of the Toleration Act, were likely to pick and mix their religious affiliations?

Some historians have suggested that the 'super-heated' vocabulary represented by the language of binary polarity inevitably deepened conflict between religious groups in the long eighteenth century.[65] The binary mode of thinking forced people to place each other into one or other of the polar opposites, and this may well have encouraged them to view matters out of all proportion, thereby intensifying hostility between religious groupings. For example, in New England, a number of influential interpretations have suggested that this heightened language was an integral cause of the American Revolution.[66] Nevertheless, it is possible to argue that the cumulative effect of the language of the 'other' was to direct religious bitterness into pre-ordained channels. In the world after 1689, all religious denominations distanced themselves from pursuing active persecution; according to one leading Church of England figure, persecution itself was a mark of popery and the anti-Christ[67] (and hence during the 1790s, some Anglicans transferred their accusation of anti-Christ from the Catholic Church to the French Revolution, with what seemed to be its far more destructive and persecutory tendencies).[68] Rather than persecution, it became much more important to preach and write against religious rivals (and by doing so to persuade people to one's own position). Thus part of the power of the Church's language of the 'other' was that in large measure it also constrained and shaped what the Church could and could not do; if it backed persecution (as some of its members did in the decades after 1660) then it could fall into the danger of itself becoming, and indeed itself being accused of being, the 'other'.[69]

If, as has been suggested, the rise of political parties helped to provide political stability by channelling political differences into the party structure and thereby stylising political conflict, much the same can be said of the ways in which the religious stereotype helped contain and stylise religious differences.[70] Ultimately, what is striking is that the polemical vocabulary of the 'other' articulated in sermons, tracts, and pamphlets did not result in more violence. Of course, in times of acute tension, violence did occur; one has only to note the persecution against Quakers and other Nonconformist groups in the decades immediately after 1660 (although as Adrian Davies and others have shown this was not necessarily the 'normal' relationship even between Quakers and the wider world, and a much more tolerant relationship was more usual).[71] There were, it is true, a number of set-piece riots, which could lead to the destruction of places of worship, such as the Sacheverell Riots in 1710 (where High-Church mobs set Nonconformist meeting houses on fire), the stoning of early Methodists (leading to the death of William Seward in 1743), the Gordon riots of 1780 (which led to the destruction of the homes of known Catholics), and the

Church and King riots of the 1790s (which again led to the destruction of Nonconformist meetings and Joseph Priestley's laboratory) . But as Jan Albers has remarked, "religious bigotry was an unpleasant fact of life, and led to occasional outbreaks of violence, but the destruction of a meeting-house and the intimidations of a mob, were hardly the rack, the stake, or the Inquisition."[72] This is suggestive of the ways in which during the long eighteenth century, at least within England, preaching and writing against one's religious rivals had become a substitute and a replacement for perse-cution and religious wars.

To an extent, the hostile language of the 'other' complicates our under-standing of the period conventionally associated with the Enlightenment. On the one hand, it might be thought that the ways of describing religious rivals outlined above hardly indicates an enlightened way of thinking, although on the other hand those attributes that were admired and were harnessed to the Church such as moderation, reason, magnanimity, and humanity certainly chime in with values central to the Enlightenment. In this, the religious 'other' can be seen to represent an anti-Enlightenment force, with its emphasis on the irrational, the violent, and the bestial.[73] Moreover, in trying to understand how the binary polarities worked out in practice, we should note that even the stereotypes could be applied discrim-inately. The vicious anti-Catholic language that led people to fight against 'Popery', which as Defoe famously remarked, they did not know "whether it be a man or a horse",[74] encouraged English men and women to hate foreign Catholics, while at the same time getting on amicably with their local Catholic neighbours for much of the time.[75] This raises interesting points about the relationship between language and 'social reality'; how far meeting and mixing with members of rival religious traditions meant that to a large extent the language of the 'other' broke down in day to day negotiations, but conversely the resilience of the discourse is testimony to the power of language to override empirical observations.

This chapter has attempted to explore some of the ways in which the Church of England articulated its own position by demarcating itself from its rivals. The patterns of discourse that I have highlighted created a set of opposites that were repeated, taken up, and used in countless printed writ-ten sources. As I suggested at the start of the chapter, the same underlining inversions could also be seen in some of the visual sources of the period too. It is in the context of the pamphlet and sermon literature that I have dis-cussed that we should locate William Hogarth's unpublished print 'Enthu-siasm Delineated' (c. 1760), the very title of which was a virtual repeat of various printed pamphlets, and a version of which was published in 1762 as *Credulity, Superstition and Fanaticism: A Medley*.[76] The original print is a very complex one to interpret. Hogarth dedicated it to the Archbishop of Canterbury, and it is unclear whether this was because this was an attack on the current archbishop (who had had a Nonconformist background and, it was suspected, some Methodist sympathies) or whether this was to mark off the Church from its rivals.[77] Like Lavington's earlier pamphlet, *The Enthusiasm of Methodists and Papists compar'd*, Hogarth's print satirised both Roman Catholicism and Methodism. Here we have a Nonconformist preacher, holding puppets of God and the devil, ranting in front of an anguished congregation, and underneath his wig (which is falling off) he reveals his monkish tonsure (highlighting the hidden connection with Rome). A scale gauges the depth of his hysterical preaching (marked on it are the words: 'Chroist [sic], Blood, blood, blood, blood') and a thermometer measures the spiritual state of the whole scene, going from Prophecy, Madness, and Despair through Revelation to Joyful, Pleased, Angry, and Wrathful. The collar on the baying dog in front of the pulpit has the name 'Whitefield' inscribed on it. Beneath the preacher an aristocrat fondles a young girl, echoing the printed attacks on the Methodists' love-feasts. At the back of the print, Hogarth has placed a Muslim looking in on the mad scene through a window, paralleling the literary trope of viewing European manners from the standpoint of the East (thereby—in an inversion of the Saidian model—neatly making the Orient the barometer of normality, to highlight the 'otherness' and peculiarity of the English situation).[78] The original version of the print was never published, supposedly because Hogarth was persuaded that this would be read as a critique not just of Methodism but of Christianity *tout court*.[79] The printed version, which was much admired by such contemporaries such as Horace Walpole (himself an enemy of Methodism), drew rather more obviously on the connections between the Methodist movement and what were deemed to be irrational beliefs in witchcraft, ghosts, and the supernatural.[80] At the bottom of the print Hogarth appended a biblical quotation that might very well have been inserted in all the written challenges to enthusiasm discussed in this chapter: "Believe not every Spirit but try the Spirits whether they are of God because many false prophets are gone out into the World" (1 John 4.1) as a warning to the credulous.

Hogarth's own religious beliefs are shadowy: the son of a Nonconformist, he himself moved in deist circles and was suspicious of clericalism.[81] Yet here the structures of his art seem to draw on the messages and antitheses articulated in many of the Anglican tracts, pamphlets, and sermons of the period. That Hogarth, who was not necessarily an admirer of the Church, could use his art to explore some of the themes and tropes I have been describing, tells us something about the reach and purchase of the Church of England's language of the 'other' during the long eighteenth century.

NOTES

1. Within a very rich literature, see J. Lieu, *Image and Reality: The Jew in the World of the Christians in the Second Century* (Edinburgh: Edinburgh University Press, 1996); J. Lieu, *Christian Identity in the Jewish and Graeco-Roman World* (Oxford: Oxford University Press, 2004); R.

1. Moore, *The Formation of a Persecuting Society: Power and Deviance in Western Europe, 950–1250* (Oxford: Oxford University Press, 1987). It should also be noted that historians of early Christianity now commonly refer to 'Christianities' rather than simply 'Christianity', and it is worth suggesting that this nomenclature should be routinely adopted by all historians of Christianity.

2. E. Lévinas, *Totality and Infinity: An Essay on Exteriority*, trans. A. Lingis (Pittsburgh, PA: Duquesne University Press, 1969 [1961]); E. Lévinas, *Otherwise Than Being, or Beyond Essence*, trans. A. Lingis (The Hague: Nijhoff, 1981[1974]), E. W. Said, *Orientalism* (Harmondsworth, England: Penguin, 1978); P. Sahlins, *Boundaries: The Making of France and Spain in the Pyrenees* (Berkeley: University of California Press, 1989).

3. L. Colley, "Britishness and Otherness: An Argument", *The Journal of British Studies* 31 (1992). Colley's points are further developed in L. Colley, *Britons: Forging the Nation, 1707–1837* (New Haven, CT: Yale University Press, 1992).

4. For criticisms of Said, see R. King, *Orientalism and Religion: Postcolonial Theory, India and 'the Mystic East'* (London: Routledge, 1999).

5. Colley (1992), especially chapter 1.

6. T. Claydon, *Europe and the Making of England, 1660–1760* (Cambridge: Cambridge University Press, 2007).

7. A. Robinson, "Identifying the Beast: Samuel Horsley and the Problem of Papal Anti-Christ", *Journal of Ecclesiastical History* 43 (1992), pp. 592–607.

8. See O. P. Grell, J. Israel, & N. Tyacke (eds.), *From Persecution to Toleration: The Glorious Revolution and Religion in England* (Oxford: Clarendon, 1991); G. Schochet, "The Act of Toleration and the Failure of Comprehension: Persecution, Nonconformity, and Religious Indifference", in D. Hoak & M. Feingold (eds.), *The World of William and Mary: Anglo-Dutch Perspectives on the Revolution of 1688–9* (Stanford: University of California Press, 1996), pp. 165–187.

9. J. C. D. Clark, *English Society, 1688–1832: Ideology, Social Structure, and Political Practice during the Ancient Regime* (Cambridge: Cambridge University Press, 1985) and the revised edition (with important change of chronology and subtitle), J. C. D. Clark, *English Society, 1660–1832: Religion, Ideology, and Politics during the Ancient Regime* (Cambridge: Cambridge University Press, 2000). See also J. C. D. Clark, "England's Ancien Regime as a Confessional State", *Albion* 21 (1989).

10. J. Parker Lawson, *History of the Scottish Episcopal Church from the Revolution to the Present Time* (Edinburgh: Gaillie and Bayley, 1848).

11. I am currently writing a study of the Church of England in New England. For now, see J. B. Bell, *The Imperial Origins of the King's Church in Early America, 1607–1783* (New York: Palgrave Macmillan, 2004).

12. For clear discussions of this point, see J. Bossy, *Christianity in the West, 1400–1700* (Oxford: Oxford University Press, 1985), pp. 97–104; E. Cameron, *The European Reformation* (Oxford: Oxford University Press, 1991), pp. 136–144. Some recent research suggests that despite the concentration on 'the Word' in the Reformation, we also need to take seriously other forms of media. See A. Ryrie, "Piety Abhors a Vacuum: The Reinvention of Devotion in the Early English and Scottish Reformations', in K. Cooper & J. Gregory (eds.), *Revival and Resurgence in Christian History, Studies in Church History* 44 (2008), pp. 87–105.

13. In forming this ideology, John Bale's *The Image of both Churches* (1545) was crucial as the first full commentary in English on the book of Revelation. Bale's book viewed the history of Christianity in terms of the fight between

the 'true' Church and the 'false' Church of Rome and the Anti-Christ. See J. N. King, *English Reformation Literature: The Tudor Origins of the Protestant Tradition* (Princeton, NJ: Princeton University Press, 1982).

14. P. Collinson, *The Birth Pangs of Protestant England: Religious and Cultural Change in the Sixteenth and Seventeenth Centuries* (Basingstoke: Macmillan, 1988), pp. 147–148.

15. P. Lake, "Anti-Popery: The Structure of a Prejudice", in R. Cust & A. Hughes (eds.), *Conflict in Early Stuart England: Studies in Religion and Politics 1603–1642* (London: Longman, 1989), pp. 72–106.

16. For example, T. Laqueur, *Making Sex: Body and Gender from the Greeks to Freud* (Cambridge, MA: Harvard University Press, 1990) argued that it was in the early modern period that understandings of the body and gender became hardened and polarised into what he calls 'the two-body model', which replaced more fluid models. For an indication of how fluid gender moles in the medieval period could be, see C. Walker Bynum, *Jesus as Mother: Studies in the Spirituality of the High Middle Ages* (Berkeley: University of California Press, 1982).

17. The classic study of the ways in which the world was turned upside down in mid-seventeenth-century England is C. Hill, *The World Turned Upside Down: Radical Ideas During the English Revolution* (London: Temple Smith, 1972). However, there has also been a historiography that has queried how widespread these ideas were. See J. C. D. Clark, *Revolution and Rebellion: State and Society in England in the Seventeenth and Eighteenth Centuries* (Cambridge: Cambridge University Press, 1986).

18. See M. G. Finlayson, *Historians, Puritanism and the English Revolution: The Religious Factor in English Politics Before and After the Interregnum* (Toronto: University of Toronto Press, 1983), pp. 132–133.

19. See the notorious chapters fifteen and sixteen of Gibbon's classic *Decline and Fall of the Roman Empire* (first published in 1776). For Gibbon's Protestant lens, see R. Porter, *Gibbon* (London: Weidenfeld and Nicolson, 1988), pp. 117–118, 133.

20. J. Gregory, "The Eighteenth-Century Reformation: The Pastoral Task of Anglican Clergy After 1689", in J. Walsh, C. Haydon, & S. Taylor (eds.), *The Church of England c. 1689–c. 1833: From Toleration to Tractarianism* (Cambridge: Cambridge University Press 1993), pp. 67–85. See also A. Pettegree, *Reformation and the Culture of Persuasion* (Cambridge: Cambridge University Press, 2005), which argues for the importance of persuasion in the sixteenth century.

21. For the role of the sermon, see T. Claydon, "The Sermon, the 'Public Sphere' and the Political Culture of Late Seventeenth-Century England", in L. A. Ferrell & P. McCullough (eds.), *The English Sermon Revised: Religion, Literature and History, 1600–1750* (Manchester: Manchester University Press, 2000). pp. 208–234.

22. See the trilogy: J. Brewer & R. Porter (eds.), *Consumption and the World of Goods* (London: Routledge, 1993); J. Brewer & A. Bermingham (eds.), *The Consumption of Culture, 1660–1800: Image, Object, Text* (London: Routledge, 1995); J. Brewer & S. Staves (eds.), *Early Modern Conceptions of Property* (London: Routledge, 1995).

23. For aspects of this, see J. Gregory, "Anglicanism and the Arts: Religion, Culture and Politics in the Eighteenth Century", in J. Black & J. Gregory (eds.), *Culture, Politics and Society in Britain, 1660–1800* (Manchester: Manchester University Press, 1991), pp. 82–109.

24. For prints, see J. Miller (ed.), *Religion in the Popular Prints, 1600–1832* (Cambridge: Chadwyck-Healey, 1986).

25. R. Fowler, *Linguistic Criticism* (Oxford: Oxford University Press, 1986), pp. 64–66.
26. R. A. Knox, *Enthusiasm: A Chapter in the History of Religion, With Special Reference to the 17th and 18th Centuries* (Oxford: Oxford University Press, 1950). A more recent study—which concentrates on the intellectual criticisms of enthusiasm and not on the pamphlet literature I discuss—is M. Heyd, *'Be Sober and Reasonable': The Critique of Enthusiasm in the Seventeenth and Early Eighteenth Centuries* (Leiden: Brill, 1995).
27. Knox (1950), pp. vi and 6.
28. For Weber's sociology of religion, see S. N. Eisenstadt (ed.), *Max Weber on Charisma and Institution Building* (Chicago: University of Chicago Press, 1968); M. Weber, *Economy and Society: An Outline of Interpretive Sociology*, ed. G. Roth & C. Wittich (New York: Bedminster, 1968), Part 2, chapter 6.
29. J. Kent, *Wesley and the Wesleyans: Religion in Eighteenth Century Britain* (Cambridge: Cambridge University Press, 2002), p. 5.
30. Knox (1950), p. 6 and G. Hickes, *The Spirit of Enthusiasm Exorcised in a Sermon Preached before the University of Oxford, on Act Sunday, July 11 1680* (London: printed for Walter Kettilby, 1680).
31. M. Casaubon, *A Treatise concerning Enthusiasme, as it is an Effect of Nature: but is Mistaken for either Divine Inspiration, or Diabolical Possession* (London: printed by R.D, 1655 [1654]).
32. T. Edwards, *The First and Second Part of Gangraena, or, A Catalogue and Discovery of many of the Errours, Heresies, Blasphemies and Pernicious Practices of the Sectaries of this Time, Vented and Acted in England in these Four Last Years also a Particular Narration of Divers Stories, Remarkable Passages, Letters: An Extract of Many Letters, All Concerning the Present Sects; Together with some Observations upon and Corollaries from all the Forenamed Premisses* (London: printed by T.R. and E.M. for Ralph Smith, 1646).
33. For example, the pamphlet attributed to Thomas Comber, prebendary of Durham cathedral, *Christianity no Enthusiasm, or, the Several Kinds of Inspirations and Revelations Pretended to by the Quakers Tried and Found Destructive to Holy Scripture and True Religion: In Answer to Thomas Ellwood's Defence thereof in his Tract, miscalled Truth Prevailing &c.* (London: printed by T.D for Henry Brome, 1678).
34. H. Wharton, *The Enthusiasm of the Church of Rome Demonstrated in some Observations upon Ignatius Loyola* (London: printed for Ric. Chiswell, 1688).
35. G. Lavington, *The Enthusiasm of Methodists and Papists compared*, 3 parts (London: printed for J. and P. Knapton, 1749–51).
36. Lavington (1749–51), preface.
37. Anon., *Enthusiasm no Novelty; or the Spirit of the Methodists in 1641 and 1642* (London: printed for T. Cooper, 1739).
38. A. T. Blacksmith (sometimes attributed to John Witherspoon), *Enthusiasm Delineated:, or, the Absurd Conduct of the Methodists Displayed in a Letter to the Rev. Messieurs Whitefield and Wesley* (Bristol, England: printed for the author and sold by T. Cadell, 1764); S. Roe, *Enthusiasm Detected, Defeated: With Previous Considerations Concerning Regeneration, the Omnipresence of God, and Divine Grace, &c* (Cambridge, England: printed for the author by Fletcher & Hodson and sold by S. Crowder, J. Dodsley and M.Hingeston, 1768); J. Eyre, *A Dispassionate Inquiry into the Probable Causes and Consequences of Enthusiasm: A Sermon, Preached July 30, 1798, in the Parish Church of St Mary's, Reading, at the Visitation of the*

Right Reverend John, Lord Bishop of Salisbury (Reading, England: printed and sold by Smart and Cowslade, 1798), pp. 6–7.

39. G. Whitehead, *Enthusiasm above Atheism, or, Divine Inspiration and Immediate Illumination (by God Himself) Asserted and the Children of Light Vindicated in Answer to a Book Entituled the Danger of Enthusiasm Discovered* (London: s.n., 1674).

40. [John Wesley], *An Advice to the People Called Methodists* (Newcastle upon Tyne, England: printed by John Gooding, 1745), p. 9, where he told his followers to "avoid enthusiasm". See the nuanced discussion of Wesley's attitude to enthusiasm in D. Hempton, *Methodism: Empire of the Spirit* (New Haven, CT: Yale University Press, 2005), pp. 32–54.

41. Said (1978), pp. 71–72.

42. Said (1978), p.72.

43. Said (1978), p.70.

44. C. Davis, *Fear, Myth and History: The Ranters and the Historians* (Cambridge: Cambridge University Press, 1986).

45. Said (1978), p.72.

46. J. Gregory, "*Homo Religiosus*: Masculinity and Religion in the Long Eighteenth Century", in T. Hitchcock & M. Cohen (eds.), *English Masculinities, 1660–1800* (London: Longman, 1999), pp. 85–110.

47. Lavington (1749–51), p. 196.

48. Lavington (1749–51), p. 196.

49. J. Moore, *Of the Truth and Excellency of the Gospel: A Sermon Preached before the Society for the Propagation of the Gospel in Foreign Parts, At their Anniversary Meeting, in the Parish Church of St Mary-le-Bow, on Friday the 20ᵗʰ of February, 1712/13* (London, 1713), p. 6.

50. G. Burnet, *Of the Propagation of the Gospel in Foreign Parts: A Sermon Preach'd at St Mary-le-Bow, Feb. 18, 1703/4, before the Society Incorporated for the Propagation of the Gospel in Foreign Parts* (London, 1704), p. 15.

51. Burnet (1704), pp. 16–22 and Moore (1713), p. 8.

52. W. Kennett, *The Lets and Impediments in Planting and Propagating the Gospel: A Sermon Preach'd before the Society for the Propagation of the Gospel in Foreign Parts, At their Anniversary Meeting, in the Parish Church of St Mary-le-Bow, 15 February 1711/12* (London: Joseph Downing, 1712), p. 8.

53. Kennett (1712), pp. 24–55.

54. Said (1978), p. 59.

55. See N. Hobart, *A Serious Address to the Members of the Episcopal Separation in New England Occasioned by Mr Wetmore's Vindication of the Professors of the Church of England in Connecticut* (Boston: printed by J. Bushel and D. Green for D. Henchman, 1748).

56. J. Mayhew, *Observations on the Charter and Conduct of the Society for the Propagation of the Gospel in Foreign Parts; Designed to Shew their Nonconformity to Each Other* (Boston: printed by R. and S. Draper, 1763); J. Mayhew, *A Defence of the Observations . . .* (Boston: printed and sold by R. and S. Draper, 1763).

57. For Anglican appeals for toleration, see W. S. Perry (ed.), *Historical Collections Relating to the American Colonial Church*, 5 vols (Hartford, CT: printed for the subscribers, 1870–78); vol. 3, *Massachusetts* (1873); "David Mossom's Petition to Governor Shute, 1722" (p. 140); "The Humble Petition of Samuel Myles, James Honeyman, James MacSparran, Matthias Plant, George Piggot and Samuel Johnson to the King's Most Excellent Majesty in Council, 1725" (pp. 191–199).

58. Lambeth Palace Library, MS 1124/1, fol. 168v, 1124/2, fol. 100.

59. C. Chauncy, *Enthusiasm Described and Caution'd Against: A Sermon Preach'd at the Old Brick Meeting-House in Boston, the Lord's Day after the Commencement, 1742* (Boston: printed by J. Draper, 1742).
60. Mayhew (1763) and Mayhew (1763).
61. See the essays in M. B. Rowlands (ed.), *Catholics of Parish and Town, 1558–1778* (Catholic Record Society, London 1999).
62. On the importance of Church Methodism, see G. Lloyd, "'Croakers and Busybodies': The Extent of the Influence of Church Methodism in the Late Eighteenth and Early Nineteenth Centuries", *Methodist History* 42 (2003), pp. 20–32.
63. For some more positive Anglican views of the emergence of Methodism, see J. Gregory, "'In the Church I will Live and Die': John Wesley, the Church of England and Methodism", in W. Gibson & R. Ingram (eds.), *Religious Identities in Britain, 1660–1830* (Aldershot, England: Ashgate, 2005).
64. J. Gregory, *Reformation, Restoration, and Reform, 1660–1828: Archbishops of Canterbury and their Diocese* (Oxford: Oxford University Press, 2000), p. 273. The pattern of 'double allegiance' to both Church of England and nonconformist places of worship continued well into the second half of the nineteenth century. See F. Knight, *The Nineteenth-Century Church of England and English Society* (Cambridge: Cambridge University Press, 1995), p. 23.
65. J. Spurr, "Religion in Restoration England", in L. K. J. Glassey (ed.), *The Reigns of Charles II and James VII and II* (Basingstoke, England: Macmillan, 1997), p. 108
66. A classic statement is C. Bridenbaugh, *Mitre and Sceptre: Transatlantic Faiths, Personalities and Politics, 1689–1775* (Oxford: Oxford University Press, 1962).
67. G. Berkeley, *Sermons: By the Late Rev. George Berkeley*, ed. E. Berkeley (London: Rivingtons, 1799), p. 245.
68. Robinson (1992).
69. For the defence of persecution, see M. Goldie, "The Theory of Religious Intolerance in Restoration England", in Grell et al. (1991). For attacks on the Restoration Church as a persecutor, see G. R. Cragg, *Puritanism in the Period of the Great Persecution, 1660–1688* (Cambridge: Cambridge University Press, 1957).
70. For the classic view of the stabilising effects of the rise of political parties, see J. H. Plumb, *The Growth of Political Stability in England, 1675–1725* (London: Macmillan, 1967). The 'Plumb thesis' has been challenged and modified in a number of ways, but the general thrust of the argument is persuasive. For a clear discussion, see G. Holmes, *The Making of a Great Power: Late Stuart and Early Georgian England, 1660–1722* (London: Longman, 1993), pp. 386–398.
71. For a general—if now rather old—discussion of persecution in the decades after 1660, see Cragg (1957). For a view of the generally tolerant relations between Quakers and Anglicans, see A. Davies, *The Quakers in English Society, 1655–1725* (Oxford: Oxford University Press, 2000).
72. J. Albers, "'Papist Traitors' and 'Presbyterian Rogues': Religious Identities in Eighteenth-Century Lancashire", in J. Walsh, C. Haydon, & S. Taylor (eds.), *The Church of England, c. 1689–c. 1833: From Toleration to Tractarianism* (Cambridge: Cambridge University Press, 1993) p. 333.
73. Although those who were labelled 'enthusiasts' were often deemed to be antithetical to Enlightenment values, recent treatments have explored the interface between 'enthusiasm' and 'enlightenment'. See D. Bebbington, "Revival and Enlightenment in Eighteenth-Century England", in A. Walker

& K. Aune (eds.), *On Revival: A Critical Examination* (Carlisle, England: Paternoster, 2003), pp. 71Paternoster Press85; Hempton (2005), pp. 32–54.

74. [Daniel Defoe], *The Great Law of Subordination Consider'd* (London: sold by S. Harding, 1724), p. 20.

75. See the essays in Rowlands (1999).

76. This is reproduced in Miller (1986), p. 199 (although it is misdated to 1739).

77. J. Gregory, "Thomas Secker", *Oxford Dictionary of National Biography* (2004).

78. Examples of the literary genre include Montesquieu's *Lettres Persanes* (1721) and Oliver Goldsmith's *Citizen of the World* (1762).

79. J. Uglow, *Hogarth: A Life and a World* (London: Faber and Faber, 1997), p. 651.

80. Uglow (1997), p. 654.

81. Uglow (1997), pp. 6, 186–188.

Part III

Struggling for the Self

8 *Christianos*
Defining the Self in the Acts of the Apostles

Todd Klutz

INTRODUCTION: FROM DICTIONARY TO DISCOURSE

For purposes of textual analysis and interpretation, dictionaries have limitations that are increasingly recognised.[1] Although dictionaries contain vast amounts of potentially useful information, their tendency is to provide brief glosses rather than proper definitions, and to show little or no interest in contextual and discursive aspects of meaning.[2] Moreover, the manner in which their glosses are typically presented, with a given category of usage often being linked for instance to a range of diverse texts from various periods, can easily give the misleading impression that the semantic potential of a given term is both essentially stable and equally accessible to all members of the pertinent speech community. Accordingly, whenever the aims of interpretation revolve around either the potential meaning or the actual usage of a single term, the pronouncements of dictionaries should never be accepted as final or beyond refinement. Instead, they are best treated as contributions to a conversation that we ourselves must construct, and that should normally be expected to go far beyond—or perhaps even against— the dictionary and its inevitably narrow interest in lexical meaning. The present chapter is a conversation of precisely that variety. Its topic is one of the most historically influential keywords in the vocabulary of Hellenistic Greek, namely the Greek noun *Christianos* (normally glossed as 'Christian'). The primary rationale for this inquiry is that previous treatments of *Christianos* in the standard tools of scholarship are plagued by difficulties like those summarised above. Both the specific character and some of the consequences of those difficulties are discussed below in my treatment of particular dictionary entries. Afterwards, the two occurrences of *Christianos* in the New Testament document known as the Acts of the Apostles are interpreted with the aid of select concepts borrowed from what has come to be known as 'critical discourse analysis' (hereafter CDA).

In general, CDA consists of a set of tools that integrates the linguistic criticism of texts and the critical study of discursive practice and sociocultural change.[3] But more tangibly and in the present context, CDA serves to heighten our awareness of the ways in which the connotations of a given word are shaped in particular utterances by the various levels of context in which it occurs and by any collocational patterns (i.e., clusters of words whose co-occurrence is habitual and thus predictable in a given field of discourse) to which it might contribute.[4] For instance, because the meaning of *Christianos* in the Acts of the Apostles and several other early Christian texts is demonstrably ramified by the word's relations to discourse concerning either Jews and Judaism or the authority of Rome, or both, a critical discourse analysis of the key passages is obligated to investigate the shape of those relations in terms of the discursive particulars of each context of usage. Within the framework of the present study, CDA plays an important role by helping to show that two of the earliest attested occurrences of *Christianos* are characterised by far greater semantic instability than is recognised in the standard scholarly treatments. By means of the same analysis, a close but largely unnoticed relationship can be observed between the keyword's semantic variation within a single well-known document and more general processes of conflict and change in that text's wider sociocultural environment. And finally, by illuminating not only the keyword's semantic variation but also its dialectical relation to social conflict and change, the study helps us to recognise some of the ways in which discursive power and social agency are instantiated in texts whose influence continues to be felt in our own time.

A CRITIQUE OF FOUR DICTIONARIES

Even the most skilful interpreters of ancient texts rely on information provided by reputable lexicographers. In ways that tend to be overlooked, and to a degree that is widely underestimated, dictionaries are, as J. A. L. Lee observed, esteemed by their users as authoritative, their terse summaries of meaning often being invested with an almost legal or even oracular weight.[5] Yet because lexicons are, like all works of scholarship, the products of imperfect knowledge, guesswork, compromise, and interaction with predecessors, they can never carry the full burden of trust that their users place in them.

With regard to the meaning of *Christianos* in early Christian writings, a critical examination of the standard lexical entries will help to remind us of both the discourse-simplifying character of lexical glossing, and of the importance of attending carefully to the lexical relations of words in their discursive contexts. With a view to examining a truly representative sample of dictionaries, I have chosen works that differ appreciably in terms of either corpus breadth, or lexicological orientation, or general layout and organisation of data, or two or more of these respects. On this basis the tools selected for scrutiny are the ninth edition of Liddell and Scott's *A Greek–English Lexicon* (hereafter LSJ); the second edition of W. Bauer's *A Greek–English Lexicon of the New Testament and Other Early Christian*

Literature (hereafter BAGD); the second edition of J. P. Louw and E. A. Nida's *Greek–English Lexicon of the New Testament Based on Semantic Domains* (hereafter Louw–Nida); and H. Balz and G. Schneider's *Exegetical Dictionary of the New Testament* (hereafter EDNT).[6]

Liddell, Scott, and Jones

Because of its comparative brevity, the entry in LSJ is the least complicated of the chosen four and the easiest to analyse critically. For starters, the LSJ entry provides a clear example of lexical glossing and some of its most serious limitations: Immediately after the printed form of the nominative-case noun with its masculine article, a single brief gloss is provided, namely 'Christian'.[7] Of course, in itself this particular gloss is not to be faulted; but what does merit criticism is the same entry's complete lack of supplementary information concerning (1) the diversity of connotations that *Christianos* conveys in the different passages cited in the same entry, (2) the nonorthogonal but semantically important relationships that obtain between *Christianos* and the varying clusters of other lexemes found in the given references (e.g., *Ioudaios*, *Hellenistes/Hellen*[8], and *mathetes* in Acts 11.19–26), and (3) diachronic factors that impinge strongly not only on the word's referent in each of its occurrences but also on distinctive aspects of its meaning (e.g., whether in any of its cited occurrences *Christianos* has connotations pertaining to Roman authority).

At least one other noteworthy fault in the LSJ entry is worth mentioning. After a brief list of the three New Testament passages in which *Christianos* occurs, only one other reference is provided, a quotation attributed to Porphyry of Tyre (the third century biographer of Plotinus) and embedded in Eusebius's *Ecclesiastical History* 6.19. Despite the expansive chronological gap between the New Testament references and the excerpt attributed to Porphyry, the single gloss 'Christian' is implied to be adequate by itself as a semantic cover for all four of the word's occurrences. This is the case even though the excerpt from Porphyry explicitly associates being a *Christianos* in his own day with criminality—an association that, as discussed below, has no parallel in the New Testament.

Bauer's Lexicon

Much of what has just been said about the entry in LSJ applies to the corresponding article in BAGD. Like LSJ, for instance, BAGD offers a single gloss—'Christian'—and says nothing about the significantly different connotations that the word conveys in different contexts. In its favour, the entry in BAGD includes a more extensive list of references to ancient texts in which the word occurs, both Christian and non-Christian; the information provided in BAGD is therefore indispensable to students wishing to analyse *Christianos* in the most efficient manner possible. Yet this same strength is also a liability; for the single gloss 'Christian' is far less likely to do justice to the variation in associative meanings of *Christianos* across the multiple occurrences cited by BAGD than it is across the smaller number of occurrences listed by LSJ. And finally, the entry in BAGD displays no more interest than LSJ does in how the meaning of *Christianos* changes through time. As indicated at several points in the analysis below, a properly nuanced interpretation of the meanings of *Christianos* in early Christian discourse cannot afford to dispense with such diachronic and wider historical types of inquiry.

Louw–Nida

In contrast to the entries in LSJ and BAGD, the information given on *Christianos* in the Louw–Nida lexicon includes not only the standard gloss (i.e. 'Christian') but also a concise and useful definition: namely, 'one who is identified as a believer in and follower of Christ'.[9] Admirably, the provision of that information fulfils expectations nurtured by the lexicon's Introduction, whose authors specify the prevailing dearth of definitions (in contrast to mere glosses) in the available dictionaries as the main rationale for the new type of lexicon they have created.[10] Moreover, the value of the definition just cited for *Christianos* in particular is enhanced by another innovative feature of the same lexicon, namely its classification of all the items it treats into semantic domains (e.g., 'Groups and Classes of Persons and Members of Such Groups and Classes'[11]) and subdomains (e.g., 'Socio-Religious [Groups and Classes]').[12] By virtue of that feature, the user of Louw–Nida can easily compare the definition provided for *Christianos* with that given for a range of semantically related terms (e.g., *ekklesia*, *ta ethne*, *Hellen*), and can thereby ascertain without difficulty how the sense of *Christianos* is both similar to and different from that of other Greek terms pertaining to socioreligious groups and classes.

Unfortunately, though, and partly because the entry in Louw–Nida treats only one of the three canonical passages in which *Christianos* occurs (Acts 11.26), it affords its users none of the diachronic types information that almost always enrich the synchronic study of words in relation to particular contexts of utterance. Furthermore, Louw–Nida's quotation of Acts 11.26 in the same article mistranslates the Greek noun phrase *tous mathetas*, which is best rendered not as 'the believers' (as in Louw–Nida) but rather as 'the disciples', in a manner that misconstrues the relationship between that expression and *Christianous*. Despite the repeated claim by the editors that the new dictionary is distinguished by interest in the connotative aspects of lexical meaning,[13] their entry for *Christianos* shows no interest either in the negative overtones stemming from the term's use by antagonistic outsiders or in the possible friction between the meaning intended by the outsiders who were the term's first users and that understood later by the narrator of Acts himself.

Exegetical Dictionary of the New Testament

In general, and like the older so-called 'theological' dictionaries edited by G. Kittel and C. Brown, EDNT has less in common with a *dictionary*—at least as that term is normally understood—than with an *encyclopaedia*.[14] For instance, the entry for *Christianos* in particular includes various types of information, ranging from the bibliographic and the etymological to matters of identity formation and the history of religio-political change in the early Roman Imperial period. It furthermore manages to provide all this helpful information while avoiding the sort of methodological sins associated with Kittel.[15] Yet the same entry suffers from weaknesses that severely limit its value for the analysis and interpretation of *Christianos* in early Christian writings. For instance, and perhaps most important, in his treatment of the Antiochene context of reference in Acts 11.26 ('The disciples were first called Christians in Antioch'), G. Schneider postulates that Jesus's followers were first labelled as *Christianoi* in a setting where they had already begun to separate themselves from the local synagogues, a proposal that combines defensible inference—conflict with Antiochene Jews is very likely—and groundless conjecture, namely, no support is given for the view that Christians separated themselves from the synagogue. Similarly, when Schneider comments on the significance of *hos Christianos* in 1 Peter 4.16 ('But if any of you suffers *as a Christian*, let him not be ashamed'), he tacitly agrees with Leonhard Goppelt in taking the phrase as presupposing 'that Christians are familiar to the public as representatives of *their own questionable religion*' (emphasis mine),[16] a judgement that interpreted in its context erroneously implies that by 64 CE the break between the Christ-cult and Jewish synagogues (or even Judaism more generally) was far advanced in the region between Rome and Asia Minor.[17] Finally, although Schneider's article has the virtue of including a list of all the keyword's occurrences in the writings of Ignatius (c. 105–107 CE), it neither comments on how the term's meaning in those contexts differs from its meaning(s) in the New Testament, nor includes a full listing of the term's occurrences in other writings by the Apostolic Fathers, the latter omission suggesting a strong possibility of arbitrariness in the selection of evidence for inclusion in the article.

The Promise of a New Approach

The present discussion has focused thus far solely on how *Christianos* is treated in representative lexical tools. Because of the trust that even the best commentators often put in lexicons, many of the shortcomings found in the dictionaries are mirrored in the major commentaries and other types of scholarly literature. Similarities between the content of the dictionary entries and what other kinds of published scholarship say about the earliest attested occurrences of *Christianos* are discussed at various points below.

But more important, at least partly as a result of applying concepts borrowed from CDA, the ensuing analysis shows that *Christianos* is used with a far greater variety of associative meanings in its earliest attested occurrences—indeed, even within a single early document—than is recognised in the standard dictionaries and commentaries. Moreover, in both of the passages analysed below the distinctive shades of meaning conveyed by the term yield information both about particular processes of social conflict and cultural change relevant to the assumed context and about the communicative agency of the text's author.

CHRISTIANOS IN THE ACTS OF THE APOSTLES

The remaining sections of this chapter are more concerned with the pragmatics and discursive effects of *Christianos* in its Lucan contexts than with the lexical relations of the term more generally. Consequently, wherever I refer below to 'lexical relations', my interest resides either wholly or largely in the ways in which *Christianos* relates, not to other lexical items that belong to the same semantic domain, but rather to other words that are collocated with it in either of its two occurrences in Acts.[18] The ensuing analysis furthermore assumes that in each occurrence, the keyword's meaning should be understood in the light of not only its intratextual relations but also its various inferred layers of extra-linguistic context.

Acts 11.26

The first occurrence of *Christianos* in the narrative sequence of the book of Acts is embedded in a comment by the text's narrator concerning where the followers of Jesus were first called 'Christians' (i.e., in Antioch). Although the narrator does not specify who it was that first used the term, the agent in the designated process of labelling is normally understood as having been one or another group of outsiders (i.e., non-Christians).[19] That understanding receives significant support from the term's only other occurrence in the same document, namely Acts 26.28, where the partly Jewish tetrarch Herod Agrippa II (c. 27–100 CE) refered to an attempt just made by the apostle Paul to persuade the ruler to become a 'Christian'. With the term being placed in that context on the lips of a character whose Jewish associations are highly significant for the force of the wider narrative, we have reason for conjecturing that the deleted agent in Acts 11.26 was likewise either Jewish or at least closely associated with Jewish culture and religion, though ultimately there is no way of achieving certainty on this point.[20]

Because the use of *Christianos* in Acts 11.26 is problematic and fascinating in several ways, it has attracted much scholarly attention and commentary.[21] But despite the attention given to this passage by previous studies, the possibility of achieving new insights into it should not be precluded.

In the first place, and especially since in Acts 26.28 Agrippa II shows full awareness that the Jewish missionary Paul is wanting to persuade the partly Jewish ruler himself to become a 'Christian', we have excellent reasons for probing into what kinds of lexical relations can be observed between *Christianos* in Acts 11.26 and other group-orientated terms—most notably *Ioudaios*, but also *Ellenistas/Ellen*, *ekklesias*, and *mathetas*—in the immediate co-text of that reference.

Near the beginning of the discourse segment that closes at the end of Acts 11.26, an event recounted earlier in the same work—namely the persecution that broke out in Judea of the so-called 'Hellenist' (i.e., Greek-speaking Jewish) members of the Jerusalem church (Acts 8.1b–3)—is represented as a condition for the next phase in the spread of the Christ movement: Many of the believers who fled from Jerusalem because of the persecution 'travelled as far as Phoenicia, Cyprus, and Antioch', and spoke about Jesus 'to no one but Jews (*Ioudaiois*, Acts 11.19)'.[22] Significantly, therefore, in this context both the missionary followers of Jesus and the audiences of their proclamation are best understood as consisting solely of Jews; and implicitly, the missionaries of the movement are represented as understanding both themselves and the most appropriate audiences for their message to be Jewish.

Thus, although the narrator proceeds to recount the successful preaching of the gospel amongst Antiochene Gentiles (Acts 11.20–24), his subsequent reference to those 'disciples' (*mathetas*) who were the first to be called 'Christians' (verse 26) must be understood as including a number of Jews. Accordingly, and as many commentators have overlooked, in Acts 11.19–26 the Greek words *Christianos* and *Ioudaios* are neither semantic opposites nor mutually exclusive referentially; instead, their referents are best construed as overlapping.[23] Neither here nor elsewhere in Acts does the text's author exemplify knowledge of terms such as *Christianismos* ('Christianity') and *Ioudaismos* ('Judaism'), terminology that does occur for instance in the writings of Ignatius,[24] and that in his context presupposes a taxonomy of socioreligious knowledge significantly different from that assumed in Acts.[25]

The Jewish flavour of *Christianos* in Acts 11.26 is strengthened by several lexical relations not yet mentioned. First, the noun *mathetes*, whose plural form has a meronymic (i.e., whole to part) relationship with *Christianous* in the same verse, is best construed in all its previous occurrences in Acts as referring to specifically Jewish followers of Jesus.[26] Thus, although in principle we must uphold the distinction between the referent of *mathetes* and its lexical sense, the referential pattern just noted serves none the less to highlight semantic continuity more than it does change between the term's use in Acts 11.26 and its occurrences in the antecedent co-text. A similar observation can be made concerning the term *ekklesia* ('church'), which, directly before its use in verse 26 as a collective reference to all the Christians of Antioch, is employed with reference to the thoroughly Jewish 'church' of Jerusalem (verse 22), and has an Israelite referent in each of its previous occurrences in the same narrative.[27] And finally, this same atmosphere of Jewish-ethnic associations would seem to be reinforced by the widely overlooked stylistic effects of the syntagm *egeneto de autois kai eniauton holon sunachthenai en te ekklesia* ('So it was that for an entire year they [i.e. Barnabas and Paul] associated with the church', 11.26), whose distinctively septuagintal syntax helps to identify this segment of the narrative with the Jewish-biblical history of God's dealings with Israel.[28]

The preceding observations therefore not only impinge on the discourse meaning of *Christianous* in verse 26 but also support the recent scholarly trend of interpreting Luke-Acts more generally as part of a broadly intra-Jewish conversation about who possesses the best claim to the Jewish-biblical heritage of Israel.[29] Furthermore, the same observations shed light on a difficulty alluded to above but never satisfactorily resolved in the history of exegesis: Namely, how to understand the instance of agent-deletion in the clause *chrematisai te protos en Antiocheia tous mathetas Christianous* ('and it was in Antioch that the disciples were first called Christians', Acts 11.26). In other words, by precisely who in Antioch were the disciples first called 'Christians'?

As hinted above, in general while a few interpreters have understood the active voice of *chrematisai* as having a reflexive middle sense (i.e., 'the disciples called *themselves* Christians), most have construed it as functioning instead like a passive with unspecified agency (i.e., 'the disciples were called Christians').[30] If the reflexive potential of the middle voice had been the main idea, the grammatical subject of the same clause (i.e., *tous mathetas*, 'the disciples') would be assigned a heightened degree of involvement in the process designated by the verb.[31] But such intensification finds no support in the immediate co-text, and none of the same verb's eight other occurrences in the New Testament—including the active-voice forms in Romans 7.3 and Hebrews 12.25—can be satisfactorily interpreted as having the force of a reflexive middle. Accordingly, the primary function of *chrematisai* in Acts 11.26 is most probably to designate a past process of naming, wherein the assumed labellers are not the same as the labellees (i.e., the followers of Jesus). The clause *chrematisai te protos en Antiocheia tous mathetas Christianous* as a whole, therefore, should be read as implying that the followers of Jesus were first called 'Christians' by people outside the circle of the Christ movement.[32] For this reason and several others, many commentators infer negative connotations from the use of *Christianos* in this clause.[33] That reading of the clause is almost certainly correct. But equally pertinent to the present discussion is whether the co-text of the key clause holds any clues that might warrant a more precise identification of the disciples' antagonistic Antiochene labellers.

At the outset, we would do well to take some grammatical advice from Porter: Namely, although occurrences of the passive with agent-deletion sometimes invite or even require interpretative speculation on the part of the reader (i.e., concerning who or what the agent of the action is), in many cases such speculation is unnecessary.[34] However, as already hinted above, the presence of *Christianos* on the lips of Herod Agrippa II in Acts 26.28—the only other Lucan context in which the term occurs—supports an identification of the outsiders in Acts 11.26 as out-group (and possibly influential) Jews.[35] To be sure, that particular source of support is not decisively strong; and if no other evidence could be offered for the same position, the question of the more specific identity of the Antiochene outsiders might best be dismissed as unanswerable. But in fact additional evidence for this position is available. More particularly, because the church in Antioch emerges in Acts 11.27 to 18.22 as the main base of operations for the Pauline mission's proselytising and related activities, any noteworthy patterns in the narration of those endeavours might shed light on the character and origins of the church on which they depend.[36] In this connection, one pattern stands out as especially relevant to the present question: namely, in nearly every locale where Paul and his associates proclaim the gospel, they begin their operations by establishing a foothold in the synagogue, which then serves as a social network for their evangelistic efforts; and in several of the settings where Paul's networking in the synagogue bears fruit in the form of converts, the consequences of his success include envy and slander from Jews who have not accepted his proclamation.

What this evidence suggests, therefore, is that although the Lucan account of the origins of the church of Jews and Gentiles in Antioch (Acts 11.19–26) includes no explicit mention of a synagogue, early audiences of the book of Acts probably would have inferred that the birth and early growth of the Antiochene community had been conditioned by the same combination of missionary tactics, social networking, and conflict that subsequently prevailed at other key sites of Christian evangelistic work. Consequently, those same audiences would probably have understood the use of *Christianos* in Acts 11.26 as part of a hostile and specifically Jewish response to the Christ movement's success in gaining converts at the expense of the Antiochene synagogue.[37]

The preceding analysis contributes not only to the recovery of the identity of the deleted agent in the clause *chrematisai te protos en Antiocheia tous mathetas Christianous* ('the disciples were first called Christians in Antioch') but also to the fulfilment of one of two closely interrelated procedural commitments articulated near the beginning of this chapter, namely to investigate in each of the keyword's two Lucan occurrences the character of its relations to terms that are both collocated with it and concerned with distinctively Jewish interests. The conflict just inferred from Acts 11.26 between church and synagogue, moreover, scarcely undermines the semantic continuities between *Christianous* and those terms that satisfy the conditions just repeated. For as studies of social conflict often point out, groups that stand close to one another either culturally or geographically are far more likely to experience intergroup hostility than are those that stand far apart.[38]

The other procedural commitment is to probe the keyword's relations to words or domains pertaining to Roman authority. The silence of Acts 11.19–26 speaks loudly in this regard, especially by comparison with the salient Jewish connection deduced above. More particularly, neither the episode itself nor its immediate co-text contains even a hint of interest—either sympathetic or antagonistic—in Rome; and the suggestion made by some to the effect that the deleted agent in verse 26 is best construed as Roman officials in Antioch has even less in its favour than the proposal that takes the agent as consisting of ordinary local gentiles.[39] The combination of this lack of interest in Rome and the strong Jewish associations inferred above gives *Christianos* in Acts 11.26 meanings that contrast sharply with its associations in several of its other early occurrences, including that in Acts 26.28.[40]

Finally, and unrelated to any theoretical principle outlined above, at least brief attention should be devoted to a feature that shows *Christianos*—especially in the first several decades of its semantic development—to have been a site of discursive struggle, which gives the usage in Acts 11.26 a heightened degree of polyphony unmatched by any of the term's other early occurrences in extant texts. The feature in question involves what is often called 'point of view'—the terms 'focalisation' and 'orientation' are often used with similar meaning—and that can be defined generally as the position from which either the narrator or other speakers in a text see what is narrated. The phenomenon can as that definition implies be contrasted with what is normally meant by 'narration', and can be usefully understood as consisting of several discrete facets. The widely used distinctions between psychological, spatio-temporal, and ideological point of view are fully adequate for purposes of the present analysis.

Psychological point of view pertains chiefly to the types of knowledge possessed by the consciousness through which the various elements of a narrative are focalised (e.g., the limited knowledge of an internal character-focaliser versus the more encompassing knowledge of an external narrator-focaliser).[41] In terms of psychological point of view, the decision by the author of Acts 11.26 not to quote directly those who first labelled the disciples as Christians but rather to summarise that past event ('the disciples were first called "Christians" [i.e., by outsiders] in Antioch') is noteworthy; for his summary tightly combines in a single clause both the retrospective angle of the narrator and the prior point of view of the (unnamed) agents in the labelling process. Two different voices can, therefore, and should, be heard in Acts 11.26.

The primary interest of this observation resides not in itself but rather in its implications for the other two aspects of focalisation in the same passage. On the plane of spatio-temporal orientation, for instance, a significant difference should be observed between the narrator and the unnamed labellers with regard to the contexts in which the word *Christianos* is used. Most importantly, where the act of labelling performed by the unnamed agents pertains solely to Christ-followers in Antioch in the early 40s CE, the circumstantial elements *protos en Antiocheia* ('first in Antioch') in the same clause imply authorial awareness of the subsequent use of *Christianos* up to the time of the composition of Acts (c. 75–85 CE), and therefore in a potentially much wider range of geographical contexts.[42] Thus, not only is the word *Christianos* in this passage focalised through two different minds; it also implies two different types of context: Namely, the narrowly defined context of reference in which *Christianos* was purportedly first used, and the later situation of an implied author who possesses at least some knowledge of the same word's usage in subsequent settings. That same distinction, moreover, creates conditions whereby different and perhaps even conflicting meanings can be generated by our keyword in this single clause.

As it turns out, strong reasons can be given for interpreting the ideological orientation of Acts 11.26 as polyphonic and more specifically as discordant. The negative overtones that *Christianos* would have conveyed in the discourse of the unnamed labellers have already been noted above, where the unexpressed agent of *chrematisai* in Acts 11.26 was identified as Antiochene Jews opposed to the Christ movement. At the same time, from a rhetorical standpoint the use of *Christianos* by the narrator makes acceptable sense only if the term had acquired potential for more positive associations by the time of the composition of Acts.[43] Finally, the envisaged shift from the negative intention of the labellers to the more positive orientation of the narrator deserves high marks for sociolinguistic realism to the extent that it illustrates a widely attested strategy of responding to charges of deviance: Namely, the device of 'neutralisation', which works chiefly by redefining either the person(s) already accused of deviance or the labels that have been applied to them.[44] Therefore, in Acts 11.26 the word *Christianous* is best understood as a polyphonic signal of ideological struggle between the Christ movement and some of its earliest Jewish opponents. As confirmed in part by the analysis below, the particular effects of that same instance of polyphony are not closely paralleled by usage attested in other Christian texts from the first two centuries CE.

Acts 26.28

The only other occurrence of *Christianos* in Luke's writings is found on the lips of Herod Agrippa II, in a passage where the ruler has just heard Paul defend himself. After Paul's speech and in response to a question about the ruler's own belief in the prophets of Jewish Scripture, Agrippa replies with an utterance whose basic sense is represented well by A. T. Robertson: 'With little argument you are trying to persuade me in order to make me a Christian.'[45] Because the keyword in this instance is embedded in a brief piece of direct discourse, it would seem to possess less potential for a non-unitary, polyphonic reading in this context than it has in Acts 11.26. Still, several aspects of the word's immediate co-text require attention if its discourse meaning in this particular setting is to be determined adequately.

First, in Acts 26.28 the embedding of the keyword in an utterance by one of the story's characters contributes to a difference of speech presentation between the verbal happenings in that passage and those represented in Acts 11.26. More particularly, in contrast to the formulation in Acts 11.26, where *Christianos* is focalised not only through the voice of the disciples' Antiochene opponents but also through the voice of the story's narrator, the use of direct discourse in 26.28 has the effect of associating *Christianos* solely with the speech of Agrippa. The attitude of the narrator toward the word in Acts 26.28 is therefore even less explicit than it is in Acts 11.26. But what about the attitude of Agrippa? Significantly, Agrippa's question constitutes neither a cooperative reply to Paul's query concerning the prophets nor an expression of faith in Paul's larger message. Instead, it conveys incredulity about the rapid pace at which Paul's message has proceeded from defence mode to evangelistic appeal, and perhaps also suspicion concerning Paul's communicative goals more generally. Agrippa's question is scarcely that of an insider; and in the response attributed to Paul in the ensuing verse, the use of the circumlocution *toioutous hopoios kai ego eimi* ('such as I myself am') as an alternative to *Christianon* might be read as expressing, amongst other things, unease on the part of the Lucan Paul with Agrippa's choice of words. Furthermore, both the negative connotations intended by the Antiochene opponents in Acts 11.26, and the absence of *Christianos* in Paul's own writings could be cited as support for the same reading. On these grounds we might understand Agrippa's use of *Christianos* in Acts 26.28 as having associations not unlike the negative ones inferred above from its earlier use in Antioch (Acts 11.26).

The difficulty is, however, that other grounds need to be covered before an adequately nuanced view can be offered concerning the connotations of *Christianon* in Acts 26.28. Most important, and as the ensuing co-text of Agrippa's utterance makes explicit, unlike the implied Antiochene labellers in Acts 11.26 the ruler is not clearly antagonistic to Paul. While he may not be immediately persuaded to embrace Paul's 'Christian' variety of Judaism, Agrippa none the less clearly identifies himself with a larger chorus of elites who judge Paul as having done nothing deserving 'death or imprisonment' (26.31), and he explicitly tells the Roman governor that Paul could have been set free if he had not appealed to the emperor (26.32). As ruler of several parts of Galilee and certain territories of the Lebanon, moreover, Agrippa stands at a much higher position in the social pyramid than either Paul or the Antiochene opponents in Acts 11.26, so that Paul's speech would most likely be construed by the ruler as a prospective client's humble (and thus positive) request for support.[46]

Thus, unlike the antagonistic use of *Christianos* by the disciples' threatened Jewish equals in Antioch, Agrippa's use of the same term in Acts 26.28

is best understood as reflecting the comparatively detached and unthreatened perspective of a social superior.[47] The contrasts in tenor between equal and superior, hostile and detached, are ignored only at the expense of adequately complicated contextualisation. Thus, even within the Acts narrative itself the term *Christianos* is far more connotatively flexible than previous treatments have tended to notice.

Two other aspects of how *Christianos* is used in Acts 26.28 need to be considered before the present analysis can be brought to a proper conclusion. First, as in Acts 11.26 as also in the context of Agrippa's question, *Christianos* is employed in a manner that implicitly gives its content a strongly Jewish flavour. Agrippa, after all, would not even be hearing Paul's defence if the distinctively Jewish nature of the key issues had been comprehensible to a pagan official such as Festus (Acts 25.18–20). But since the dispute revolves largely around matters of the Jews' 'own religion' (*tes idias deisidaimonias* Acts 25.19), and since by his own admission Festus is 'at a loss how to investigate these questions' (25.20) the Roman governor is hoping that Agrippa—a figure praised by the Lucan Paul as 'especially knowledgeable in regard to all the customs and controversies of the Jews' (26.3)—might be able to interpret the case for the benefit of both Festus himself and ultimately the emperor (25.26–27).[48] Just as important, Agrippa's subsequent inference that Paul's arguments about the prophets, Moses and the Jewish Messiah are designed at least partly to serve as a case for becoming 'a Christian' (26.28), indirectly attributes to the key category a thoroughly Jewish set of cultural associations. Indeed, from the standpoint of the narrative's implied author, Agrippa's question in 26.28 not only exemplifies a fundamentally accurate grasp of the link between becoming a 'Christian' and believing Jewish biblical prophecy, it also suggests—like so much else in the Lucan narratives—that secure understanding of what it means to become a 'Christian' depends on a more encompassing knowledge of 'the customs and controversies of the Jews' (26.3).

Finally, what about the relationship between Agrippa's concept of a 'Christian' and the representation of Roman authority in the immediate co-text? One of the best ways of approaching that question is to recognise it chiefly as an inquiry into how the Lucan Paul—as a representative of the socioreligious category 'Christian' (26.28–29)—is treated by various agents of Roman authority in the events leading up to and directly following the key utterance by Agrippa. Approached from that angle, our question has already been answered in part: to the extent that Agrippa is a puppet of Rome and a friend of the Roman governor over Judea (25.13–27), his judgement that Paul is innocent (26.30–31) serves as an indicator of Roman opinion more generally.[49]

The commitment of the narrator of Acts to that particular portrayal of Rome's disposition is reinforced at several points in the same section of the narrative. For instance, in Festus's attempt to prepare Agrippa for his hearing of Paul, the governor explains that the missionary has already been found innocent of charges relevant to Roman law (25.13–27); and later, Festus is among those who agree with Agrippa that Paul 'is doing nothing to deserve death or imprisonment' (26.30–31). Numerous other details in the wider narrative co-text—for instance, the portrayal of Paul as having been born a Roman citizen; as having been rescued from the Jews of Jerusalem and then declared innocent by the tribune Claudius Lysias; and later as having been treated kindly by a centurion of the Augustan cohort during his sea-voyage to Rome—point to the same lack of tension between Roman authority and being a 'Christian'.[50] To be sure, this facet of the Lucan narrative deserves at least some of the critical suspicion to which it is nowadays often subjected.[51] Furthermore, it should not be allowed to blind us to other, less favourable images of empire in this and other sections of Luke-Acts.[52] But most importantly for the present inquiry, the emphasis in Acts 21–28 on the innocence of Paul does impact on the discourse meaning of *Christianos* in 26.28 in a manner suggesting that the word conveys no connotation of enmity with Rome. Thus, despite several differences in orientation between the two Lucan occurrences of *Christianos*, a high degree of discursive continuity between them is discernible in at least one vital respect: As in Acts 11.26 so also in the discourse of Agrippa II, the word lacks the overtones of conflict specifically with Roman authority that reverberate in several other early (but slightly later) contexts.[53]

Unfortunately, space does not allow those other contexts to be treated here. But for purposes of understanding the meaning and context of the term's usage in Acts, a brief reflection on its absence in the letters of Paul may prove not merely appropriate but illuminating. For instance, the negative overtones intended by the word's first users, in Antioch, go a long way toward enabling us to understand why Paul might not have considered the word useful in his own efforts to define the identity of the Christ cult; whereas the mere willingness of the narrator of Acts 11.26 to mention the word, even where the context of reference involves anti-Christian polemic, suggests that by the time Acts was composed, the term had acquired potential for more positive uses, and that Acts itself was therefore most probably written a decade or more after the writings (or even the death) of Paul.[54]

Thus, if only momentarily and for the sake of argument we assume the historical reliability of the key narratives in Acts and also understand the absence of *Christianos* in Paul as stemming from the word's earliest use by outsiders as a negative label, then the evidence treated in the present study can be summarised diachronically by the following outline:

Date of Usage	Passage	Speaker/Writer	Connotations
Early 40s CE	Acts 11.26	Antioch opponents	Negative
50–57 CE	Term's absence in Paul's letters		Negative?
57–59 CE	Acts 26.28	Herod Agrippa II	Neutral or ambivalent
75–85 CE	Acts 11.26	Narrator	Positive

The most interesting aspect of this outline is its suggestion that as time passes from the early 40s CE to the most probable range of dates for the composition of Acts, around 75–85 CE, *Christianos* evolves from a term whose meaning is perhaps exclusively negative, and is therefore probably used solely by out-group critics, to one that depending on context can also convey either neutral or positive associations.

Now because the meaning potential of many culturally salient keywords is likely to be especially unstable during periods of intense sociocultural struggle and rapid change, the story told by the preceding outline deserves to be seen as plausible to the extent that the Christ movement was born and raised in a context of religious conflict, innovation and change.[55] Of course, plausibility in such matters can never ensure the historical reliability of our primary sources; and for purposes of the present essay, issues of historicity have been subordinated at most points to questions concerning the discourse semantics of *Christianos*.

CONCLUSION

The foregoing analysis of Acts 11.26 and 26.28 indicates that both the semantic potential and the actual usage of *Christianos* in early Christian texts are far more complex than previous studies have tended to allow. Far from conveying a single basic meaning in all its attested occurrences, *Christianos* varies considerably in meaning—especially in regard to connotative aspects of usage—from one context of usage to another. Even within a single document such as the book of Acts, the connotations of *Christianos* can be seen to vary in subtle but important ways depending, for instance, on the social status of the speaker on whose lips the term is placed (e.g., anti-Christian Jews from Antioch in Acts 11.26 or the tetrarch Herod Agrippa II in Acts 26.28).

However, my present interest in highlighting the keyword's semantic variation should not be understood as a denial of continuity between its various occurrences. On the contrary, although *Christianos* is far more semantically unstable than is usually recognised, in the book of Acts and in other early Christian texts it invariably serves to denote one follower or more of Jesus Christ. Furthermore, although the cultural tension between the referent of *Christianos* and its given social environment varies in degree across the different contexts of usage, in no instance can the measure of tension be characterised as low. Both in the New Testament and in the Apostolic Fathers, people designated by the term *Christianos* are always involved in social conflict. The *Christianoi* are not merely different; they are deviant in ways that invite opposition and abuse. And as suggested at many points in the analysis above, the cultural tension entailed by that opposition and abuse conditions the discourse meaning of *Christianos* in its particular contexts of usage.

Another interesting implication of this essay involves the interface between polyphony, struggle, and diachronic change in lexical usage. More particularly, of the various passages mentioned above, the one that gives best access to the earliest use of *Christianos*—namely, Acts 11.26—proves on reflection to instantiate the strongest sense of struggle and heteroglossia; for in addition to reflecting the deviance-labelling discourse of some of the Christ movement's earliest critics, the use of *Christianos* in that passage also realises the agency of later Christ followers (including the narrator of the text himself) who struggled against lexical precedent to invest the term with positive significance. That struggle was scarcely decided in a flash; for it could still be overheard a few years later in the situation implied by 1 Peter, whose emphatic attempt to strengthen the positive meaning of *Christianos* (4.16) presupposes a context in which the word continues to be used by outsiders as a label of abuse. Unfortunately, 1 Peter 4.16 cannot be analysed here; but were it interpreted by means of the tools applied above to Acts 11.26 and 26.28, it would almost certainly be found to partly colour *Christianos* with tints perceptible neither in the Lucan occurrences nor in second-century writers who took up the word only a few decades later.

NOTES

1. The criticisms outlined here are adapted from N. Fairclough, *Discourse and Social Change* (Cambridge, England: Polity, 1992), p. 186; J. P. Louw & E. A. Nida, *Greek–English Lexicon of the New Testament Based on Semantic Domains*, 2 vols (New York: United Bible Societies, 1988–89), vol. 1, pp. vii–ix.
2. The difference in brief is that between the briefest possible listing of translation 'equivalents' in the receptor language and information about what the word shares, semantically, with other words, how it differs from those words, and what connotative meanings it may have. See Louw & Nida (1988–89), vol. 1, pp. vii–ix.
3. See e.g., N. Fairclough, *Critical Discourse Analysis: The Critical Study of Language* (London: Longman, 1995), p. 2.
4. The theoretical framework for this type of analysis is broadly sociolinguistic and has been strongly influenced by the Neo-Firthian linguist M. A. K. Halliday. For recent discussion of the theory and its methodological procedures, see N. Fairclough, *Analysing Discourse: Textual Analysis for Social Research* (London: Routledge, 2003); N. Fairclough, *Language and Power*, 2nd ed. (Harlow, England: Longman, 2001).
5. J. A. L. Lee, "The Present State of Lexicography of Ancient Greek", in P. R. Burton et al. (eds.), *Biblical Greek Language and Lexicography* (Grand Rapids, MI: Eerdmans, 2004), pp. 66–74.
6. H. G. Liddell, R. Scott, & H. S. Jones, *A Greek-English Lexicon*, 9th ed. (Oxford, England: Clarendon, 1968); W. Bauer, W. F. Arndt, F. W. Gingrich, & F. W. Danker, *A Greek-English Lexicon of the New Testament and Other Early Christian Literature*, 2nd ed. (Chicago: University of Chicago Press, 1958); Louw & Nida (1988–89); H. Balz & G. Schneider, *Exegetical Dictionary of the New Testament* 3 vols (Grand Rapids, MI: Eerdmans, 1990–93).

7. LSJ, s.v. *Christianos*.

8. Some Greek manuscripts for Acts 11.20 (e.g., Vaticanus and the Byzantine text) have the word *Hellenistas* ('Hellenists', i.e., Greek-speaking Jews), whereas others (e.g., p[74] and Alexandrinus) read *Hellenas* ('Greeks'). The latter reading makes far better sense of the contrast with 'Jews' in verse 19, but for that very reason looks more like a scribal correction than its more awkward alternative does.

9. Louw–Nida, vol. 1, p. 127, §11.35.

10. Louw–Nida, vol. 1, pp. vii–ix.

11. Louw–Nida, vol. 1, p. 121.

12. Louw–Nida, vol. 1, p. 123.

13. Louw–Nida, vol. 1, pp. vi, x–xi, xvi–xix.

14. G. Kittel & G. Friedrich (eds.), *Theological Dictionary of the New Testament*, trans. G. W. Bromiley, 10 vols (Grand Rapids, MI: Eerdmans, 1964–76); C. Brown (ed.), *New International Dictionary of New Testament Theology* 3 vols (Exeter, England: Paternoster, 1975).

15. On the lexicological shortcomings of Kittel and similar wordbooks, see the critiques in J. Barr, *The Semantics of Biblical Language* (Oxford, England: Oxford University Press, 1961); P. Cotterell & M. Turner, *Linguistics and Biblical Interpretation* (Downers Grove, IL: InterVarsity. 1989), pp. 109–123.

16. L. Goppelt, *Der Erste Petrusbrief* [Literally, 'The First Letter of Peter', but translation in English is entitled 'Commentary on First Peter'], 8th ed. (Göttingen, Germany: Vandenhoeck & Ruprecht, 1978), p.309, cited in G. Schneider, 'Christianos', in EDNT, p. 478.

17. The so-called 'parting of the ways' between ancient Christianity and Judaism is increasingly recognised as having been a gradual process that stretched across several centuries. See e.g., J. Siker, "Christianity in the Second and Third Centuries", in P. F. Esler (ed.), *The Early Christian World* (London: Routledge, 2000), vol. 1, pp. 232–235; C. Setzer, *Jewish Responses to Early Christians: History and Polemics, 30–150 C.E.* (Minneapolis, MN: Fortress, 1994), pp. 182–190.

18. This approach to analysing lexical relations is adapted from S. Eggins, *An Introduction to Systemic Functional Linguistics* (London: Pinter. 1994), pp. 101–105.

19. See e.g., C. K. Barrett, *The Acts of the Apostles* (Scotland: Clark, 1994), vol. 1, p. 557.

20. On the exegetical issues and options, see J. A. Fitzmyer, *The Acts of the Apostles*, AB, vol. 31 (New York: Doubleday, 1998), pp. 477–478.

21. For bibliography see e.g., Fitzmyer (1998), pp. 478–479.

22. In this context, *Ioudaios* functions as the ethnic name of a group of persons who belong to the Jewish nation; see Louw–Nida, vol. 1, pp. 824–825, § 93.172.

23. cf. T. Penner, *In Praise of Christian Origins: Stephen and the Hellenists in Lukan Apologetic Historiography* (London: Clark, 2004), pp. 262–263, note 1.

24. See e.g., Ignatius, *Magnesians* 10.1, 3; *Philadelphians* 6.1; and *Romans* 3.3.

25. The contrast is obscured by G. Gilbert, "Roman Propaganda and Christian Identity in the Worldview of Luke-Acts", in T. Penner & C. Vander Stichele (eds.), *Contextualizing Acts: Lukan Narrative and Greco-Roman Discourse* (Atlanta: Society of Biblical Literature, 2003), p. 234. Gilbert neglects the differences between the Lucan, Petrine, and Ignatian usages of the cognate term *Christianos*.

26. See Acts 6.1, 2, 7; 9.1, 10, 19, 25, 26 (twice),38.

27. See Acts 5.11; 7.38; 8.1, 31; 9.31.

28. As *egeneto de* + a substantive in the dative + an infinitive is frequently attested in the ancient Greek translation of Hebrew biblical narrative as a way of rendering the *waw*-consecutive construction in classical Hebrew, but is almost never found in writings by pagan authors, its use in Acts and other New Testament writings possesses distinctively Jewish-biblical overtones.

29. See e.g., T. E. Klutz, *The Exorcism Stories in Luke-Acts: A Sociostylistic Reading* (Cambridge: Cambridge University Press, 2004), pp. 239–242; D. Moessner (ed.), *Jesus and the Heritage of Israel: Luke's Narrative Claim upon Israel's Legacy* (Harrisburg, PA: Trinity, 1999).

30. cf. J. Moreau, "Le nom des chrétiens" ["The name of the Christians"], *La nouvelle Clio* 1–2 (1949–50), pp. 190–192; E. J. Bickerman, "The Name of Christians", *Harvard Theological Review* 42 (1949), pp. 122–124. Occurrence of *chrematizo* in active form with middle force is rare but may be exemplified in Plutarch, *De mulierum virtutibus* 248.D, where the active form *chrematizein* can be construed as either middle in force (cf. LSJ, s.v. '*chrematizo*') or passive.

31. On the potential of the middle voice to heighten the involvement of the grammatical subject, see S. E. Porter, *Idioms of the Greek New Testament*, Biblical Languages: Greek, 2 (Sheffield, England: JSOT, 1992), pp. 67–68.

32. cf. H. Karpp, "Christennamen" ["Name for Christians"], in *Reallexikon für Antike und Christentum* (Stuttgart, Germany: Hiersemann, 1950–66), vol. 2, column 1132; H. Conzelmann, *Acts of the Apostles*, trans. J. Limburg et al. (Philadelphia, PA: Fortress, 1987), p. 88.

33. See e.g., I. H. Marshall, *The Acts of the Apostles: An Introduction and Commentary* (Grand Rapids, MI: Eerdmans, 1980), p. 203.

34. Porter (1992), p. 65.

35. *Contra* Elliott, *1 Peter*, p. 790, the hypothesis of a specifically Jewish coinage of *Christianos* would entail neither an acknowledgement by those Jews that Jesus was the Christ/Messiah nor a level of proficiency in Latin incommensurate with Jewish culture in the Diaspora. The antagonists would almost certainly have known that *Christos* was often used by Jesus' disciples as a proper name rather than as a title. And the currency of Latin suffixes in Hellenistic Greek vocabulary (cf. F. Blass, A. Debrunner, & R. W. Funk, *A Greek Grammar of the New Testament and Other Early Christian Literature* [Chicago: University of Chicago Press, 1961], p. 5), including the use of *-ianus* in the formation of party names (e.g., *Kaisarianoi, Neronianoi, Herodianoi*), would have required minimal knowledge of Latin on the part of the labellers.

36. See especially Acts 11.27–30; 13.1–3; 14.24–28; 15.22–40; 18.22–23.

37. *Pace* E. Haenchen, *The Acts of the Apostles: A Commentary*, trans. B. Noble & G. Shinn (Oxford: Basil Blackwell, 1971), p. 371, who sees the postulate of gentile identity for the labellers as needing no defence.

38. See e.g., L. Coser, *The Functions of Social Conflict* (London: Routledge & Kegan Paul, 1956), pp. 67–72.

39. In favour of Roman officials is E. Peterson, "Christianus", in E. Peterson, *Frühkirche, Judentum und Gnosis: Studien und Untersuchungen* [*Early Church, Judaism and Gnosticism: Studies and Investigations*], (Freiburg im Breisgau, Germany: Herder, 1959), pp. 73–86. On the side of the gentile populace of the city more generally is Conzelmann (1987), p. 89.

40. See also 1 Peter 4.16; Ignatius, *Romans* 3.2–3; *Magnesians* 4; *Martyrdom of Polycarp* 3.2; 10.1–2; and *Diognetus* 1; 2.6, 10; 4.6; 5.1; 6.1, 2, 3, 4, 5, 6, 7, 8, 9.

41. cf. M. Toolan, *Narrative: A Critical Linguistic Introduction* (London: Routledge, 1988), p. 73.

42. The date suggested here of the early 40s CE is extrapolated from the chronology provided in R. Jewett, "Introduction to the Pauline Corpus", in J. Barton & J. Muddiman (eds.), *The Oxford Bible Commentary* (Oxford: Oxford University Press, 2001), p. 1073.

43. As it happens, and *pace* Elliott, *1 Peter*, pp. 791 & 794, positive semantic potential is realised through the use of *Christianos* in 1 Peter 4.16, a passage that was probably composed only a short time after the writing of Acts.

44. On 'neutralisation', see B. J. Malina & J. H. Neyrey, "Conflict in Luke-Acts: Labelling and Deviance Theory", in J. H. Neyrey (ed.), *The Social World of Luke-Acts: Models for Interpretation* (Peabody, MA: Hendrickson, 1991), pp. 97–122.

45. A. T. Robertson, "The Meaning of Acts xxvi.28", *The Expository Times* 35 (1923–24), pp. 185–186. Robertson's suggestion has the virtue of not only doing justice to the grammar but also making appropriate discourse sense of Paul's reply in 28.29 ('Whether with a little or with a lot, I pray to God').

46. On the significance of inequality in social status more generally for understanding exchanges like that between Paul and Agrippa II, see B. J. Malina, *The New Testament World: Insights from Cultural Anthropology*, 3rd ed. (Louisville, KY: Westminster John Knox Press, 2001), pp. 35, 95.

47. *Contra* Elliott, *1 Peter*, pp. 790–791.

48. The English noun 'religion' has acquired a great variety of meanings, over fifty of them recognised by 1912, according to J. Z. Smith, "Religion, Religions, Religious", in M. C. Taylor (ed.), *Critical Terms for Religious Studies* (Chicago: University of Chicago Press, 1998), pp. 269–284. None of these corresponds precisely to the sense of the Greek noun *deisidaimonia* in Acts 25.19. However, the discourse meaning of the Greek word in this passage can be understood satisfactorily as relating closely to the reference in Acts 25.8 to 'the law of the Jews' and 'the [Jerusalem] temple'. Thus, while considerations of 'faith' or 'theology' are not necessarily outside the frame, matters of cult, ritual practice, and conduct are more focal.

49. On the unwavering loyalty of Agrippa II to Rome, see F. O. Garcia-Treto, "Agrippa II", in P. J. Achtemeier (ed.), *Harper's Bible Dictionary* (San Francisco: Harper & Row, 1985), pp. 15–16.

50. On Paul as Roman citizen, see Acts 16.35–39; 22.25–29; 23.27. On the rescue of Paul by Claudius Lysias, see Acts 23.6–35. And on the kind treatment of Paul by the centurion Julius, see Acts 27.1–3, 42–44.

51. See e.g., P. F. Esler, *Community and Gospel in Luke-Acts: The Social and Political Motivations of Lucan Theology* (Cambridge: Cambridge University Press, 1987), pp. 201–219.

52. See e.g., D. R. Edwards, "Surviving the Web of Roman Power: Religion and Politics in the Acts of the Apostles, Josephus, and Chariton's Chaereas and Callirhoe", in L. Alexander (ed.), *Images of Empire* (Sheffield, England: JSOT, 1991), pp. 179–201.

53. In addition to the references listed above in n. 44, see *Kerygma Petrou* 2 [Clement of Alexandria, *Stromateis* 6.5.39–41].

54. On the date of Acts, see Fitzmyer (1998), pp. 51–55.

55. Fairclough (1992), p. 186.

9 Attributing and Rejecting the Label 'Hindu' in North India

Mary Searle-Chatterjee

ACADEMIC USE OF THE WORD 'HINDU'

Much academic usage of the word 'Hindu' presumes that it refers to an identifiable community of people who share 'membership' of a 'religion', 'Hinduism'. This usage is particularly pronounced in Religious Studies circles. Neither they nor anthropologists and sociologists have shown much interest in the way Indians use the label 'Hindu'. Anthropologists who have attempted to go beyond detailed description of local practice have usually addressed some aspect of the debates generated by Louis Dumont's generalised account of *homo hierarchicus*.[1] They have attempted to delineate the key ideas and practices of what they see as the Hindu world, though others have rejected the idea that there is any kind of shared system. Chris Fuller, in a valiant attempt to synthesise the multiplicity of 'Hinduism', admitted that he doubted if 'Hinduism corresponded to any concept or category that belongs to the thinking of a large proportion of ordinary people'.[2]

Historians have shown much more interest in the use of the words 'Hindu' and 'Hinduism'. There were cognate terms in ancient Persian, though there is no evidence of the word 'Hindu' appearing in the subcontinent before the eighth century CE.[3] 'Hindu' was first used by Muslim Arab traders, then by Persian and Central Asian immigrants and warlords, not surprisingly, since identities and labels emerge in the encounter with people who are different. Initially, the term denoted any people of the region beyond the Indus. Later it referred to those who were not Muslim. The main indigenous terms for divisions among what we might now call religious groups were Brahmana and Shramana, the latter term referring to those (including the Buddhists) who denied the authority of the Brahman priests and the Vedic texts.[4] Finer subdivisions of the Brahmanas included Vedantins, Mimamsakas, Nyayakas, and so on, as discussed by Jacqueline Suthren Hirst in this volume. Elsewhere, Syed Farid Alatas states on the basis of a re-reading of the eleventh century scholar al-Biruni in the original Arabic that he referred to the *adyan* ('religions' in the plural) of India or al-Hind, one of them being that followed by the Brahmans.[5] Until about the fourteenth century the word 'Hindu' was one used by Muslims, and after that, only sparingly by others at first.[6] This does not, of course, mean that cultural complexes that are now labelled Hindu had not yet come into being. For the purposes of this chapter, the significance of this historical discussion is that one of the key conceptual indigenous distinctions made until at least the end of the first millennium CE was between followers of Brahmans and others. By the fifteenth century, the poems of the radical *nirguni* sects (particularly popular among lower castes, though sometimes written by Brahmans) drew contrasts between Hindus and Turks, or Hindus and Musulmans, in contexts that made it clear, and sometimes even specified, that something akin to 'religion' was meant rather than mere ethnic or geographic identity.[7] However, without clear documentary evidence, it should not be presumed that this use of the word 'Hindu' included 'untouchable' castes. Recent studies of the Mughal Empire during its decline in the eighteenth century have shown that upwardly mobile groups or conquering chieftains often adopted Brahmanic ritual and symbolism to gain legitimacy for a new-found status through association with prestigious older elites.[8] This led to much wider diffusion of Brahmanic ideas.

Heated debates now rage about the genesis of both the idea and the word 'Hinduism'. I refer only to some of the highlights of this debate. In a controversial but very influential work, Heinrich von Stietencron argued that the idea of 'Hindu*ism*' as a monolithic entity was a late creation, almost entirely a creation of Western Christian perspectives. It depended on the prior notions that 'religion' is a phenomenon and that there is an identifiable number of specific 'religions'. He argued that it would be more accurate in reference to the period prior to the arrival of the British to speak not of 'Hinduism' but of religions such as Vaishnavism, Saivism, and Shaktism. In his view, the word 'Hinduism' emerged in British writing as late as the nineteenth century, and was gradually internalised by Indian reformers.[9] Among others, Wagle argued against the extreme view of Stietencron, showing that in Maharashtra there was a strong awareness of unity and distinctiveness as early as the sixteenth century, though the term 'Hinduism' was never used. However, *maharashtra dharma* ('Maharashtrian law/religion/order') appeared in some texts.[10]

Having ruled the roost of Indianist academic debate for a few years, Stietencron now faces a cat among the pigeons in the form of Will Sweetman. Through careful study of seventeenth century texts in four European languages, Sweetman has not merely shown that the term 'Hinduism' appeared in the eighteenth century, but also that the idea of a specific Indian religion had emerged in Europe well before the actual term 'Hinduism' was coined. Its roots were in the early 1600s, and it had become explicit by the beginning of the eighteenth century in the work of French Jesuits whose practice of sending letters to one another from the four corners of the subcontinent had led them to the idea there was a region-wide 'religion' that could not just be subsumed under the older, wider category of 'heathenism' (or gentilism). The most important of Sweetman's arguments has been that

European observers were not imposing their own categories ('religion'/ 'religions') on practice and belief in India, since it was their encounter with Indian informants that led them to develop the idea of Hinduism (even though the word came later). Far from imposing Western concepts on others, it was this engagement with Indians that had a major role in generating the *modern* use of the English words 'religion'/'religions'. This new usage was not an outcome of Christian ideas; on the contrary, it implied a certain detachment from Christian tradition. A similar usage had emerged in Europe several times before, in periods when contact with other cultures had engendered a more sceptical climate. Sweetman refered to Peter Biller's work, showing that in the twelfth and thirteenth centuries something like the modern notion of 'religions' is apparent in the development of nouns such as 'Christian-ismus', 'Judaismus', 'gentilitas' and 'Saracenia'. The rise of Waldensian and Catharinian sects within Christendom and the advance of the Mongols combined to create an awareness of religious plurality.[11] Graham Ward has discussed examples of this in texts of the thirteenth century.[12] Sweetman also pointed out that the idea of 'India' as we now think of it was only emerging in the seventeenth century. Without the idea of a unitary 'India' there could hardly be any idea of a specific Indian religion.

Talal Asad and Timothy Fitzgerald argued some time ago that the development of the modern usage of the word 'religion' was primarily part of a process that enabled emerging capitalist markets to be seen as separate from, and hence unimpeded by, the constraints of moral values.[13] They now have to line up against those who stress the role of engagement with unfamiliar peoples and cultures. Asad's later work had shifted towards an emphasis on the role of cultural encounter.[14] Debates on the emergence of the modern Western idea of 'religion' and 'religions' are also discussed in the chapter in this volume by Francesca Tarocco. Nonetheless, historians and anthropologists alike have generally assumed that whatever the situation in the past, today Indians and Euro-Americans use the label 'Hindu' in roughly similar ways.

'UNTOUCHABLE' SWEEPERS IN 1970S VARANASI/BANARAS

In 1971 when I started several years of fieldwork among 'untouchable' urban Sweepers in Varanasi, the 'holy city of the Hindus', I assumed that I was studying a *Hindu* caste. I was aware that Sweepers in some other neighbourhoods had become Muslims and that in some parts of India Sweepers were Christians. My Sweepers were clearly neither Muslim nor Christian, so I was puzzled when I heard them talking about 'Hindus' as if they were people other than themselves, for example, 'the people who live across the road'. Luckily I was able to stop myself saying, 'But aren't you

Hindus?' and instead asked in classic ignorant outsider fashion, 'Who are Hindus?' Their reply astounded me. 'Hindus', they said, 'are Brahmans and Thakurs' (Thakurs are local land-owning castes).[15] At first I could hardly believe the evidence of my ears. It was some time before I found an earlier reference to something similar elsewhere in North India.[16] For Sweepers, 'Hindu' was a status term. It was used as part of a binary set. '*Choti*' ('small') powerless people or castes like themselves were contrasted with '*Hindu*' or '*bari*' ('big') people of power and prestige associated with Brahmanic values. This was the usage of ordinary, nonpoliticised sweepers. 'Hindu', then, for the low castes was a class or status term. It was a term applied only to others.

It is not uncommon for minority subgroups to refer inadvertently to majorities, or dominant groups (in this case, the 'twice-born', 'high' castes) as though they constitute the whole. The British sometimes class themselves as European, sometimes not. Such terms are segmentary and may be more or less inclusive in reference. However, in the case of the 'low' caste reference to Hindus as people other than themselves, something more is involved. Even when Muslims were present, Sweepers did not shift to referring to themselves as 'Hindus' as I shall show later.

'HIGH' CASTES IN 1970S VARANASI

The 'high' castes in 1970s Varanasi did in some contexts think of themselves as *Hindus* and many would fairly quickly identify themselves as such to foreigners. However, for them, 'Hindu' did not mean the same as it did to the 'low' castes. It was used in terms of a different set of binary oppositions. Hindus were contrasted with foreigners, or with people with foreign links, rather than with people of low status. The 'low' castes were not so much excluded from the category as forgotten or invisible. Hindus were Indians who were neither Musulman nor Christian. At first sight this resembles common Western usage. The word 'Hindu' appears to denote a 'religious' group. However, the term is used broadly and often subsumes traditions that foreigners would see as non-Hindu, but that have their origins on Indian soil, such as 'Jainism', 'Buddhism', and 'Sikhism'. Everyone in India is, by default, a Hindu, except those who identify with some tradition whose geographical origin is outside South Asia. Parsees are a partial exception in that their origin was outside India yet they are often subsumed under the label 'Hindu'. They no longer look to a geographical region beyond India, having arrived as refugees. Even so, a Parsee identity is sometimes contrasted with a 'Hindu' or Indic one such as 'Marathi', even though many Parsees live in Marathi-speaking areas, and speak Marathi. A 'Hindu' then is not someone with a particular set of beliefs and practices, but rather someone who is a true son of the soil, not in any way a foreigner. The term 'Musulman' is often counter-posed to a regional, or territorial, rather than 'religious' identity. Someone not hostile to Muslims might say, 'She is not Muslim, she is Indian', or in Bengal, the question 'Is he Bengali?' could receive the answer, 'No he is Muslim', even though the Muslim in question was Bengali-speaking, born and bred in Bengal. In urban usage, such geographic terms are often replaced with the term 'Hindu'. 'Hindu', then, for the 'high' castes is a territorial or ethnic term. It refers to those whose commitments are only to what are seen as indigenous traditions. It is a term applied to the self.

THE NINETEENTH CENTURY

In the nineteenth century there was less difference between 'high' and 'low' caste usage than there was in 1970s Varanasi. The 'high' castes used the word *Hindu* to refer to people who paid respect to Brahmanic values rather than to traditions that had originated outside India, but only if they were of 'high' caste. *Hindus* were contrasted with Chamars ('Leatherworkers') or some other such term indicating low status quite as much as they were with Muslims or Christians. A 'Hindu' was a person 'from a good family' who, even if not making much use of Brahman priests, did at least not challenge their authority in the way that Muslims or Christians did. In the early 1900s, and no doubt much later too, 'high' castes were still using *Hindu* in contrast to Chamar.[17] This was the same as the 1970s Sweepers' usage. In Bengal even today the main conceptual opposition for both high and low castes is between *boro/bhadra lok* and *choto lok* ('big' and 'small' people). This resembles low caste usage in the Uttar Pradesh region around Varanasi. There was also an alternative nineteenth century high caste usage whereby the label 'Hindu' was applied to any Indian, including Muslims and Christians. This resembled the purely geographic usage of the Arabs and Turks when they first arrived in India; it also reveals the continuing importance of a notion of territoriality in 'high' caste understanding.[18]

In the 1930s neither Gandhians nor members of the paramilitary nationalist organisation the Rashtriya Sevak Sangh (RSS, a 'Hindu' nationalist movement known in the United Kingdom as the Hindu Sevak Sangh or HSS) took the Hindu identity of 'untouchables' for granted. It had to be created.[19] During Gandhi's 1932 fast against the 'untouchable' activist Dr. Ambedkar's insistence on separate electorates for 'untouchables', his supporters urgently called a conference for 'Hindu and untouchable leaders'.[20]

British understanding of the word 'Hindu' was altogether different. By the mid-nineteenth century Britons took it for granted that all individuals have a separate and identifiable 'religion' that is central to their identity and derives from a longstanding, scripturally-based tradition adhered to by large numbers of people. A 'religion' was a 'packaged' entity, a system of practice and belief.[21] When they began in the Indian Census of 1871 to classify people in terms of 'religion', they were surprised to find how difficult this was. It was tiresome that many Indians did not seem to know what their 'religion' was, perhaps just one more illustration, they thought, of how muddled the place was. The British assumed that anyone who was neither Muslim nor Christian should be classed as 'Hindu'. Census takers in the Punjab were instructed that Chuhras ('low' castes) who were not Muslims or Christians and who did not classify themselves as any other religion should be classified as 'Hindus'. Many high caste census collectors had initially refused to classify 'low' castes as Hindus, contrary to British expectations.[22]

During the nineteenth century, in a context of internal elite competition, movements for nation formation and self-determination, both the denotation and connotation of the word 'Hindu' for the high castes began to change due to the influence of British systems of categorisation. Eventually, electoral considerations would become paramount. Nationalist 'high' caste 'Hindus' began in some public contexts to label 'low' castes as 'Hindus' in opposition to Muslims and Christians. This usage involved at least partially taking on board the nineteenth-century British assumption that all individuals have a distinct primary identity that can be classified as 'religious' and that 'Hindu', 'Muslim', and 'Christian' are examples of such identities. Categories like Ravidasi, Vaishnava, or Shakta were not as acceptable; Chamar ('leatherworker') or Banarsi ('resident of Varanasi') even less so. Further discussion of the way that nationalist leaders in colonised countries have often taken on board some of the assumptions of the imperial powers is found in the essays in this volume by Andreas Christmann and Francesca Tarocco.

CENSUS DISTORTIONS IN BRITAIN TODAY

History repeats itself and a new version of the old problems of census categorisation has emerged in Britain today. Ravidasis and Valmikis find they are not listed under 'religions'.[23] Gujerati or Hindi are seen as even less acceptable responses to questions about 'religion', whether in the census, by teachers, or even by researchers. The cake of identity and community can be cut in many different ways and 'religion' may not be the obvious knife to use. This was seen in my discussions in English in the 1990s with Punjabi Dalits (the term for former 'untouchable' castes initially used by activists and now used more widely) now living in Britain. A Ravidasi coach driver, born in the Punjab, but living in Southall, produced the following comment. 'I never was a Hindu but I do have a friend who is an Indian' ('Indian' here means what the British would call 'Hindu'). A Ravidasi travel agent in Southall said 'My clients are from all communities. They are my friends; I see them regularly, Muslims, Sikhs, Hindus, Gujeratis'. Here regional/linguistic origin is seen as being of the same order of classification as 'religion'. According to Parmila in Manchester, 'The *Hindus* wear sarees and speak Hindi, not like Punjabis'. A woman clerical worker in Southall commented that, 'English people have no idea how many religions there are in India. They know about Punjabis or Gujeratis or Muslims but not about Ravidasis'.

An advice worker in Birmingham brought out even more of the complexities. 'How I think of myself depends on who I'm talking to. To English people, I'm an Indian and a Punjabi. In Punjab, I'm someone from England. When Indians ask I say I'm Valmiki. You could say my religion is Valmiki but English people say Valmiki is not a religion. You could say I'm Hindu. But really the Hindus were Aryans. We were descended from the Nagas who were defeated and tortured by the Aryans so we had to do jobs like sweeping. My father was born a Hindu, then he became a Sikh then an *Arya Samaji* [a member of a reformist 'Hindu' organisation], then a Communist'.

In these quotations we see that nationality, region, language, 'religion', and politics are used interchangeably as examples of identity, as a single set of categories. Gujerati is a category of the same order as Muslim. It was, and still is, as difficult to label Indians in terms of an alien concept ('name your religion') as it is for Britons to respond to such injunctions as 'name your guru', 'name your paternal *gotra*', or 'of whom are you a devotee?' Defenders of a 'religion' question in the modern British Census need to think long and hard about the distortions it produces. Many of us not of Indian origin also find no home in the straitjacket of categories provided.

NORTH INDIA FROM THE 1970S TO THE PRESENT

For the 'high' castes by the 1970s the 'lowest' castes, unless they clearly specified otherwise, were now 'Hindus' by default, that is 'of the soil', though still seen as of doubtful character and inferior worth. They were thought to be linked, albeit loosely, if only as inferior clients or appendages. Activists from the RSS, a right-wing 'Hindu' nationalist organisation, would visit Sweeper slums for 'uplift' work and would assure the residents that they now were or could be Hindus, especially if they became cleaner and stopped eating meat.

Yet culture, of course, is not the same as identity. Sweepers may or may not have previously been part of the same shared cultural world as the 'high' castes (this is a matter of some controversy). But they were now being pressured to adopt a new identity, to label themselves as Hindus in contrast to Muslims and Christians. They were being asked to use the word Hindu in a new way, to adopt the 'high' caste territorial usage. Missionaries from the RSS encouraged them to avoid any personal names with Arabic or Persian roots. Some 'low' caste individuals or groups saw this as an opportunity for acceptance and assimilation; others simply persisted with their older linguistic usage. In adjacent neighbourhoods, Muslim activists were similarly urging residents to adopt names with Arabic, Persian, or Turkish roots.

For the 'low' castes, use of the term Hindu is not now a neutral descriptive act but is associated with stereotyping and divisiveness. In 1986 I spent six months studying Hindu/Muslim relations in Varanasi. In the course of a rather rushed exploration of the links between caste and 'religion', I neglected the professional anthropological rule of using only the concepts produced by my informants. I asked several groups of Sweeper children in a non-Muslim neighbourhood whether they were Hindu or Muslim. Their clothing bore no mark of any particular identity. They were unable to answer. Adults showed disapproval of my questions and said such things as, 'It is not good to talk like that', 'We are not like that', or 'We are all mixed up'. By the 1990s, 'high' caste 'religious' nationalists of the Sangh Pariwar, the Hindu Mahasabha, the Rashtriya Sevak Sangh, and the Vishva Hindu Parishad, would sometimes refer to Hindus as a single *jati*, that is, a single caste or species. This was a reversal of the old idea by which only 'high', 'clean' castes were Hindus, but a continuation of the idea that a Hindu is a person who is not in any sense foreign. For the 'high' caste nationalists, Hindus would in the natural state of affairs be dominant, while others, such as Muslims and Christians, would be in a client relationship. Non-Hindus are by definition aliens, lacking respect for the ancestors and the traditions of the past, and hence potentially subversive towards the status quo and the rightful social order. That is why communists are often classified with Muslims and Christians. A Hindu can be an atheist; his beliefs are not important. Nor is his private behaviour important. But he cannot be someone who flaunts disrespect in public by expressing commitment to Gods, teachers, or traditions originating from outside the subcontinent. To be Hindu is to show respect. 'High' castes object to religious conversion not because they want to police the private domain, but because they see it as a public expression of defiance and insubordination, as indeed it often is.

This new more inclusive usage has now become entrenched among many of the upper castes and classes in the context of growing right-wing nationalism that seeks to mobilise a large constituency to resist pressures, not as in the nineteenth century, from rival elite Muslim landowners, but now from the lower classes, a sizable chunk of whom are Muslim. The new usage is also an expression of the elites' search for self-respect in a globalised world economy dominated by English classifications and in which Euro-American arrogance is only too evident. 'Modern Westerners' (or at least mid-twentieth century ones) appear to have clear religious labels, core scriptures, centralised religious leaders, and defined institutions, and to have also abandoned 'superstitions'. A 'proper' religion, it is thought, is needed if one is to hold one's head high; a nuclear bomb is needed for the same reason. It is not surprising, then, that heavy pressure to change practice comes from the new middle classes of high caste origin, particularly expatriate Indians in Britain and the United States. Drastic measures are needed to numb the running sore of racial stigma. Nonresident Indians find their anti-Muslim prejudices confirmed by the British public.

In recent decades there has also been a great increase in the visibility of 'low' castes both in politics and in literature. India's massive programme of positive discrimination, the largest in the world, has now produced an educated class of 'untouchables' or Dalits. The disappearance of India's single party system and the growth of electoral competition have given new clout to numerically large low caste groups and voting blocs.[24] For some Dalit activists, the taken for granted, private, usage of 'Hindu' as a term applying only to the high castes has been made the basis of a polemical and *public* challenge to the status quo. Kancha Ilaiah's book *Why I am Not a Hindu* is perhaps the best-known example of this.[25] Here the word 'Hindu' is not just used to denote elite groups but also to refer to a posited 'religion' (in the modern Western 'packaged' sense) with specific beliefs and practices. The writer delineates what he considers to be the distinct traditional values and 'religion' of the Shudra 'low' caste communities.

A study of Punjabi villages published in 1988 showed that patterns of 'low' caste self-identification varied with their economic situation. Groups described themselves as 'untouchables' rather than as 'Hindus' in villages where they were extremely poor, but also in villages where prosperity had given birth to rebelliousness. In villages where there was a 'middling' situation they were more likely to describe themselves as 'Hindus,' probably a mark of assimilationist aspirations.[26] The Sweepers of Varanasi fit this pattern. Though their income as municipal sanitation workers is not bad, given the visibly polluting nature of their work any hope of raising their social status is nonexistent. Their approach was similar to that of the very poor rural Sweepers in the Punjabi study. Other Dalits assert a non-Hindu identity by pursuing the alternative path of 'conversion,' mainly to Buddhism though occasionally to Christianity, Islam, or guru-led 'sects'. But the word 'conversion' may not be appropriate if 'low' castes never thought of themselves as 'Hindu' in the first place.

CONNOTATIONS OF THE WORD 'HINDU'

It is sometimes useful to distinguish between denotation and connotation. Changes in connotation often lead to a redrawing of group boundaries, and hence of the group denoted. That has been true of high caste usage of the word 'Hindu'. For some members of 'low' castes, on the other hand, the denotation of 'Hindu' has remained unchanged even though the connotation of the word is now different. I shall now discuss the connotations of the label 'Hindu' and related representations in a particular set of narratives concerning the early history of the subcontinent.

As I have shown, in the nineteenth-century nationalist 'high' castes (or 'big' people) began to widen the denotation of the label 'Hindu', as well as to adopt new ideas about what were appropriate ways of performing and thinking about rituals. They also began to make use of new narratives produced by British scholars and writers. According to these narratives, nomadic invaders from Central Asia to the north-west who were named Aryans descended on the subcontinent in the second millennium BCE, bringing complex literatures and philosophies in the Sanskrit language. These narratives were speculative constructions derived from linguistic evidence showing that Sanskrit and the languages of northern India had affinities with languages from the north-west, including those of Europe. Western orientalists waxed lyrical on the glories of the ancient culture revealed in Sanskrit texts, a world so different, they thought, from the modern mess that had justified the British in taking over. A racist tendency to assume that peoples from the north and west were culturally superior undoubtedly made these theories of ancient invasion more plausible to Europeans. Undeterred by this, many of the 'high' castes felt a new sense of pride from these scholarly discoveries and adopted the view that the presumed Aryan invaders were the ancestors of the 'high' castes. By extension, the 'low' castes must be the descendants of the culturally inferior indigenous people who had not produced a vast poetic and philosophic literature. A vivid and contentious expression of the idea that all great things originated outside the subcontinent appeared in the mid-1960s in Nirad Chaudhuri's book, *The Continent of Circe*.[27]

It was not long before some radical 'low' caste activists picked up on a contradiction between 'high' caste narratives of origin and labelling of groups. If 'Hindus' are defined territorially as indigenous people (unlike Muslims and Christians) with true commitment to their homeland and hence rights to the land, how is it that the 'high' castes adhered to the myths of alien Aryan Central Asian origin? If the narratives are correct, then Dalits are the true indigenous people who have lost their rightful position due to the oppression of the alien invader 'high' castes. This view was encouraged by missionaries who claimed that Brahman priests were alien oppressors. Mahatma Jotirao Phule, an extraordinarily dynamic and creative nineteenth-century Maharashtrian polymath and 'low' caste (though not 'untouchable') campaigner was the first to create major structural transformations in the meaning of the Aryan myths. He did this by highlighting one muted element in the mythic structure and using it as the basis for a new version of the narrative. Invasion, rather than culture, now became the key term. The cultured Aryan colonist was now the brutal alien conqueror who oppressed the indigenous people and their cultures. The low castes now become the upholders of the true and suppressed Indic religion.[28] This is a modification of the older 'low' caste usage in which Hindus were the elites allied with the Brahmans. But it is not quite an inversion of the kind produced by the marginal groups discussed by Philip Alexander elsewhere in this volume. Phule's ideas continue to resurface periodically. Outside Maharashtra they have been known mostly only by educated activists or by politicised 'untouchable' groups, particularly Leatherworkers who have been influenced by the Mahars, the large Maharashtrian 'untouchable' group into which Dr. Ambedkar was born.[29]

In the 1920s similar ideas emerged in the Punjab. It had become a highly politicised region with four potential blocs of voters with rough numerical parity, comprising Sikhs, Muslims, 'high' caste Hindus, and 'low' castes. Who would the 'low' castes side with?[30] The Arya Samaj began a purification (*shuddhi*) movement to 're-admit' the fallen 'low' castes back into the 'Hindu' fold. All manner of sects and groups were players in the field. The 'untouchable' Ad-Dharmis (followers of the 'original' rule, order, or 'religion') insisted they were the descendants of the indigenous inhabitants of India who had preserved the original *dharma* in the face of Aryan ('Hindu') 'high' caste oppression. 'We are not Hindus, and we are not part of Hinduism'.[31] By 1931 they had succeeded in getting themselves classified as a 'religion' in the Census of India.[32] In Uttar Pradesh, a similar group described itself (and continues to do so) as Adi-Hindus. In this last usage there is a complete reversal of denotation. The Dalits now are the 'Hindus'.

Juergensmeyer argued that the idea that the 'low' castes were descendants of the original inhabitants was new, and inspired by the Adi-Dravida ('original Dravidian') movement of South India, in which Brahmans were seen as alien North Indian oppressors. He states that the earliest records of such a usage of *adi* are from the early twentieth century.[33] Phule's writings were of course earlier, though not widely known. It is possible that there are yet older roots to this. In rural areas Dalits are often night watchmen and are thought to have an ancient knowledge of the boundaries of village land.

In 1970s Varanasi, Sweepers were more interested in Trade Union activity as a means of improving their lot than in myths of Aryan origin. This was not the case among Chamars ('leatherworkers'), a numerically much larger group, many of whom called themselves Ravidasis and regularly visited Ravidasi temples. The largest temple on the Ganges riverfront is now dedicated to the saint Ravidas. It was financed with the help of contributions from Ravidasis in Britain, particularly in Birmingham. It is, then, not only groups with power who use, and change, labels. Public challenges to the labels used by the powerful are expressed when the possibility of political change arises. The spread of new media, enabling communication across vast distances, and changes in self-perception, the growth of a large educated class of 'low' caste origin, and the growing importance of elections have led to changes in India in labelling and representation of both self and others.

The sacred myth of Central Asian Aryan origin has been attractive to many Indians of 'high' caste as it implied a racial affinity with Indo-Europeans, including the prestigious British rulers. Radical 'low' caste writers' reconstructions of these narratives have exposed the contradiction in 'high' caste mythology and reasoning. Those who claim to be the descendants of ancient invaders cannot use the argument of alien origin to question the citizenship rights of Muslims, some of whom are the descendants of more recent immigrants or colonists. So the religious nationalist 'high' castes are moving on again. As early as the 1920s, Gowalkar was arguing that the original home of the Aryans was not in Central Asia, but in the sub-continent.[34] The myth of alien origin is increasingly being abandoned. It is argued that the early Sanskrit Vedic scriptures were all composed in India and that the 'Aryans' were actually indigenous. This new narrative is now appealing because it enables Hindu nationalists to be logically consistent in their argument that only the truly indigenous deserve full civic rights. They, the supposed descendants of the Aryans, they can now argue, are, and have always been, indigenous (see Table 1: 'Who is Hindu?').

There is in any case now general agreement among reputable historians of India that there was no single cataclysmic invasion of people speaking a different language in early times, but more likely many small migrations over long periods of time. Languages can even spread to new areas without any large migration of people, though this is unusual. The view that Sanskrit is linked to languages of the north-west rather than to those of South India is still accepted by scholars. The fact that the early texts contain references to flora, fauna, ecology, and technologies not found in the North Indian plains does pose problems for those who wish to claim that all great things developed within the subcontinent, hence the death threats to Sanskritists and archaeologists engaged in this area of debate.

As seen in Table 1, the changing narratives about the Aryans in ancient India, with their inversions and structural transformations, contain a debate about citizenship and dominance, rights to reside on the land, and rights to dominate the land and its residents.[35] I use a Lévi-Straussian structuralist method of representing inversions and transformations in basic 'sacred' narratives.[36] Unlike Lévi-Strauss, I show that variations can be linked to particular classes and political groups, and that they change, interactively, over time, in the course of political struggles. The table is a heuristic device to highlight key changes in the use of the label 'Hindu'; inevitably it simplifies a multitude of complex processes.

Can one say that that since the participants in this debate share a vocabulary they are part of the same bounded cultural or even 'religious' world, whether or not they describe themselves as 'Hindu'? If we adopt such a fluid notion of culture we would have to include the British as part of that culture or 'religion'. The British in India in the nineteenth and twentieth centuries were major players in the emergence of the ideas discussed in this essay, although their contribution sometimes took the form of a monologue that was deaf to anything else. They were certainly heard by others. They were not 'invisible' or 'ignored' others, like the *mlecchas* to whom the eighth-century Shankara referred, as Jacqueline Suthren Hirst discusses in this volume. Even now the British (and Americans) continue to be an influential, if invisible, presence at debates among 'Hindus'. They are what might be called 'effective' others, even if not always 'opponent' others. The fact that a particular group such as the nineteenth-century British did not always hear what their opponents were saying cannot be considered a criterion for regarding them as external to the magic ('Hindu'?) circle of those who debated Indian 'sacred' narratives since a similar deafness was also found in 1970s Varanasi among the 'high' castes, many of whom were unaware of 'low' caste usage of the word 'Hindu'. It is not uncommon for lower status groups to be much better informed about their superiors than the latter are about them. This has been demonstrated in studies of 'race relations' in the American South, and in gender studies elsewhere. It is inconsistent to say that the 'high' castes were in some way more party to the debate than the British. Yet this is what conventional use of such reifying concepts as 'religion', culture', 'tradition', and 'Hindu' would seem to imply. It might be argued, though not convincingly I feel, that despite such inequality in comprehension the different castes understand the conversation in a way that the British did/do not, that as soon as the possibility of public argument developed with the growth of electoral democracy and the spread of new media enabling communication across vast distances, there was shared understanding of what was at stake so that where there was misunderstanding it was wilful and strategic.

The notion of 'religion' is as problematic as the notion of 'society'. Marilyn Strathern argued that the idea of 'society' makes us think in terms of entities. It obscures the fact that all action and thought is relational and it makes it seem as if relationships are secondary not primary to human existence. 'The concept of society has existed in anthropological accounts as a rhetorical device, as a closure on ethnographic narrative'.[37] The practice of the Western academic discipline of Religious Studies, in so far as it has reified 'religions', has a similar effect. In this case, it makes us see the British as external rather than as central to debates about the use of the word 'Hindu'. By inadvertently using modern 'high' caste usage of the word 'Hindu', itself partly a product of nineteenth-century British influence, it has also provided useful ammunition for right-wing groups in political contests in the subcontinent. It is anything but neutral.

Like any one else, English speakers from outside the subcontinent will naturally use their own indigenous categories, such as 'religion', to describe what they find in India. It is more problematic when they use a term such as 'Hindu' in their own way without recognising that it was and is used in a variety of different ways in the region where it emerged.

In summary, then, Hindu has had a different denotation at different levels of the status system, with some groups using it to refer to a status category, others to refer to a territorial group. However, both the denotations and connotations of the label continue to change, since it is formed in the context of a political struggle involving other sets of labels. As the meaning of the label changes, so too do the numbers of those applying it to themselves. The main parties to the conflict over this label are the 'high'

Table 1. Who is Hindu?

	1600s	1800s	1920s	1970s	1990s/2000s
Low caste usage	Hindu = (1) High caste follower of Brahmans	Hindu = (1) High caste follower of Brahmans	Hindu = (1) High caste follower of Brahmans	Hindu = (1) High caste follower of Brahmans	Hindu = (1) High caste follower of Brahmans
Low caste radical usage			Hindu = (1) High caste follower of Brahmans, + (2) of Aryan + (3) Foreign + (4) Brutal Conqueror origin	Hindu = (1) High caste follower of Brahmans + (2) of Aryan + (3) Foreign + (4) Brutal Conqueror origin	Hindu = (A) (1) High caste follower of Brahmans, + (2) of Aryan + (3) Foreign + (4) Brutal Conqueror origin OR = (B) (6) Indigenous people who are the lowest castes
High caste usage	Hindu = (1) High caste follower of Brahmans	Hindu = (A) (5a) Indian even if Muslim or Christian OR = (B) (1) High caste follower of Brahmans +(2) of Aryan + (3) Central Asian origin.	Hindu = (5b)True Indian, Loyal to Indian Traditions that is not a Muslim or Christian + (2) esp. of Aryan + (3) Central Asian origin	Hindu = (5b)True Indian, Loyal to Indian Traditions that is not a Muslim or Christian + (2) esp. of Aryan + (3) Central Asian origin	Hindu = (5b)True Indian, Loyal to Indian Traditions that is not a Muslim or Christian + (2) of Aryan + (7) (for Hindutva) of indigenous origin
British usage	N/A	Hindu = (8) follower of Hindu religion	Hindu = (8) follower of Hindu religion	Hindu = (8) follower of Hindu religion	Hindu = (8) follower of Hindu religion

castes, 'low' castes, and the British. Thus we see that it is not only groups with power who change classifications, since challenges to the labels used by the powerful are expressed when there are changes in self-perception, in this case with the growth of a large educated class of 'low' caste origin with the possibility of political change through elections. However, except in the diaspora, none of these usages of the word 'Hindu' are linked with ethics, the search for peace, or transcendence of the self, even though South Asian culture is extraordinarily rich in the exploration and discussion of such matters. Such discussion would be more likely to take the form of 'How may I find peace?' or 'Who or where or what is god?' or 'Who is fit to be a guru?' and not 'What does my religion require?' or 'What does it mean to be a Hindu?'

NOTES

1. L. Dumont, *Homo Hierarchicus: The Caste System and Its Implications* (London: Vikas, 1970).
2. C. Fuller, *The Camphor Flame: Popular Hinduism and Society in India* (Princeton, NJ: Princeton University Press, 1992), p. 10.
3. R. Thapar, *Early India: From its Origins to 1300* (Delhi, India: Penguin, 2002).
4. R. Thapar, "Imagined Religious Communities: Ancient History and the Modern Search for a Hindu Identity", *Modern Asian Studies* 23, 2 (1989), pp. 209–31.
5. S. F. Alatas, "Problematising the Construction of Hinduism and the Concept of Religion: Al-Biruni and the Religion of Hind" (University of Singapore, unpublished manuscript, 2005).
6. R. M. Eaton, *The Rise of Islam and the Bengal Frontier, 1204–1760* (Berkeley: University of California Press, 1996) and Thapar (2002), pp. 439–440.
7. D. N. Lorenzen, *Bhakti Religion in North India: Community Identity and Political Action* (Albany: State University of New York Press, 1995), p. 12 and D. N. Lorenzen, "Who Invented Hinduism?" in J. E. Llewellyn (ed.), *Defining Hinduism* (London: Equinox, 2005), pp. 70–73.
8. S. Bayly, *Caste, Society and Politics in India from the Eighteenth Century to the Modern Age* (Cambridge: Cambridge University Press, 1999).
9. H. von Stietencron, "Hinduism and the Proper Use of a Deceptive Term", in G. D. Sontheimer & H. Kulke (eds.), *Hinduism Reconsidered* (Delhi, India: Manohar, 1989, pp. 11–27. See also H. von Stietencron, "Religious Configurations in Pre-Muslim India and the Modern Concept of Hinduism", in V. Dalmia & H. von Stietencron (eds.), *Representing Hinduism: the Construction of Religious Traditions and National Identity* (Delhi, India: Sage, 1995), pp. 51–81.
10. N. Wagle, "Hindu-Muslim Interactions in Mediaeval Maharashtra," in Sontheimer & Kulke (1989), pp. 134–52.
11. W. Sweetman, *Mapping Hinduism: 'Hinduism' and the Study of Indian Religions, 1600–1776* (Halle, Germany: Franckeschen Stiftungen, 2003), pp. 14–30, especially pp. 19–20.
12. G. Ward, "The Politics of Paradise: Language and Power in the Formation of Religion" (Manchester University, unpublished manuscript, 2005).
13. T. Asad, *Genealogies of Religion: Discipline and Reasons of Power in Christianity and Islam* (Baltimore: John Hopkins University Press, 1993);

T. Fitzgerald, "'Hinduism' and the 'World Religion' Fallacy", *Religion* 20 (1999), pp. 108–118.

14. T. Asad, *Formations of the Secular* (Stanford, CA: Stanford University Press, 2003).

15. M. Searle-Chatterjee, *Reversible Sex Roles: The Special Case of Banaras Sweepers* (Oxford: Pergamon, 1981), p. 48.

16. O. Lynch, *The Politics of Untouchability: Social Mobility and Social Change in a City of India* (Columbia: Columbia University Press, 1969), p. 162.

17. G. Pandey, "Which of us are Hindus?", in G. Pandey (ed.), *Hindus and Others* (Delhi, India: Viking, 1993), pp. 238–269, especially p. 246.

18. An example of this is 'Hindu-Muhammadan' in the 1911 Census, cited in D. Ludden (ed.), *Contesting the Nation* (Philadelphia: University of Pennsylvania Press, 1996), p. 279.

19. P. Van der Veer, *Religious Nationalism: Hindus and Muslims in India* (Berkeley: University of California Press, 1994), p. 28.

20. C. Jaffrelot, *Dr. Ambedkar and Untouchability: Analysing and Fighting Caste* (London: Hurst, 2005), p. 65.

21. R. King, *Orientalism and Religion: Postcolonial Theory, India and 'The Mystic East'* (London: Routledge, 1999).

22. *Report on the Census of British India, taken on 17th February, 1881*, 1–17 (London: HMSO, 1883); M. Juergensmeyer, *Religious Rebels in the Punjab: The Social Vision of Untouchables* (Delhi, India: Ajanta, 1988), p. 72.

23. E. Nesbitt, "Pitfalls in Religious Taxonomy: Hindus, Sikhs, Ravidasis and Valmikis", *Religion Today* 6, 1 (1990), pp. 9–12.

24. L. I. Rudolph & S. H. Rudolph, *In Pursuit of Lakshmi: The Political Economy of the Indian State* (Chicago: Chicago University Press, 1987); C. Jaffrelot, *India's Silent Revolution: the Rise of the Lower Castes in North India* (London: Hurst, 2003).

25. K. Ilaiah, *Why I am Not a Hindu* (Calcutta, India: Samya, 1996).

26. Juergensmeyer (1988), pp. 16–17.

27. N. Chaudhuri, *Continent of Circe* (Oxford: Oxford University Press, 1966).

28. R. O'Hanlon, *Caste, Conflict and Ideology: Mahatma Jotirao Phule and Low Caste Protest in Nineteenth Century Western India* (Cambridge: Cambridge University Press, 1985), p. 141.

29. Dr. Ambedkar, scholar, lawyer, campaigner, and cabinet minister of 'untouchable' origin, was one of the giants of early twentieth-century India. He also wrote the Indian constitution.

30. Juergensmeyer (1988).

31. Quotation from Ad Dharm Mandal cited in J. Leslie, *Authority and Meaning in Indian Religions: Hinduism and the Case of Valmiki* (Aldershot, England: Ashgate, 2003), p. 56.

32. Juergensmeyer (1988), pp. 24–26.

33. Juergensmeyer (1988), p. 25.

34. G. Omvedt, *Dalit Visions: the Anti-Caste Movement and the Construction of an Indian Identity* (Hyderabad, India: Orient Longman, 1995), p. 10.

35. See the similarities in structural analyses of the Old Testament in E. Leach & D. A. Aycock, *Structuralist Interpretations of Biblical Myth* (Cambridge: Cambridge University Press, 1983).

36. C. Lévi-Strauss, *Structural Anthropology* (Harmondsworth, England: Penguin, 1973).

37. M. Strathern, "The Concept of Society is Theoretically Obsolete", in T. Ingold (ed.), *Key Debates in Anthropology* (London: Routledge, 1996), pp. 60–66, especially p. 64.

10 Idiom, Genre, and the Politics of Self-Description on the Peripheries of Persian

Nile Green

BETWEEN SOURCES AND SOCIETIES

Like paintings that attempt to mimic the reality of the world on canvas, the written source materials used by historians may be understood as attempts to capture the nature of the social world in the fundamentally different world of writing.[1] For writing creates a world in which language, genre, authorial intent, and context conspire to shape the appearance of its inhabitants. The challenge put forward by literary and critical theory to the working practice of historians and other scholars of 'religion' has led them to reassess the relationship between writing and the world, forcing them to question whether written accounts should be seen as sources on 'events' or merely as part of an autonomous realm of intertextuality. This debate, which has provoked the so-called literary and linguistic 'turns' in historical studies, has been highly effective in finally shattering the illusory mirror that positivist historians once assumed their written 'sources' held up to the past. Historians have been encouraged to reconsider the old philosophical question of the relationship between representations (art, writing, discourse) and reality (however this is conceived), and hence to reconsider the epistemological foundations of historical knowledge. It is not my intention to iterate a position of radical historical uncertainty, nor to suggest that writing occupies a platonic and self-sufficient world of its own, for the articulation of some kind of connection between texts and the societies that produce them must remain a prerequisite of the project of history. But discerning the nature of that connection so as to sense the world beyond the text requires a suitable method of reading source materials, and it is in this field of hermeneutics that the most profitable engagement between historians and theorists can emerge.

Offered in this essay is a sketch of the ways in which language and its entrapment in the power relations of its users have affected the written representation of different holy men and their associated cultural practices in societies whose literatures have been shaped by the discursive tradition of Islam.[2] By discursive tradition I mean here a body of terms, concepts and categories for rendering the world knowable, but which however influential or even hegemonic is never the sole frame of reference for any society. Given the close links between Muslim institutions and written learning in so much of Asian history, the discursive traditions of Islam and their originally Arabic literary expression exerted vast influence on the development of a whole series of Asian literatures, from Turkish and Persian through to Punjabi, Bahasa Indonesian, and Pashto. These traditions have also exerted influence on the self-definition of non-Muslim groups in Africa and Asia; the examples of the Yazidi and the Ahmadiyya are briefly examined in the last section of this essay. However, the discussion focuses mainly on the use of the Persian language among Pashtun Afghans and Kurds to show the ways in which the discursive traditions of Perso-Islamic writing shaped the representation of 'religious' practice among two social groups located originally on the mountain fringes of the Persian linguistic world, which before the modern era encompassed and connected Iran, Central Asia, and India.[3]

Like many other social or ethnic groups in this vast area, the Afghans and the Kurds possessed distinct languages of their own, but at times adopted the more powerful medium of Persian for the description of their own social worlds, in so doing painting their own pasts with a palette and techniques originally developed by other groups in quite different social settings. While several of the other contributors to this volume demonstrate the ways in which sociolinguistic groups have employed 'religious' language as a means of creating 'others', this essay illustrates a complementary process by which culturally or politically marginal groups have used the established language of the discursively powerful to paint themselves as 'sames' rather than 'others'. Linguistic power is in this sense as important to the creation of self-identities as it is to the manufacture of 'others'.

The dilemmas of description are particularly acute with regard to those multifaceted and complex figures we might broadly term as saints (in universal Arabo-Islamic terminology, *awliya*). In all literate cultures such figures inhabit two realms simultaneously, enjoying social lives among other living people and parallel but by no means identical careers in the texts that describe them. Since many living holy men engage with texts in some way during their lives—reading, writing, or otherwise mimicking their normative examples—the world of the saintly text and the saintly event can rarely be neatly separated. Given the investment of collective meaning that saints personify, in text or in flesh, if we accept the proposition that writing does not simply mirror the world, then ascertaining the multiple social roles and personae of a saint is no simple matter. Such supernatural men of power were present in all of the societies of premodern Islam and continue to exert influence in the present day. But despite their considerable diversity of style and substance, written sources have long persisted in presenting them with reference to the homogenising Islamic discourse of 'Sufism' (*tasawwuf*).

In formulating a hermeneutics suitable for re-examining the historical roles of language and power in Islamic societies, this essay draws attention to two particular features of written discourse. The first is the pan-regional descriptive lexicon of originally Arabic terms that is broadly identical in a series of languages which writers in many African and Asian societies have used to describe their holy men and the cultural practices that surround them. The second is the standardised written genres whose norms have been adopted in these various social settings over long periods of time. What I suggest is that these features of writing have disguised the social realities of different Asian societies by homogenising a range of activities and institutions through the employment of common lexicons and genres. This focus on writing must also alert us to the partisan nature of language in much of Asian history in which learned languages of power such as Persian, associated with states or hegemonic groups connected with them, have been adopted.

The remit of this approach is defined less by time, place, or 'religious' group than by commonalities of terminology and genre. The result is a re-ordering of the world into regions of writing; not I emphasise of language as such, but of the specific commonalities of genre, norms, and terminology that are concomitant with written communication as discourse. Of course, what we see in such regions of writing is very often a shared ordering of the world, since this is precisely what writing does: it creates written realms of order and perfection, giving shape, reason, and the dignity of meaning to the world. But at the same time as creating normative and self-replicating nets of texts, writing has also been the medium of innovation, controversy, and rebellion. By looking at several of the genres that present the history of different holy men in the Persianate (here, 'Persian-using') region, we explore a two way process in which the adoption of common idioms and genres have made the histories of certain groups conform to the norms of others, while at the same time these commonalities have served to undermine certain forms of hegemony by disguising local social systems or cultural practices in the respectable genres and language of the power-ful. The use of shared languages, idioms, and genres for the description of different societies and their distinct histories is in this way a twin process of hegemony and resistance. In recognising this process, we may develop a hermeneutics of suspicion that is capable of recognising the variant social and cultural realities that lie hidden beneath the homogenising tendencies of written traditions.

THE SUFI IDIOM

The terminology created by the early Muslim theorists and commentators on Islamic sainthood (*wilayat*) and its accompanying ideology (*tasawwuf*, 'Sufism') and adopted by hundreds of later writers in a variety of settings has disguised a wide variety of ideas and activities beneath its common nomenclature. From its early formulation by Arab writers in Iraq during the ninth and tenth century, the terminology of Muslim sainthood laid the basis for what we may term as a Sufi idiom that gradually spread to almost every corner of the Muslim world. This led to the near universality of the originally Arabic terminology of Islamic sainthood in the regional languages of the Muslim world, while the existence of such literary lingua francas as Arabic and Persian (and in a more restricted way such literatures as Urdu) created a more closely aligned inner ring of learned and so likened minds. This terminology—what Louis Massignon called the *lexique technique* of Sufism—was capable of being shared between different Muslim groups while other (social, political or moral) aspects of a wider 'worldview' remained quite different.[4] This Sufi idiom was to provide a compliant but nonetheless common way in which divergent social facts could be given sense. The written discourse of Sufism (*tasawwuf, 'irfan*) thus provided a way in which local Muslim identities could be connected to the *umma*, the imagined transregional community of the entire reach of Islam. Through recourse to the conceptual model provided by the written works of *tasawwuf*, a local holy man, pilgrimage centre or body of customs could be explained in such a way as to place local practice within a conceptual system that was intelligible to people identifying themselves as Muslims from places that were distant and different.[5] This notion of an idiom rather than an actual 'worldview' is important, for I am suggesting that this created a common terminology for what were often very different social phenomena. With the high level of movement and communications between the vastly different peoples and places that made up the premodern world civilisation of Islam, such a unifying idiom was necessary to explain the presence of the supernatural men of influence that characterised the many social worlds of Islam no less than other premodern societies. What was crucial to the success of this idiom was not its metaphysical abstraction, but its identification with living persons. Less the rarified mysticism of nineteenth-century orientalists, this was an embodied Islam that was firmly rooted in its variant social worlds but represented through homogenising traditions of writing.

A shared Sufi terminology served to disguise the diversifying localisation of Islam into different regional contexts through the identification of a wide variety of quite distinct holy men as members of the same transcendental Sufi community (*ta'ifa, qawm*) into which their followers could also be initiated. These bonds between the local and the universal, between practice and theory, were cemented through recourse to the genealogical models that constituted the Sufi networks of the *silsila* (literally 'dynasty, ancestral group', hence a lineage of masters) and *ta'ifa* (literally 'people, tribe', hence a Sufi order). In formulating a spiritualised model of social relations based on initiation (*bay'at*) into the community of the '[chosen] people' (*ta'ifa, qawm*), the early Sufi theorists of the tenth and eleventh centuries and their countless successors in the centuries that followed were able to create a meta-genealogy that transcended the actual bonds of kinship through which their societies were in their different ways all structured.[6] This idiom therefore provided an ideational means of connecting people with no ties of kinship over vast areas by adopting the terminology of kinship to reinforce alternative social bonds based on (or at least reified by) voluntary association with a new social formation given power through its association with transcendental attributes (salvation, perfect knowledge, supernatural power) and written learning.

HISTORIOGRAPHY: THE *TARIKH-E-KHAN JAHANI*

The first genre that I wish to examine is that of *tarikh* ('[annalist] history'). Following earlier Arabic models, history writing developed in Persian in the tenth century, before making its way to India alongside the wider importing of Persianate court and literary culture during the Delhi Sultanate (1206–1526).[7] By the time of the rise of the Mughal Empire, Persian historiography in India had a strong tradition behind it that was replenished by the continued migration of literary savants from Central Asia and Iran. Among the many literary genres that flourished under the Mughals, the genre most closely connected with the court was that of historiography. As the Islamic millennium approached during the reign of Akbar (1556–1605), this long-standing royal pastime became something of an obsession, with a whole series of dynastic and totalising 'world' histories being patronised. Against this background there emerged a number of comparable historical works of subimperial patronage shaped by the tastes of the various ethnic groups sheltering under the umbrella of Mughal power. While for some of these groups (Turanis, Iranis), the use of literary Persian was echoed by the use of different dialects of Persian as a spoken language, for others (Rajputs, Afghans) this was not necessarily the case.[8] One of the texts that appeared during this period of the extravagant patronage of history was the *Tarikh-e-Khan Jahani*, the earliest comprehensive history of the Afghans that was patronised by Khan Jahan Lodi (d. 1631), the Afghan boon companion of the emperor Jahangir (r. 1605–1627).[9] Beginning with the ethnogenesis of the Afghans and continuing right through to the early seventeenth century, the *Tarikh-e-Khan Jahani* long served as the most influential text of Afghan history.[10] Yet for all the polish and professionalism of the team of researchers and writers who compiled it, there remains something paradoxical about the *Tarikh-e-Khan Jahani*. For though devoting an appropriate number of pages to the glorious era of Afghan power in India during the reigns of the Afghan Lodi and Sur rulers, much of the text is devoted to legends located in the less edifying settings of the high pastures of their tribal homelands and their precarious early settlements in India. The text was at once a signal of the arrival of the Afghans at the inner locus of cultural and political power and at the same time a testament to their longstanding marginality as a tribal people inhabiting the fringes of powerful states.

Dedicated to the history of a marginal tribal people for whom Persian was at best a learned language and whose own language would be scarcely used for writing history for two centuries to come, the *Tarikh-e-Khan Jahani* marked several of the boundaries of the Persian written world. But in spite of the 'difference' of Afghan history (its location, social structure, language), its written expression was shaped in accordance with a genre that made specific demands of its own. The past (history) was in this sense shaped by the demands of writing (historiography). In the courtly context in which the *Tarikh-e-Khan Jahani* emerged, the principal textual models were the series of historical works sponsored by the Mughal rulers themselves. Even the story of the Afghans' ethnogenesis from the Prophet Muhammad's companion Qays 'Abd al-Rashid first found textual expression in the imperial Mughal *A'in-e-Akbari* of a generation earlier.[11] Drawing on the 'world histories' of earlier Islamic tradition, particularly in its Persian tradition passing from Juwayni (d. 1283) through Khwandamir (d. 1535) and on into Mughal India, required a trajectory taking the history of peoples from their primogenitors, through their conversion to Islam (preferably by a saint) and on through the field of battle to political glory. In competition with these other historical works that dignified the Mughals and other stake-holding groups within the Mughal imperium, the patron of the *Tarikh-e-Khan Jahani* sought a similar accolade for his own people by recounting their history according to the generic norms of *tarikh*.

The aspect of the *Tarikh-e-Khan Jahani* on which I wish to focus is its lengthy section on the holy men of the Afghans. This final section (*khatima*) of the text was itself a reflection of the importance of narratives of the holy men of given peoples or political territories in other Persian historical works. For as strongholds of historical memory, the saints were connected to many kinds of narrative in Indo-Persian historiography; with their abundance of tales of the miraculous the historians of the Afghans were no exception. Saints were considered a kind of supernatural capital, and the more a people or dynasty possessed the better. The primary comparison is found in the imperial *A'in-e-Akbari*, which contains a section devoted to the great Sufi saints whose shrines and so spiritual power (*barakat*) was located in the Mughal realm.[12]

Genre, and the shape it was given by the imperial power of patronage, was therefore the first mould into which the memory of the Afghan past was poured. In the *Tarikh-e-Khan Jahani* we find the same kinds of Sufi tropes found in earlier histories of other Indo-Muslim dynasties. Yet in order to see the more subtle distortions of social reality wrought by writing, we need to turn to the relationship between the holy men of the Afghan tribes and the shaping influence of the Sufi idiom. In the *Tarikh-e-Khan Jahani*, we find numerous Afghan holy men described with the familiar terminology of the Sufis and yet there seems to be a fundamental dissonance in the text between the literary norms that it follows and the social reality to which it referred. Given the overall rhetorical purpose of the text to glorify (and indeed systematise and strengthen) the tribal social structure of the Afghans, it is a dissonance that the text is never able to fully resolve. For the Sufi saints are not organised in accordance with their Sufi orders (*ta'ifa*) in the text, but in accordance with their tribes (also *ta'ifa*), for such was the semantic range and indeed ambiguity of the classical Sufi lexicon that the word for 'tribe' and 'Sufi order' was the same. From the period of the earliest Sufi commemorative works (*tazkirat*), the reordering of the world found in such Sufi writings had painted the Sufis as a transcendent community of individuals whose ties to God, and to one another, surpassed any other social ties. As a result, they were described through an appropriation of ordinary terms of social organisation as a people (*qawm*) divided into their own distinct tribes (*ta'ifa*), which in turn featured particular lineages or dynasties (*silsila*). In principle, this was a revolutionary vision of social relations, as it was also at times in practice. Yet the picture of social relations that was sacralised in the saintly sections of the *Tarikh-e-Khan Jahani* is quite the opposite of this model of ties of 'religious' affiliation, a picture whose form may have been influenced by the spectacular failure of the Rawshaniyya movement among the Afghans in the decades prior to the text's composition. The loyalties of the Sufis of the *Tarikh-e-Khan Jahani* are not primarily to the transregional tradition that we know of as Islam, nor are they to the alternative '[chosen] people' (*qawm*) envisioned by the ideologues of *tasawwuf*. Instead, the *Tarikh-e-Khan Jahani* presented the Afghan saints as the ancestors and supernatural protectors of their fellow tribesmen, so alerting us to the variety of social functions masked beneath the universalising Perso-Arabic terminology of Sufism. For this was not a neutral lexicon, but one dignified with social respectability and supernatural prestige. The language of Sufism served to disguise a more complex social reality of supernatural men of influence whose mentality and practices often owed much more to their local milieux than to the any serious level of participation in the transregional and standardising body of beliefs and practices described in the doctrinal and practical writings of the many scholarly Sufis from elsewhere. For the tribal saints of the *Tarikh-e-Khan Jahani* do not seem primarily to have been participants in the textual world that was shared across the time and space by Sufi writers and readers communicating through a tradition of normative writings. At least as portrayed in the *Tarikh-e-Khan Jahani*, these saints were devoted to more practical activities, from discovering water sources and protecting cattle in the tribal homelands to founding settlements and leading trade missions in the Afghan diaspora in India.[13]

In the *Tarikh-e-Khan Jahani*, we are therefore caught between the rhetoric of Islam, the court, and the tribe. As a result, the underlying social reality to which the text referred remains opaque, such that it is ultimately unclear whether the saints described in the *Tarikh-e-Khan Jahani* were really sanctified tribal leaders or representatives of the pan-regional Islamic discourse and terminology of *tasawwuf* ('Sufism'). Among the shifting sands of the power games of patronage, genre, and idiom, what we can examine with more certainty is the nature of the text itself. For amid the forces wrestling for mastery of the *Tarikh-e-Khan Jahani*, we see the birth pains of a culturally marginal group attempting to write their own history. The presentation of the holy men and the wider Afghan past within the text took shape in association with the power relations of its context as represented by the political power of the Mughals and the older discursive powers of *tarikh* and *tasawwuf*. It is through the flaws in this rhetoric—the fissures between the demands of inherited tradition and the intransigence of the social world that the text sought to depict—that we have the possibility of hearing the echoed voices of the past.

EPIC VERSE: THE *SHAHNAMA-YE-HAQIQAT*

Turning from the Indo-Afghan frontiers of the Persianate world, I now address the similar themes of history and holy men at the other end of the written realms of Persian among the Kurds of western Iran. As in the case of the *Tarikh-e-Khan Jahani*, here too I examine how a mountain people whose language and social structure differed considerably from those of the powerful states that surrounded them adopted the Persian language of their neighbours to formulate a written history of their own. The classic example of this is the *Sharafnama* written in 1597 by the Kurdish Prince Sharaf al-din Bitlisi.[14] As the primogenitor of Kurdish historiography in Persian, in its attempts to articulate the history of a people recently absorbed into the expanding Ottoman state the *Sharafnama* is in many ways the twin text of the *Tarikh-e-Khan Jahani*. However, to move on from the genre of *tarikh* I now turn to a later example of Kurdish self-expression in the form of Persian epic verse. The text in question is the early twentieth-century *Shahnama-ye-haqiqat* of Hajj Ni'matullah, in which were first systematised the history and doctrines of the Kurdish nativisation of Islam whose followers are known as the Ahl-e-haqq ('People of Supreme Truth').[15]

Hajj Ni'matullah was born around 1871 in the village of Jayhunabad in Iranian Kurdistan, but brought up in the nearby city of Kirmanshah. Receiving a good education, he learned to read and write Persian in addition to his native Kurdish.[16] In the first decades of the nineteenth century, Kirmanshah had flourished under the governorship of the Qajar Prince Muhammad 'Ali Mirza (d. 1821), who endowed the city with bazaars, caravanserais, and palaces.[17] But though situated on the main route between Tehran and Baghdad, under the auspices of successive governors Kirmanshah fell into a longstanding decline and for the remainder of the century its bazaars lay empty and its buildings in decay. Hajj Ni'matullah's lifetime coincided with a series of local uprisings in Kirmanshah, along with serious outbreaks of cholera and occupations by foreign troops. Despite the considerable independence that Kurdish tribesmen continued to enjoy

further to the west, Kirmanshah remained an important outpost of centralised Qajar authority. However, the Kurdish Ahl-e-haqq inhabitants of
the villages of Hajj Ni'matullah's home region were peasants rather than
tribesmen like the Ahl-e-haqq to the west and for over half a century before
his birth the region and its political and economic structures had become
closely tied to the Iranian state. Reflecting the region's integration within
the state, Hajj Ni'matullah's education helped him gain employment as a
scribe and landlord's agent, and he may also have worked at the royal court
of justice in the city. His occupation during these years fits in well with the
wider social structure of the locality of his birth, for the Sahneh region
around Jayhunabad was surrounded by extremely fertile agricultural land
that was owned partly by landlords and partly by the central government
as state-owned (*khalisa*) property.[18] However, in 1900 Hajj Ni'matullah
decided to withdraw from the world of affairs and return to his native
village as a renunciant *faqir*. There he gathered a large number of followers, designated as dervishes, eventually arousing the suspicion of the local
hereditary leadership of the Ahl-e-haqq. After a period of enforced exile
from Jahyunabad, he returned to spend the final years of his life in quietist contemplation. Claiming to have had the true esoteric (*batini*) world
revealed to him during extended bouts of ecstasy, some time between 1912
and 1919, Hajj Ni'matullah wrote his *Shahnama-ye-haqiqat* in which the
hidden meanings of world history were unveiled. Yet as a history placing
the divine epiphanies and incarnations of the Ahl-e-haqq at centre stage,
this was nonetheless a distinctly Kurdish vision of the world and its past.

Hajj Ni'matullah was by no means the only innovator in the Kirmanshah region in the late Qajar era. His teenage years had seen the city's
first conversions to Baha'ism take place, with several Ahl-e-haqq apparently among them. Kirmanshah had also become an important centre for
the Ni'matullahi order after the reintroduction of Sufism to Iran in the
late eighteenth century and at the turn of the twentieth century remained
an important Sufi centre, associated with the new Shi'ite suborders of the
Ni'matullahiyya.[19] Among the Ahl-e-haqq themselves, the decades prior
to Hajj Ni'matullah's birth had seen the emergence of a millenarian movement headed by Taymur of Banyaran, who claimed to be an incarnation
of God in the lineage of the earlier localised incarnations revered by the
Ahl-e-haqq.[20] Propagating his doctrines in Kurdish verse, Taymur gathered
a large number of followers in Kirmanshah and its surroundings before his
movement was eventually suppressed by the Qajar state and Taymur himself executed.[21] In the early 1890s another millenarian Ahl-e-haqq revolt
was led by a holy man who adopted the name of 'Alamgir ('world-seizer'),
but his movement was similarly defeated by government troops.

It is against this background that we should see the career and writings of Hajj Ni'matullah, whose *Shahnama-ye-haqiqat* in many senses
attempted a literary reversal of the hegemony of the Qajar state while at the
same time reaching an accommodation with some of its discursive forms.

For in contrast to the older tradition of Ahl-e-haqq literature, which was composed in Kurdish and not written down before the nineteenth century, Hajj Ni'matullah adopted Persian for his exposition of the sacred history of his people. Hajj Ni'matullah was not the first Ahl-e-haqq poet to write in Persian as such, and in the urban environment of Kirmanshah such figures as Sayyid Ya'qub Mahaydashti (d. 1883 or 1906) had earlier written Persian verse.[22] Yet Hajj Ni'matullah's decision to compose the first systematic exposition of Ahl-e-haqq history and doctrine in Persian rather than Kurdish was an important break with tradition. As in the case of the *Tarikh-e-Khan Jahani* of three centuries earlier, the language and genre adopted by Hajj Ni'matullah was therefore that of the state that he had earlier served and the state's totalising narratives were echoed in the systematisation of history in both texts.[23] More than a Kurdish self-history in the tradition of the *Tarikh-e-Khan Jahani* or the *Sharafnama*, the *Shahnama-ye-haqiqat* took a step further by writing a history of the Kurds not as an ethnic or tribal group but as a transcendental community of the 'people of the Truth' (*ahl-e-haqq*).

Spurning the indigenous poetic forms of the Ahl-e-haqq *kalam* in Kurdish, the genre that Hajj Ni'matullah chose for his exposition of sacred history was that of the epic *Shahnama* of Firdawsi (d. *c*. 1020). Hajj Ni'matullah was by no means the first writer to rework the *shahnama* genre for celebrating figures other than the ancient kings of pre-Islamic Iran. The poet Qasimi (*fl*. 1534) had earlier written a *shahnama* in honour of Shah Isma'il Safawi, while in India the genre was adapted by numerous writers for the celebration of the deeds of different rulers.[24] But in his literary as in his professional career, Hajj Ni'matullah was more closely connected to contemporary developments. For the nineteenth century in Iran had witnessed a tremendous elevation of the importance of Firdawsi's original *Shahnama* that was connected to a profound re-envisioning of the Iranian past.[25] Incumbent upon the birth of nationalism, this new vision of history employed the perceived glory of Iran's pre-Islamic past to forge a distinctly Iranian history that could not be subsumed within a wider Islamic vision of history. Concurrent with this proto-nationalist promotion of Firdawsi's epic was the creation of imitative *shahnamas* by a number of Qajar poets. The *Shahnama-ye-haqiqat* of Hajj Ni'matullah thus represented a continuation of this revival that at the same time repudiated the Iranocentric vision of these other *shahnamas* by adapting the most important literary celebration of the Iranian past for the history of a marginal people inhabiting the mountainous western limits of Iran.[26] In its choice of genre no less than language, the *Shahnama-ye-haqiqat* represented an accommodation with a form of modernity that was experienced through the prism of the new Iranian nation state amid whose birth pangs it was written.[27]

Through the language and genre of others, the *Shahnama-ye-haqiqat* contested the hegemonic histories of the discursive (Islamic) and statist (Iranian) neighbours of the Kurds by locating the master narrative of

Islamic, Iranian, and even ancient Greek history in events taking place in the mountains of Kurdistan. This was achieved through presenting the great rulers, sages and prophets of the surrounding civilisations as companions or adjutants of a God whose full revelation only occurred in the high valleys of Kurdistan with the divine incarnations of Shah Khushin and Sultan Sahak, the 'founders' of the community of the Ahl-e-haqq. For woven around the lives of these two figures in the *Shahnama-ye-haqiqat* were accounts of a whole series of better known figures—the rulers of ancient Iran; Muhammad, 'Ali, and the Shi'a imams; the great Sufi poets; the pagan philosophers of classical antiquity—who were all co-opted into a Kurdish reversal of world history whose master key was held solely by the Ahl-e-haqq.[28] As with the disparate strands of written historiography and tribal memory collated and systematised in the *Tarikh-e-Khan Jahani*, the narratives brought together in the *Shahnama-ye-haqiqat* were by no means original, with many of them having featured in the Kurdish *kalam* in oral or manuscript form.[29] While the *Shahnama-ye-haqiqat* wrote the history of the Kurdish Ahl-e-haqq in the linguistic and generic norms of Iran, it at the same time sought to reverse this power relationship by claiming Iranian history as a mere chapter of a universal history of the Kurds.

Yet in the *Shahnama-ye-haqiqat* local cultural practices were legitimised and related to wider 'Islamic' schemata through their linguistic identification with Sufi practices, even if the Kurdish practices differed in considerable degree. A notable example is this is the initiation ceremony in which a young member (*murid*, *talib*) of the community is fully accepted into the Ahl-e-haqq by accepting an elder as his spiritual master (*pir*).[30] Like the terminology for the participants in this rite of passage, the designation of the ritual itself as 'the entrustment of the head' (*sar sepordan*) is another appropriation from the lexicon of Sufism. Building on this key social ritual, the loyalty between commoner and *sayyid* families that was the traditional backbone of Kurdish Ahl-e-haqq communities was conceptualised through the Sufi vocabulary of 'master-discipleship' (*piri-muridi*). Perhaps most significant of all is the way in which the Ahl-e-haqq have adopted the Sufi idiom to term themselves as the '[chosen] people' (*ta'ifa*). Despite belonging to the classic lexicon of *tasawwuf*, as with the use of the term in connection with the Afghan saints of the *Tarikh-e-Khan Jahani*, among the Ahl-e-haqq the word actually referred to a distinct local form of social organisation. However, we might also draw attention to the importance of the ritual use of music and pilgrimage, for again in the *Shahnama-ye-haqiqat* these practices are identified with the *sama'* and *ziyarat* of the Sufis. While there were substantial similarities between the practices of the Ahl-e-haqq and those of the Sufi orders, to assert a simple identification between the two is to miss the way in which the language of Sufism afforded an accommodation between local practices and pan-Islamic categories of ritual behaviour. For it was precisely through their musical repertoire that the Ahl-e-haqq were able to maintain and pass on in song the body of Kurdish oral traditions (*kalam*) describing their localised vision of the world and its history, while through pilgrimage to the tombs of Baba Yadgar and Sultan Sohak were they able to forge a sacred geography within their own mountainous domain. To assert, as some scholars have, that the Ahl-e-haqq represent an outgrowth of an ill-defined 'Sufism' is to render them passive recipients of tradition rather than to gauge the innate adaptability of Sufism *as an empowering lexicon* used for a variety of cultural practices on the ground. At the same time, to regard the Ahl-e-haqq as a fossilised version of pre-Islamic Iranian culture is quite plainly to lack a sense of history.

A similar adaptation of the vocabulary of Sufism to a local context may be seen among the non-Muslim Kurdish Yazidis of Iraq, showing how linguistic power slips unchallenged through the frontiers that are proposed by models of 'religious' identity. Although possessing a distinct theology and sacred history of their own, the terminology of social organisation used among the Yazidis is entirely synonymous with that of the Sufis. The different ranks of Yazidi society are thus classified as *shaykhs*, *pirs*, *faqirs*, *mujawirs*, *qawwwals* or *murids*.[31] Despite this linguistic equivalence, the social functions of these figures remain specific to the social conditions of traditional Yazidi society in the rural highlands. As with the *sayyid* families of the Ahl-e-haqq, the Yazidi shaykhs form an endogamous social unit with a strong prohibition on intermarriage with the families of their followers (*murids*). Nothing could contrast more strongly with the longstanding custom of *murids* marrying into the families of their shaykhs in the history of the Sufi orders.

While the centrepiece of the *Shahnama-ye-haqiqat* is the account of the divine mountainside manifestations of Shah Khushin and Sultan Sohak, the text is thus of interest for its adaptation of the idiom of Sufism. As we have seen, the lexicon of the Islamic discourse of *tasawwuf* provided a flexible, edifying, and broadly respectable means of labelling a variety of individuals and social institutions. While the *Tarikh-e-Khan Jahani* adapted the idiom of Sufism to reify bonds of loyalty to the Afghan tribes, for its part the *Shahnama-ye-haqiqat* reflected a comparable adaptation among the Kurds of the Ahl-e-haqq. Sufi orders among the Kurds in general were embedded in tribal and clan structures, such that it was often difficult to separate the two.[32] The organisation of the Ahl-e-haqq continued this coalescence of the language of Sufism with the structures of kinship, such that a number of families (*khandan*) emerged as the hereditary leaders of the other Kurdish Ahl-e-haqq, who were regarded as their initiates (*murids*). According to tradition, although known as *sayyids*, the leadership of these families was inaugurated with their ancestors' association with Sultan Sohak, the fourteenth / fifteenth-century incarnation of the eternal Truth (*haqq*). For these families, as well as for the whole gamut of figures associated with the Ahl-e-haqq, the idiom of the Sufis was used in abundance. From the terminology of leadership to the more abstract language of speculative mysticism, the whole lexicon of the Sufis was employed in the *Shahnama-ye-haqiqat* to describe a set of doctrines and social institutions that bore little similarity with the *tasawwuf* envisaged by the Sufi writers of medieval Iraq and Iran. Hajj Ni'matullah was in fact a Kurdish nonconformist who regarded spiritual ecstasy as superior to the hereditary authority of the Ahl-e-haqq *sayyids*. But this model of authority was no less articulated through a Sufi linguistic framework than the *sayyids*' rival system of *piri-muridi*, and both positions reflected points on the Sufi spectrum between organisation and charisma. For Hajj Ni'matullah, the spiritual message of his epic of the Kings of Truth was the authentic form of the Sufi idiom of *shari'at-tariqat-haqiqat* (Divine Law—Sufi Path—Absolute Truth). In this way, the *Shahnama-ye-haqiqat* was able to lay claim to the much older discursive tradition of the Sufis in Arabic and Persian, but re-work it to the advantage of the marginal group of mountain peoples whose history and institutions it described.

In being written in Persian epic verse, the *Shahnama-ye-haqiqat* echoed the power of the Iranian state and the ongoing institutional impoverishment of Kurdish letters. As the Ahl-e-haqq moved still closer into the orbit of the state with the modernisation of Iran under the Pahlavi regime (r. 1925–1979), greater moves towards compromise and accommodation with the state and its Shi'ite institutions were made by Hajj Ni'matullah's son, Ustad Ilahi (d. 1974), whose Persian *Burhan al-haqq* brought Ahl-e-haqq doctrine into line with Shi'ism in terms of both content and style.[33] In this way, in gradually shifting the Ahl-e-haqq towards accommodation with mainstream Shi'ism, the writings of Hajj Ni'matullah and his son echoed the series of Iranian Sufi texts during the nineteenth century that brokered the same compromise between the Sufis and the Shi'a clerics. As part of the political process itself, doctrinal writings formed a public sphere of communication between Iran's different power seekers. In these ways, in the *Shahnama-ye-haqiqat* we see a negotiated encounter between a wider discursive tradition (Islam), an expanding state (Iran) and the local cultural environment of the Kurdish highlands. Having formulated their own vision of the world through a dynamic encounter with the more powerful cultural system of the urban Islamic centres of the surrounding states, the disparate oral history and practices of this stateless group found codification, order, and written mandate in the Persian *Shahnama-ye-haqiqat* that Hajj Ni'matullah wrote in imitative reversal of the royal histories of Qajar Iran.

LOOKING FURTHER AFIELD

The nineteenth and early twentieth century in Iran witnessed the evolution of Baha'ism as well as the formation of a written literature for the Ahl-e-haqq, with text producers among both communities adapting existing genres in Persian for the articulation of identities distinct from the dominant mainstream of Shi'ite Iran. During the same period, India witnessed a similar series of social and intellectual upheavals closely linked with shifts in the technology of communication that were incumbent upon language change and the coming of print. An interesting comparison with the *Shahnama-ye-haqiqat* can be made with the writings of Hajj Ni'matullah's contemporary, the Punjabi visionary and self-proclaimed successor to the Prophet Muhammad, Mirza Ghulam Ahmad (d. 1908). The movements associated with both these figures occupy an ambiguous position with regard to wider Islamic tradition, at once reinvigorating older strands of metaphysical speculation that had long inhabited the fringes of Muslim respectability while at the same time being forced to clarify their relationship with the Islamic *fiqh* and *kalam*.[34] Both movements represented attempts to reformulate Islam through their respective visions of divine incarnations in the Kurdish highlands and a prophetic succession to Muhammad in the plains of Punjab and in so doing to re-position the geography of the master narratives of Islamic tradition. Like Hajj Ni'matullah's decision to use Persian for his *Shahnama-ye-haqiqat*, Mirza Ghulam Ahmad's use of the transregional languages of Arabic, Persian, and Urdu signalled a similar gaze beyond the geographical and linguistic borders of his immediate Punjabi environment. Here Ghulam Ahmad's attempt to Indianise Islam by drawing on the Quranic tradition of God sending prophets to all the peoples of mankind begs comparison with the series of earlier Sufis and gurus in Punjab whose vernacular verses had allowed their followers to gradually detach themselves from Muslims entirely as members of the fraternities and sororities of the Sikh *khalsa*, a localised social formation only classified in the terms of 'religion' under colonial influence. As among those members of the Ahl-e-haqq for whom the existence of a sacred (oral) scripture in Kurdish was proof of their separation from Islam, so in the formation of the Sikh communities did the linguistic character of scripture serve as a charter for their gradual social detachment from their Muslim neighbours. Like the Baha'is in Iran, with their self-evident generic and linguistic continuity with Islamic tradition the Ahmadiyya have not had this option. The decision whether to employ local vernaculars or the transregional written languages already claimed by older or stronger discursive traditions therefore bears important consequences.

The process outlined in this sketch of the roles of lexicon and genre in the written description of cultural practice is by no means unique to Persian. Given that the starting point for much of this terminology and its associated genres was Arabic, parallel processes also occurred in the Arabic written world, which covered a no less diverse geographical and social area. Once again these processes are most clearly observed in diglossic regions in which local and vernacular social worlds have been depicted through the medium of written Arabic. A useful example is Sudan, whose rich Muslim tradition comprised a wide spectrum of holy men whose affiliation with the transregional Islam of Arabic book-learning varied considerably. When we look at the historical sources for the study of the holy men of Sudan we therefore face the same problem of standardising terminology being used to describe a range of people with multiple-cultic personae and social functions. A good example of this is the *Tabaqa* of Wad Zayfullah (d. 1809), one of the principal sources on the history of Islam in Sudan.[35] Like all of the texts we have discussed, the presentation of the past in Wad Zayfullah's *Tabaqa* was shaped in accordance with the character of the present, and in large part the contents of the *Tabaqa* echoed the chronology and political geography of the Funj dynasty (1504–1821) of Nilotic Sudan. In this text we again witness the influence of the norms of genre—in this case the biographical dictionary or 'book of classes' (*tabaqa*)—in shaping the presentation of social life according to the demands of writing. Given the varied and complex tribal milieux of Sudan, the 'flat' perspective of the *Tabaqa* is suspicious. We know from ethnographic studies that like the practice of Islam elsewhere, Sudanese Islam contains many localised features centring on the activities of holy men, yet in Wad Zayfullah's *Tabaqa* we find the same classic Sufi terminology used in abundance. However, glimpsed amid the *Tabaqa*'s presentation of a series of normative virtues in standardised vocabulary are a number of distinctive and local customs. When we attempt to gain some kind of thick description of Sudan's complex past, we are therefore faced with the same linguistic tension between writing and the world in which difference is muted by a homogenising received idiom of respectability and power.

CONCLUSIONS

After the eleventh or twelfth century, the social, intellectual, and at times political respectability of Sufism as both social formation and discourse made its terminological lexicon an attractive—and for many apparently natural—means of labelling a variety of holy men and the practices associated with them. Having at times veiled the qualitative differences in the social history of different groups, the false homogeneity suggested by this universal terminology was further reinforced by the literary norms of shared genres of writing. In the previous sections we have seen how written languages of power—and specific idioms and genres within them—act as fields of contest between different social groups, particularly between hegemonic states and their discourses and tribal or subaltern groups lacking a written vernacular literature of their own. In such contexts these dis/continuities of idiom and genre form a more useful mode of analysis than such blunt heuristic devices as either the 'World Religions' or even their constituent parts (in this case, 'Sufism'). Where language, idiom, and genre flatten out the distinctions of the lived world, this approach helps us recognise difference in pasts which textual sources too easily present in terms of unity and equivalence, and so as uniformly 'Islamic'. In a discussion of "the normative vocabulary which any society employs for the description and appraisal of its social life", Quentin Skinner has argued that "to see the role of . . . evaluative language in helping to legitimate social action is to see the point at which . . . social vocabulary and . . . social fabric mutually prop each other up."[36] Skinner's adage would suggest that the legitimate language of *tasawwuf* therefore had the power to protect or promote whatever practices it was used to describe.

NOTES

Earlier versions of this essay were presented at 'History and Indian Studies', Maison Française, Oxford, 2005; 'Moving Literatures', South Asia Triangle Consortium, North Carolina, 2006; and the Middle Eastern History Seminar, School of Oriental and African Studies (London), 2007. I am very grateful for these invitations and for the astute comments of their audiences.

1. For a problematisation of the relationship between Sufi writings and their historical contexts, see N. S. Green, "Emerging Approaches to the Sufi Traditions of South Asia: Between Texts, Territories and the Transcendent", *South Asia Research* 24, 2 (2004), pp. 123–148.

2. My starting point here in Talal Asad's work should be obvious. See T. Asad, *The Idea of an Anthropology of Islam* (Washington DC: Center for Contemporary Arab Studies, Georgetown University, 1986).

3. On the linguistic and intellectual coherence of this Persophone region, see F. C. R. Robinson, "Ottomans-Safavids-Mughals: Shared Knowledge and Connective Systems", *Journal of Islamic Studies* 8, 2 (1997), pp. 151–184.

4. L. Massignon, *Essai sur les origines du lexique technique de la mystique musulmane* [*Essay on the Origins of the Technical Lexicon of Islamic Mysticism*] (Paris: Geuthner, 1922).

5. cf. E. Gellner, *Muslim Society* (Cambridge, England: Cambridge University Press, 1981), p. 103: "Sufism provides a theory, terminology, and technique of leadership".

6. In one important case study, Jürgen Paul analysed the social functions of the regional *ta'ifa* formed by the Central Asian Sufi master Khwaja Ahrar (d. 1490) in terms of the formation of a 'faction' (*ta'ifa*) of peasants, craftsmen and merchants. See J. Paul, "Forming a Faction: The *Himāyat* System of Khwaja Ahrar", *International Journal of Middle East Studies* 23, 4 (1991), pp. 533–548.

7. J. S. Meisami, *Persian Historiography: To the End of the Twelfth Century* (Edinburgh, Scotland: Edinburgh University Press, 1999).

8. M. Alam, "The Pursuit of Persian: Language in Mughal Politics", *Modern Asian Studies* 32, 2 (1998), pp. 317–349.

9. Ni'mat Allāh ibn Habīb Allāh Harawī, *Tarikh-e-Khan Jahani wa Makhzan-e-Afghānī* [*The Khan Jahan's History and the Afghan Coffers*], ed. S. M. Imām al-Dīn, 2 vols (Dacca, Bangladesh: Asiatic Society of Pakistan, 1960–1962), hereafter *TKJ*. A translation of a single manuscript of the early abridgement of the *TKJ* known as the *Makhzan-e-Afghānī* was published by B. Dorn (trans.), *History of the Afghans* (London: Murray, 1829–1836).

10. N. S. Green, "Tribe, Diaspora and Sainthood in Afghan History", *Journal of Asian Studies* 67, 1 (2008).

11. Abū'l Fazl, *Aīn Akbarī*, ed. H. Blochmann (Calcutta, India: Asiatic Society of Bengal, 1875), vol. 1, p. 591.

12. Abū'l Fazl (1875), vol. 2, pp. 207–225.

13. *TKJ*, vol. 2, pp. 644–645, 743–744, 754–755, 764, 843–870.

14. Sharaf Khān Bidlīsī, *Sharafnāma: Tārīkh-e-mufassal-e-Kurdestān* (Tehran, Iran: Muʻassasa-e-Matbuʻat-e-ʻIlmī, 1964), also translated by M. R. Izady, *The Sharafnāma, or, The History of the Kurdish Nation* (Costa Mesa, CA: Mazda, 2005).

15. Niʻmat Allāh Jayhūnābādī, *Shāhnāma-ye-haqīqat: Tārīkh-e-manzūm-e-buzurgān-e-Ahl-e-Haqq* [*The Book of the Kings of Truth: A Versified History of the Great Ones of the Ahl-e-Haqq*], 2 vols, ed. Mohammad Mokri (Tehran, Iran: Anstitūʼī-ye-Farānsavī-ye-Pezhūhishhāʼī ʻIlmī dar Īrān, 1966–1971), henceforth *SNH*. On the Ahl-e-haqq, see M. R. Hamzehʼee, *The Yaresan: A Sociological, Historical and Religio-Historical Study of a Kurdish Community* (Berlin: Schwarz, 1990).

16. On the life of Hajj Niʻmatullah, see S. Safīzāda, *Mashāhīr-e-ahl-e-haqq* [*Famous Figures of the Ahl-e-Haqq*], (Tehran, Iran: 1360/1981), pp. 160–161. I am grateful to Ziba Mir-Hosseini for providing access to this work. A shorter account is also given in Mokri (1966–71), vol. 1, p. 7. A fifth book of the *Shahnama-ye-haqiqat*, entitled *Naʻim* and dealing with events in Hajj Niʻmatullah's own life and times, was not included in Mokri's edition, but has appeared in later editions. See Hāj Niʻmat Allāh Jayhūnābādī, *Haqq al-haqāʼiq yā shāhnāma-ye-haqīqat* [The Truth of Truths, or Book of the Kings of Truth], (Tehran, Iran: Intishārāt-e-Jayhūn, 1373/1994), pp. 369–429. It is unclear whether this section is all the genuine work of Hajj Niʻmatullah or partly that of his son, Ustad Ilahi. The biography of Hajj Niʻmatullah is also discussed in Z. Mir-Hosseini, "Breaking the Seal: The New Face of the Ahl-e Haq", in K. Kehl-Bodrogi, B. Kellner-Heinkele, & A. Otter-Beaujean (eds.), *Syncretistic Religious Communities in the Near East* (Leiden, The Netherlands: Brill, 1997), p. 182.

17. G. R. G. Hambly, "The Traditional Iranian City in the Qājār Period", in P. Avery, G. Hambly, & C. Melville (eds.), *The Cambridge History of Iran, Vol. 7, From Nadir Shah to the Islamic Republic* (Cambridge, England: Cambridge University Press, 1991), pp. 542–589, especially pp. 559–562.

18. Z. Mir-Hosseini, "Inner Truth and Outer History: The Two Worlds of an Iranian Mystical Sect", *International Journal of Middle East Studies* 26, 4 (1994), pp. 267–285, especially p. 279.

19. M. van den Bos, *Mystic Regimes: Sufism and the State in Iran, from the Late Qajar Era to the Islamic Republic* (Leiden, The Netherlands: Brill, 2002), pp. 68–69.

20. Jayhūnābādī (1373/1994), pp. 345–349. On these millenarian movements, see Hamzehʼee (1990), pp. 136–145.

21. On Taymur, see S. Safīzāda, *Buzurgān-e-Yāresān* (Tehran, Iran: ʻAtaʼī, 1361/1983), pp. 137–142. The significance of the revolt is interpreted in Mir-Hosseini (1994).

22. Safīzāda (1360/1981), pp. 161–162.

23. On these themes in Iranian history, see W. O. Beeman, *Language, Status and Power in Iran* (Bloomington: Indiana University Press, 1986); S. Meskoob, *Iranian Nationality and the Persian Language*, trans. M. C. Hillmann (Washington, DC: Mage, 1992).

24. One example was the *Shahnama-ye-ahmadi* written by Nizam al-din of Sialkot (d. unknown) as a history of his patron, the Afghan ruler Ahmad Shah Durrani (r. 1747–1773). As in Iran, the twentieth century in South Asia saw a revival of the *shahnama* genre, as in the Urdu *Shahnama-e-hind* of Hafiz Jhalandari, best known as the composer of the Pakistani national anthem.

25. M. Tavakoli-Targhi, "Refashioning Iran: Language and Culture during the Constitutional Revolution", *Iranian Studies* 23 (1992), pp. 78–86. Even among the Iranian literary modernists of the first decades of the twentieth

century, Firdawsi's *Shahnama* was spared their wider criticism of traditional literary forms; among others, Ahmad Kasravi (1888–1945) regarded the work as embodying an earlier era of Persian national revival.

26. The tribal and mountainous setting of the Hajj Ni'matullah's and his Ahl-e-haqq ancestors' revelation is alluded to frequently in the poem. See e.g., *SNH*, pp. 274, 286 (where the tribe—*qawm, īl*—of the Lors receive the revelation of Shah Khoshin) and p. 323 (where Truth appears on a Kurdish mountain).

27. On more general political dimensions of Iranian poetry during this period, see M. Rahman, "Social and Political Themes in Modern Persian Poetry, 1900–1950", in T. M. Ricks (ed.), *Critical Perspectives on Modern Persian Literature* (Washington DC: Three Continents Press, 1984).

28. On being the heir to the ancient Greek and Persian sages and Muhammad, see *SNH*, pp. 18–19 and on the Shi'a imams pp. 23–25. Stories of no fewer than twenty-seven earlier heroes and prophets, serving to place Hajj Ni'matullah in continuation of their lineage, are found in *SNH*, pp. 120–174 and pp. 285, 294. A re-reading and appropriation of Islamic sacred history appears in *SNH*, pp. 182–208; and of the great early Sufis (such as Hallaj) on pp. 232–233, 239–252, 261–265.

29. One source seems to have been in the *Dawra-ye-dīwāna-gawra*, which shares several stories with the *Shahnama-ye-haqiqat*. See M. Mokri (ed. & trans.), *La Grande assemblée des fidèles de vérité au tribunal sur le Mont Zagros en Iran* [*The Great Assembly of the Loyal Ones of Truth (Ahl-e-haqq) at the Court on Mount Zagros*] (Paris: Librarie Klincksieck, 1977). The editor has chosen to describe these originally oral poems as "un compte rendu mythico-historique de renouvellement du Pacte éternel entre le Roi du monde et ses fidèles compagnons" (p. 90).

30. *SNH, passim*, especially pp. 284, 317–319, 462–465.

31. P. G. Kreyenbroek, *Yezidism—Its Background, Observances and Textual Tradition* (Lampeter, Wales: Mellen, 1995), pp. 125–143.

32. M. M. van Bruinessen, *Mullas, Sufis and Heretics: The Role of Religion in Kurdish Society* (Istanbul, Turkey: Isis, 2000).

33. H. Algar & J. W. Morris, "Elāhī, Hājj Nūr 'Alī", in *Encyclopaedia Iranica;* S. Weightman, "The Significance of the *Kitāb Burhān-ul haqq*", *Iran: Journal of the British Institute of Persian Studies* 2 (1964), pp. 83–103. For a reform-centred approach to these writings, see Mir-Hosseini (1997).

34. In both cases the principal difficulty was the undermining of the unique status of the Prophet Muhammad. As the Persian proverb warns, 'Be crazy with God, but cautious with the Prophet' (*bā khodā dīwāna bāsh, valī bā payghāmbar hūshyār*)!

35. Much of the section of the Arabic text dealing with the Sudanese holy men has been published, with parallel translation, in S. Hillelson, *Sudan Arabic Texts* (Cambridge, England: The University Press, 1935), pp. 172–203. For a detailed study, see S. Hillelson, "Tabaqāt of Wad Ḍayf Allah: Studies in the Lives of the Scholars and Saints", *Sudan Notes and Queries* 6 (1923).

36. Q. Skinner, "The Idea of a Cultural Lexicon", *Essays in Criticism* 29, 3 (1979), pp. 221–222 (reprinted in Q. Skinner, *Visions of Politics*, vol. 1, *Regarding Method* [Cambridge, England: Cambridge University Press, 2002], pp. 158–174).

Contributors

Philip Alexander is Professor of Post-Biblical Jewish Studies at the University of Manchester, codirector of the Manchester Centre for Jewish Studies and a Fellow of the British Academy. He has worked on a wide range of topics in early Judaism and has a strong interest in the problem of how to contextualize Rabbinic Judaism in the Graeco-Roman world of late antiquity. His publications include *Mystical Texts* (Clark, 2006) and *Textual Sources for the Study of Judaism* (ed. & trans.; Manchester University Press, 1984).

Andreas Christmann is Senior Lecturer in Contemporary Islam at the University of Manchester. His research interests focus in religious thought and practice in twentieth century Islam and modern Qur'anic hermeneutics. His publications include "The Form Is Permanent, But the Content Moves: Text and Interpretations in the Writings of Mohamad Shahrour", in S. Taji-Farouki (ed.), *Modern and Postmodern Approaches to the Qur'an* (Tauris, 2003) and "Islamic Scholar and Religious Leader: A Portrait of Muhmmad Sa'id Ramadan al-Buti", in J. Cooper et al. (eds.), *Islam and Modernity: Muslim Intellectuals Respond* (Tauris, 1998).

Nile Green is Associate Professor of History at the University of California at Los Angeles and was previously Lecturer in South Asian Studies at the University of Manchester. He specialises on the history of Islam in South Asia, Iran, and Afghanistan and has published around forty articles and book chapters, as well as *Indian Sufism Since the Seventeenth Century: Saints, Books and Empires in the Muslim Deccan* (Routledge, 2006).

Jeremy Gregory is Senior Lecturer in the History of Modern Christianity at the University of Manchester. His research has contributed to the debates concerning the role of the Church of England, and religion in general, in English social, cultural, political, and intellectual history. His publications include *Restoration, Reformation, and Reform, 1660–1828:*

Archbishops of Canterbury and their Diocese (Oxford University Press, 2000) and (with John Stevenson) *The Longman Companion to Britain in the Eighteenth Century, 1688–1820* (Longman, 1999; second edition Routledge, 2007).

Todd Klutz is Senior Lecturer in New Testament Studies at the University of Manchester. He specialises on the interrelations between linguistic style, situation, and culture in early Christian literature, but has also worked on ancient demonology and the application of contemporary linguistics, literary theory, and social science to interpretation of early Christian and comparative texts. His publications include *Rewriting the Testament of Solomon: Tradition, Conflict and Identity in a Late Antique Pseudepigraphon* (Clark, 2005) and *The Exorcism Stories in Luke-Acts: A Sociostylistic Reading* (Cambridge University Press, 2004).

Mary Searle-Chatterjee is an anthropologist based at the Centre for South Asian Studies at the University of Manchester. She specialises in caste, gender, and religious ethnicity in North India. Her many publications include *Reversible Sex Roles: The Special Case of Banaras Sweepers* (Pergamon, 1981), *Contextualising Caste* (co-edited, Blackwell, 1994) and "'World Religions' and 'Ethnic Groups': Do These Paradigms Lend Themselves to the Cause of Hindu Nationalism?" reprinted in J. E. Llewellyn (ed.), *Defining Hinduism* (Equinox, 2005).

Jacqueline Suthren Hirst is Senior Lecturer in South Asian Studies at the University of Manchester. Her research in South Asian religious traditions is concerned with questions of pedagogy and hermeneutics in the Vedanta traditions of Indian philosophy and in the works of the great Advaitin commentator Shankara. The second strand of her research relates to issues of gender, education, and representation. Her publications include *Samkara's Advaita Vedànta: A Way of Teaching* (Routledge Curzon, 2005) and *Playing for Real: 'Hindu' Role Models, Religion and Gender* (co-edited with Lynn Thomas; Oxford University Press, 2004).

Francesca Tarocco is Leverhulme Trust Research Fellow and Lecturer in Buddhist Studies at the University of Manchester. Her primary research interests are the history of modern Chinese Buddhism, China-Europe relations, and the history of the Chinese religious press. Her publications include several articles on Chinese religions and *The Cultural Practices of Modern Chinese Buddhism* (Routledge, 2007) and *Karaoke: A Global Phenomenon* (with Zhou Xun; Reaktion, 2007).

Alan Williams is Reader in Iranian Studies and Comparative Religion at the University of Manchester. His publications include books and articles on pre-Islamic Iran (*The Pahlavi Rivayat Accompanying the Dadestan* *i Denig*, Royal Danish Academy of Sciences, 1990), Islamic Iran (*Rumi: The Spiritual Verses The First Book of the Masnavi-ye Ma'navi of Jalaloddin Rumi*, Penguin Classics, 2006), Diaspora Studies (*Parsis in India and their Diaspora Abroad*, co-edited with John R. Hinnells, Routledge, 2007) and Translation Studies ("New Approaches to the Problem of Translation in the Study of Religion" in Peter Antes et al. (eds), *New Approaches to the Study of Religion*, de Gruyter, 2004).

John Zavos is Lecturer in South Asian Studies at the University of Manchester. His research interests focus on the relationship between religion and politics in South Asia and the South Asian diaspora. He is the author of *The Emergence of Hindu Nationalism in India* (Oxford University Press, 2002) and has co-edited *The Politics of Cultural Mobilization in India* (Oxford University Press, 2004).

Index